Customer Experience FOR DUMMIES®

A Wiley Brand

by Roy Barnes
and Bob Kelleher

FOR DUMMIES®
A Wiley Brand

Customer Experience For Dummies®

Authorized reprint by Wiley India Pvt. Ltd., 4436/7, Ansari Road, Daryaganj, New Delhi – 110002.

Reprint: 2019

Printed at: Nice Printing Press.

ISBN: 978-81-265-5435-5

Contents at a Glance

Table of Contents

Introduction

After graduating from college, I (coauthor Roy) spent five years in Alaska, thanks to a research grant from the National Endowment for the Humanities. During that time, I spent one summer working at a fish camp with a 70-year-old Athabascan Indian named Al Frank. Al and I passed our days catching and drying salmon. He used the salmon to feed his family and his team of 18 sled dogs throughout the year. When the salmon were spawning (that is, swimming upriver to lay their eggs), Al had to catch and store as many fish as he could to survive the fall and long winter.

One windy afternoon, I was standing on a bluff overlooking the Yukon River, watching Al work. Suddenly, a black bear burst from the brush at the river's edge and galloped straight at Al. Sensing the threat, Al looked up, dropped his gutting knife, and took off running as fast as his legs could carry him. But he didn't run away from the bear. Instead, he ran *toward* it, waving his arms and hollering. Mystified, the bear skidded to a stop. Then it turned tail and headed back the way it had come. I was dumbfounded! For his part, Al walked back down the riverbank, picked up his gutting knife, and got back to work as if nothing had happened.

I scrambled down the bluff and ran to Al. Wide-eyed and excited, I asked him what in the world had made him run at the bear. Completely calm, Al answered, "What were my choices?" He explained, "If I'd stayed where I was, he would have gotten me. If I'd waded into the river, he would have gotten me. If I had tried to run away, he would have come after me and taken me down." Then, with a smile on his face, he said, "Roy, sometimes you have to be the one to decide to control events. You have to decide the outcome. *You have to control the experience.*"

I've never forgotten what Al said that day — and it applies to nearly every aspect of life. Not surprisingly, that includes customer experience.

This book is all about designing, monitoring, and controlling experience — specifically, customer experience. In it, you'll find out what customer experience is, why it matters, and the essential steps to controlling it and making it stick. As you read this book, you'll quickly discover that in customer experience, as in life, you have to charge at the bear!

About This Book

Above all, *Customer Experience For Dummies* is a reference tool. You don't have to read it from beginning to end. If you prefer, you can turn to any part of the book that gives you the information you need, when you need it.

In addition, you can keep coming back to the book over and over. If you prefer to read things in order, you'll find that the information is presented in a natural, logical progression.

Sometimes we have information that we want to share with you, but it relates only tangentially to the topic at hand. When that happens, we place that information in a *sidebar* (a shaded gray box). Even though it may not be mission-critical, we think you'll find it worth knowing. But you don't have to read it if you don't want to.

Within this book, you may note that some web addresses break across two lines of text. If you're reading this book in print and want to visit one of these web pages, simply key in the web address exactly as it's noted in the text, pretending as though the line break doesn't exist. If you're reading this as an e-book, you've got it easy — just click the web address to be taken directly to the web page.

Foolish Assumptions

You don't need an MBA to understand the contents of this book. It's written in conversational, jargon-free prose. However, you'll note that much of the advice in this text is geared toward those in management.

That said, the principles and best practices outlined in this book apply to everyone. So even if you manage no one, you'll find loads of tips and ideas in this book that will help you boost customer experience in your organization.

Icons Used in This Book

Icons are those little pictures you see in the margins throughout this book, and they're meant to draw your attention to key points that can help you along the way. Here's a list of the icons we use and what they signify.

When you see this icon in the margin, the paragraph next to it contains valuable information that will help make your life easier.

Some information is so important that it needs to be set apart for emphasis. This icon — like a string tied around your finger — is a friendly reminder of info that you'll want to commit to memory and use over the long haul.

This icon highlights common mistakes and pitfalls to avoid. An important part of achieving success is simply eliminating the mistakes; the information marked by this icon helps you do just that.

On occasion, we use real-world examples to illustrate the point at hand. Those examples are called out with this icon.

Beyond the Book

In addition to the material in the print or e-book you're reading right now, this product also comes with some access-anywhere goodies on the web. Check out the free Cheat Sheet at `www.dummies.com/cheatsheet/customerexperience` for tips on the key steps to implementing a customer experience program, the best tactic for dealing with angry customers, and 20 questions you can ask to begin your own customer experience diagnostic. You'll also find links on each of the Part intro pages for accessing additional content, including articles on managing larger-scale touchpoint redesign efforts, an example of great customer experience in action, a discussion of using a text analysis tool to sort through customer feedback, and more.

Where to Go from Here

This book isn't linear. Although you can certainly read it from cover to cover, you don't have to. You can start anywhere!

Glance through the table of contents and find the part, chapter, or section that flips your switch. That's the best place to begin. If you're already sold on customer experience and want some ideas for launching your own program, turn straight to Part II. If you're keen to discover customer experience killers — those things that ruin customer experience — start with Chapter 3. If you're in hiring mode, Chapter 13 — which discusses the traits and behaviors you need to build a workforce of customer experience advocates — is a great place to start. Or you might turn to Chapters 15 and 16 to find out how to measure your progress.

When you're finished reading this book, expand your knowledge by reading the books listed in Chapter 21. A free online article that accompanies this book also cites LinkedIn groups, summits and conferences, and blogs that focus on customer experience. You'll quickly discover that customer experience is a big and growing field, and there's a lot to learn!

Part I

What Is Customer Experience?

web extras

For Dummies can help you get started with lots of subjects. Visit www.dummies.com to learn more and do more with *For Dummies.*

In this part...

- Get clear on what customer experience is and what it means for your organization.
- Assess the impact of customer experience on your business's bottom line.
- Identify practices and behaviors that kill customer experience.
- Diagnose customer experience problems in your own organization.
- Discover how best to handle angry customers.

Chapter 1

Basic Training: Customer Experience Basics

In This Chapter

- Looking at eight essential steps to creating a great customer experience program
- Understanding why little things mean a lot
- Considering why the "low-hanging fruit" approach doesn't work
- Appreciating the importance of "owning" customer experience
- Thinking of customer experience as the ultimate competitive advantage

Before you can work to improve customer experience, you need one key piece of information: what customer experience *is*. The best definition we've seen comes from customer experience thought leader Colin Shaw:

> Customer experience is the sum of all interactions between a customer and your organization. It's the blend of your organization's physical performance [and] the emotions that you create all measured against customer expectations across all of your points of interaction.

Or to put it another way: Customer service is an attitude, not a department.

Simple, right? Well, maybe not. If you begin to dissect Shaw's observations, you quickly discover the daunting nature of the challenge in front of you.

Start with the first part of Shaw's statement. If customer experience really is "the sum of all interactions between a customer and your organization," that means it's a big problem if a customer's interaction with you is off the charts but merely okay with the next person in your organization that he deals with.

For customer experience to be great, every interaction at every customer touchpoint must be exceptional. In other words, the whole organization must work together to deliver a great customer experience. This is surprisingly rare, however. In our experience, organizations are pretty fragmented. Marketing is its own domain, separate from sales, which is separate from operations, which is separate from customer service, and so on. If your goal is to significantly improve your customer experience, you have to ensure these functional areas start communicating and working together.

Now move on to the second part of Shaw's definition: "It's the blend of your organization's physical performance [and] the emotions that you create all measured against customer expectations across all of your points of interaction." By "physical performance," Shaw refers to your organization's ability to produce and deliver a good quality product or service. The takeaway here is that if you want to deliver good customer experience, then offering a product or service that works, is reliable, and isn't a pain in the neck to use is a given. It's the bare minimum.

What about "the emotions you create"? Yes, great customer experience means creating and effectively managing your customers' emotions. The fact is, there's not a single interaction that occurs between an organization and its customers that doesn't foster an emotion of some kind. Whether that emotion is deep frustration or sheer delight is largely up to you and how thoughtfully you design, plan, and execute your customer experience.

And of course, there's the "measured against customer expectations across all of your points of interaction" bit. In other words, in delivering a great customer experience, you must consider your customers' expectations. Realize that each of your customer touchpoints affirms or negates the expectations that each customer brings to an interaction.

Moreover, be aware that consumers are quick to transfer their expectations of great customer experience from one industry to another. That means when it comes to delivering a great customer experience, you're not just competing with the store down the street . . . you're up against everyone, everywhere. (And to make matters worse, your customers are likely discussing your shortcomings on every social media channel possible!)

Over the next 300+ pages, this book delves more into what customer experience is and how best to deliver it. In this chapter, we discuss the eight essential steps to creating a great customer experience program, why "the little things" are a big deal, and a few other important topics that you need to understand before you begin the work of creating and consistently delivering a great customer experience.

Eight Steps to Creating a Great Customer Experience Program

There are eight essential components to building a great customer experience program:

1. Developing and deploying your customer experience intent statement
2. Building touchpoint maps
3. Redesigning touchpoints
4. Creating a dialogue with your customers
5. Building customer experience knowledge in the workforce
6. Recognizing and rewarding a job well done
7. Executing an integrated internal communications plan
8. Building a customer experience dashboard

We talk about each of these in detail throughout the book. For now, we give you a quick overview of each step.

Step 1: Developing and deploying your customer experience intent statement

The process of building your customer experience program starts here, with a formal declaration of your desired customer experience through an intent statement. The intent statement directs all subsequent work. Although the intent statement is related to and supportive of brand positioning, it's not a marketing slogan. The intent statement is more akin to a set of engineering schematics. It's a formal, defined set of criteria against which the organization can manage and monitor the delivery of customer experience. For more information on developing your customer experience intent statement, flip to Chapter 6.

Step 2: Building touchpoint maps

If you want to provide excellent customer experience, you need a deep understanding of how your customers interact with your business at each of your individual touchpoints as well as across your entire organization. To gain this understanding, you must map your customer's journey and the touchpoints they interact with along the way. This analysis provides you with a clearer understanding of your customers' experience with your organization. You can find out more about building touchpoint maps in Chapter 7.

Step 3: Redesigning touchpoints

You'll likely need to redesign one, some, or even all of your customer touchpoints to improve the experience your customers are receiving. Fortunately, the redesign process for each touchpoint requires just four weeks, or 20 workdays. No more, no less. (Due to an alarmingly prevalent bureaucratic condition — CADD, or corporate attention deficit disorder — redesign efforts must be very tightly scoped and time-limited.) During this period, the touchpoint redesign team brainstorms, proposes change, and executes on its proposal. In addition to creating change fast, this process also results in a widely dispersed set of enthusiastic customer experience change leaders. For details on this redesign process, turn to Chapter 10.

Step 4: Creating a dialogue with your customers

When it comes to getting feedback from customers, annual surveys are *out,* and constant listening and providing real-time dialogue is *in.* That means you need to inventory where you are listening effectively today, prioritizing your highest-value listening and dialogue touchpoints, and creating a governance model for managing and responding to customer feedback. The end game here is to be able to converse with your customers in near real-time and to respond to customer concerns, problems, and suggestions as they happen. For more on getting feedback from customers, see Chapter 11.

Step 5: Building customer experience knowledge in the workforce

Employees who regularly interact with customers need to understand not only what customer experience your organization intends to deliver (your intent statement), but also how to deliver that experience. Most employees are trained only on the specific functions needed to execute their individual part of their siloed business process. Very few are given real-world, hands-on, practical experience in exactly *how* to deliver great customer experience. That has to change! Chapter 12 discusses the ins and outs of building customer experience knowledge in your workforce.

Step 6: Recognizing and rewarding customer experience done well

Your organization's compensation system telegraphs to all employees what's really important and what isn't. If rewards (compensation and so forth) and recognition programs don't reflect your focus on customer experience, then even your very best efforts to turn your company's culture customer-centric will ultimately fail. The program will also fail if you reward individuals who "make their numbers" but act in a way that ignores or injures the customer experience. Chapter 13 covers the rewards of rewarding correctly.

Step 7: Executing an integrated internal communications plan

If your organization's leaders rarely mention customer concerns, issues, or opportunities, then all the best internal marketing will fall short of fostering significant cultural change. The fact is, making your organization customer-centric is an uphill battle. It is winnable, but significant resources — both financial and philosophical — need to be brought to bear, including a robust internal communications effort. For more on executing an integrated internal communications plan, see Chapter 14.

Step 8: Building a customer experience dashboard

Feel-good customer initiatives are a no-go. These must be replaced with laser-guided projects supported by clear and formal performance metrics with assigned and owned commitments. Real metrics and aggressive goals drive accountability for improvement and help kill misaligned initiatives. To help you keep track of your metrics and data, you'll want to build a highly visible customer experience dashboard and to regularly monitor, review, and discuss each measure it contains. Chapter 15 covers building a customer experience dashboard in more detail.

Little Things Matter More Than You Think

When I (coauthor Roy) was growing up, we spent our summers in rural New England, in the small village of Post Mills, Vermont (population 346). Post Mills didn't have a lot of people, but it did have a tiny airport, which consisted of two grass runways and an old wooden hangar that housed the mechanic's shop and the office for the local flight school.

The flight school was run by a guy named Bob Burbank and his wife, Janie. Bob provided instruction in both powered and sail planes, and also taught aerobatic flying. Janie, a great aviator in her own right, piloted the tow plane whenever Bob took the glider out.

I worked for the flight school for many summers — paid not in cash, but in flight time. It was my job to mow the lawn (including all 2,900 feet of each runway), and to gas and wash the planes. I was also responsible for vacuuming out the dust, dirt, and gravel that inevitably collected in the cockpits of each Cessna and Piper Cub, as well as in the Citabria, which was Bob's stunt aerobatic plane.

Every morning, I rode my bike down to the airport. One day, as I coasted to a stop and leaned my bike against the hangar, Bob was outside waiting for me. This was unusual.

"What'd you have for breakfast?" Bob asked.

"Rice Krispies and a banana," I replied.

"Okay," he said. "Let's go."

This was not the normal routine. But being 14 and having a thirst for adventure, I did as I was told. I climbed into the back seat of the two-seater Citabria stunt plane.

Bob started the fabric-skinned plane and taxied to the head of the grass runway. Then he turned the plane's nose into the wind and applied full throttle. In short order, the plane was in the air. At about 8,500 feet, Bob called out, "All buckled in?"

"Yes!" I replied.

Bob quickly rolled the plane to the right, until we were completely upside-down.

It's an amazing feeling, being upside-down. I don't know — maybe it's all the blood sloshing around in your noggin. Whatever it is, everything slows down and becomes magnified. But this time, something else happened, too: The air in the cockpit became clouded with dust, dirt, and airborne bits of gravel. Clearly, I'd done a poor job vacuuming the cockpit of the plane!

Still upside-down, with the heavier pieces of dirt and gravel now resting on the ceiling, Bob turned around and grinned at me. "Roy," he said. "Sometimes the smallest thing you do can make a really big difference." He went on: "When I'm trying to teach someone to do stunts in the plane, it makes the experience a lot less enjoyable when we have to wait for the air to clear." Lesson learned!

REMEMBER

In customer experience, as in aircraft maintenance, the little things matter a lot — disproportionately so. In fact, they often make the difference between a loyal customer and one who unabashedly takes to the Internet to criticize your company. Be warned!

Avoiding the "Low-Hanging Fruit" Approach

We hear it all the time: "Let's identify the low-hanging fruit and pick that first." In other words, let's figure out which customer experience problems are simple to solve, and deal with them first.

REMEMBER

The problem? Although a few customer experience problems *are* simple to solve, the vast majority aren't. That's because most customer experience problems are the result of complex issues that affect the entire enterprise. Customer experience is a holistic thing, created by many different individuals, processes, and departments, company-wide. Problems with customer experience are overwhelmingly systemic in nature.

Still, taking the quick-fix approach may seem like a good idea — after all, who doesn't want to see results, like, pronto? But this approach often causes yet more problems downstream. It's far more effective to develop comprehensive solutions to your customer experience problems, even if doing so takes more time.

Defining Who Owns the Customer Experience

Does your organization have a chief customer officer — one person who is responsible for ensuring that your customers enjoy a great customer experience? Or is there an ombudsman of sorts — someone who has the power and "air cover" to strongly advocate for the customer's best interest? Probably not.

Only a very few organizations have this role, but most should. In most companies, no one is responsible for managing customer experience in its entirety. In fact, most businesses are so siloed, so internally focused, that the customer — his issues, perspectives, and problems — is rarely even discussed!

Typical employees — whether they're in the executive suite or deep in the trenches — are paid to focus on their discrete slice of the business. Whether they're in IT, HR, operations, sales, marketing, accounting, or what have you, their job is to optimize their piece of the pie, becoming more efficient and effective. This naturally leads to an inside-out, company-centric view, rather than an outside-in, customer-centric focus. If there's no individual or team to formally steward the customer's interest, then over time, customers — individually or collectively — will find themselves neglected or abused.

Customers are a common resource/asset and must be managed as such. Just as most organizations have dedicated asset managers to manage their inventories, physical structures, portfolios, and so on, so, too, should they have employees dedicated to managing customers — making sure their needs are met and their long-term sustainability is ensured.

The "tragedy of the commons"

This phenomenon is not new. In the late 1960s, ecologist Garrett Hardin described it as the "tragedy of the commons." According to Hardin, individuals acting independently and rationally according to their own self-interest will, over time, act in a way that is contrary to the whole group's long-term best interest by depleting common resources. If you replace "individuals" with "departments" (think marketing, sales, or field operations), replace "group" with "company," and replace "common resource" with "customer base," Hardin's theory still applies. (The "customer as common resource" analogy is a good one.) Think about a group of cattle owners, all pasturing their stock on the same piece of land. Or of two or three cities drawing their water from the same aquifer. Eventually, the common resource is going to be in trouble.

REMEMBER

The bottom line? Someone in your organization has to "own" the customer experience. Someone must have a vision of what the customer experience will be and the tools to execute that vision. That's the only way to ensure that the experience will be consistently great.

Think of this person as being like a film director — similar to Steven Spielberg, James Cameron, or Nora Ephron. Just as a film director is responsible for producing a cohesive and engaging film, your "director" of customer experience is in charge of building a cohesive and engaging customer experience program. (Like a film director, some "directors" of customer experience even use storyboards to help others visualize the customer journey. You find out more about the use of storyboards in Chapter 8.)

The Ultimate Competitive Advantage

Not long ago, a client in the Midwest hired us to teach a customer experience training class. As usual, we started the session by going around the room and asking the attendees — about 40 in all — to introduce themselves.

Typically, in this type of exercise, we see two types of people. The first type tells you every last detail about themselves — who they are, where they grew up, the names of their cats, and so on. On the other end of the continuum are the second type — people who mumble their name and little else.

On this particular day, we discovered a third type, in the form of a young woman named Raven. When her turn came around, she stood up, smiled broadly, and declared, "Hi. My name is Raven, and I am awesome." She took a measured breath, completely in control of the room, and continued. "I love my customers, and by the time I'm done with them, they love me too." For a moment, there was complete silence in the room. Then someone laughed. "That is so true," the person said. "Everyone loves her!"

Employees like Raven represent your organization's competitive advantage. In an era when almost every part of your business can be quickly copied by a competitor, your ability to consistently deliver a great experience represents a key competitive advantage. Raven, and employees like her, enable you to do just that.

In their excellent book, *The Discipline of Market Leaders,* authors Michael Treacy and Fred Wiersema identify three distinct points of competitive differentiation:

- **Operational excellence:** Companies dedicated to operational excellence focus on superb operations and execution. Often, they do this by providing a reasonable quality product or service while leading their industry in price and convenience. The focus is on increasing efficiency, effectively managing the supply chain, streamlining operations, minimizing overhead costs, and optimizing processes. Examples of companies that take this approach include Wal-Mart and Federal Express.
- **Product leadership:** Companies who seek product leadership focus on strong product and service development; innovation; creative design; and crisp, current, and exciting brand marketing. Companies who strive to compete in this area seek to churn out a steady stream of state-of-the-art products and services. Examples of companies that take this approach include Apple and Google.
- **Customer intimacy:** Companies seeking customer intimacy focus on customer attention, service, and experience. They work to deliver highly personalized products and services. The goal for these companies is to deliver products and services that exceed the customer's expectations and to create deep and lasting relationships. Examples of companies that take this approach include Nordstrom, USAA, and The Ritz-Carlton.

According to Treacy and Wiersema, every company should focus on one of these three points of competitive differentiation. That doesn't mean that the other two points can be ignored, just that when a strategic investment is made, it should be done to strengthen the principal competitive differentiator.

The only problem? Treacy and Wiersema published their book in the mid 1990s — and a lot has changed since then! Gone are the days when a company can put customer intimacy, or experience, on the back burner.

In the 20 years since the release of *The Discipline of Market Leaders,* customers have become more sophisticated, and their expectations have continued to rise. Customers expect to be remembered, recognized, and treated as *the* most important aspect of your organization's success, not to be viewed as a number, a transaction, or merely a part of a company's processes.

Consistently delivering a compelling customer experience is the ultimate competitive advantage. An organization of customer-focused employees, processes, and touchpoints is nearly impossible to defeat. This book's objective is to reveal the tools and strategies you need to achieve this, as well as how to convince key decision-makers of the need to do so.

Are you ready to provide an incredible experience for your customers? Then read on!

Chapter 2

Dollars and Sense: The Financial Impact of Customer Experience

In This Chapter

- Recognizing the customer/financial results logic path
- Getting a high-level view of the benefits of an excellent customer experience
- Looking at key customer metrics and using correlation analysis
- Using customer experience to mold the "perfect customer"
- Understanding the high price of poor customer experience

The late, great Peter Drucker — world-renowned management consultant and prolific author — once said, "The purpose of business is to create and keep a customer." Which is why you see so many CEOs, CFOs, and others in the upper ranks of business leadership take to the podium during the quarterly meeting to exhort their troops to deliver the best customer service and experience possible.

And yet, when push comes to shove — when hard decisions, including ones that pertain to financial investments, need to be made — these same leaders are often reluctant to put their money where their mouth is. They'll spend millions of dollars on infrastructure rebuilds, marketing campaigns, and other miscellaneous initiatives, but nothing on the customer. Why is that?

In large part, the answer to this question lies in the short-term financial view forced by Wall Street's incessant short-term focus on quarterly earnings. But in reality, financial results are nothing more than an output that reflects the company's activity as a whole. If you want to produce better, sustainable financial results in the long-term, you must work to improve each of the individual elements that produce those results — including customer experience.

In this chapter, you discover how to build a business case for investment in customer experience and prove its value — both in the long term and the short term.

Follow the Arrows! The Business Logic Path

As we said, focusing only on finances misses the point. This view that only finances matter, often referred to as "short-termism," was the subject of an article in the *Washington Post* by journalist Neil Irwin, titled "How the Cult of Shareholder Value Wrecked American Business." Irwin writes:

> The imperative to boost near-term profits and share prices is a self-reinforcing cycle in which corporate time horizons have become shorter and shorter . . . And the willingness of executives to sacrifice short-term profits to make long-term investments is rapidly disappearing . . .
> A recent study by the consultants at McKinsey & Co. and Canada's public pension board found alarming levels of short-termism in the corporate executive suite. They reported that nearly 80 percent of top executives and directors reported feeling most pressured to demonstrate a strong financial performance over a period of two years or less, with only 7 percent feeling pressure to deliver a strong performance over a period of five years or more. They also found that 55 percent of chief financial officers would forgo an attractive investment project today if it would cause the company to even marginally miss its quarterly earnings target.

Translation: No one wants to think long-term. But if all you're concerned about is appeasing shareholders on a quarterly basis, then you won't be able to focus on anything but the financials. It's a little like focusing on the tip of a dog's tail but overlooking his overall health.

So what do we recommend? Keep an eye on the entire value chain that produces the financial results your organization is seeking. Financial results don't just happen — they're the result of a logical set of interactions among your employees, the business processes they operate, the technology that enables their work, and your customers' outcomes. At the very end of this synergist path are the financial results. The business logic path isn't rocket science. It's more like cooking. You need all of these ingredients in place to make sure the recipe comes out right. The business logic path is illustrated in Figure 2-1.

In more than 30 years of working with dozens of different companies from all sorts of industries, we've never had anyone dispute the logic of this diagram. No one. So why don't leaders pay more attention to all the inputs, like customer experience, instead of just focusing on financial results? The likely reason is that improving inputs is boring. Worse, making *real* progress improving them takes substantive and detailed effort over a fairly long period of time.

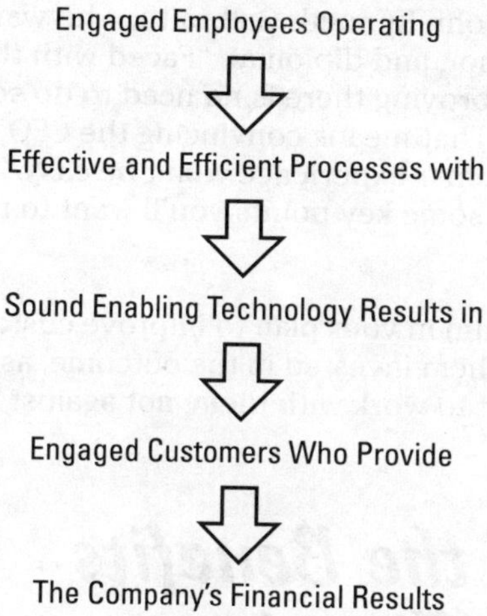

Illustration courtesy of Roy Barnes.

Figure 2-1: The financial results logic path.

Unfortunately, sustained and substantive work — even when proven to substantially move the financial needle — is not the forte of most CEOs. Nevertheless, *someone* in senior leadership has to pay attention to these inputs, including customer experience. Otherwise, it will never become a priority. But who?

Heavens to Bestie: Making the CFO Your BFF

Who should you enlist to support your customer experience efforts? Simple. The chief financial officer (CFO).

Yes, we know. *Nobody* likes the CFO. After all, the CFO's very job is to shoot down hare-brained ideas generated by people like us. But they're not bad people; they just require you to prove the return on investment for any idea you propose.

No one — especially not your CFO — is going to take it "on faith" that improving customer experience will deliver better financial results for your organization. To get your CFO onboard, you must put together a logical, reasoned, coherent, and quantifiable business case for investment in customer experience. Think of your CFO as a venture capitalist. You have to tell her a compelling story, and you must have the numbers to back up your ideas.

Be warned, however: As noted by John Kenneth Galbraith, who was an economist, author, Harvard professor, and diplomat, "Faced with the choice between changing one's mind and proving there is no need to do so, almost everyone gets busy on the proof." That means convincing the CFO — or anyone else — of the value of customer experience won't be easy. To help you, the following sections outline some key points you'll want to make in your business case.

TIP

Try to involve your CFO and her team in your plan to improve customer experience as early as possible. To get them invested in the outcome, ask for their input and advice up front. You want to work with them, not against them!

A High-Level View of the Benefits of Excellent Customer Experience

In 2011, Forrester Research built a model that predicted what would happen if a company improved its customer experience from below average to above average. Incredibly, this model revealed that in certain industries, a better customer experience could result in $1.3 billion in additional annual revenue. More than a billion dollars! Annually!

In 2013, Watermark Consulting took Forrester's research a step further. It studied the total returns for two model stock portfolios composed of the top ten customer experience companies. Here's what it found:

> For the 6-year period from 2007–2012, the Customer Experience Leaders outperformed the broader market, generating a total return that was three times higher on average than the S&P 500 Index. Furthermore, while the (top ten) Customer Experience Leaders handily beat the S&P 500, the (bottom ten) Laggards trailed it by a wide margin.

According to Jon Picoult, Watermark's founder, leaders in customer experience had better retention rates, greater wallet share, and all-around more cost-efficient processes and services. We'll leave it to you to imagine the poor results for those companies at the opposite end of the spectrum!

Along similar lines, the Temkin Group also performed a large-scale study pertaining to customer experience — in this case, proving the high correlation between customer experience and loyalty. The Temkin team found that customer experience leaders enjoy a 15 percent advantage over customer experience laggards in consumers' willingness to purchase, their *stickiness* (that is, their reluctance to switch to a competitor), and their likelihood to recommend your offerings to others.

Metric System: Key Customer Metrics

You need more than a high-level view to sway your CFO to your way of thinking about customer experience. You also need some hard facts about customer experience in your own organization.

First and foremost, you want to convey how your customers rate you on three key metrics. (Note that you glean these ratings by conducting regular customer surveys. Ideally, these should occur at least quarterly, although more frequent feedback enables you to address customer issues more quickly.)

- **Likelihood to recommend:** This measures how likely a customer is to recommend your company to friends or colleagues. Customers who respond with a high rating are among your most loyal. Not only do they basically provide you with free advertising when they recommend your company to others, but they're also less likely to share negative feedback about you on your website or on social media.
- **Likelihood to switch to a competitor:** This reveals how likely a customer is to take his business elsewhere. These days, customers can switch from you to your competitor with the click of a mouse. That makes your efforts to retain customers even more important! It only takes one bad experience to drive a customer away . . . and if a competitor responds by providing that customer with an excellent customer experience, rest assured he will be even less likely to return to you.
- **Likelihood to repurchase:** This reveals how likely a customer is to purchase from you again. If a customer has a good experience with your company, that customer will be much more willing to buy from you again!

By themselves, these three key metrics offer a good indication of how your customers feel about their experience with your company. But they get even more interesting when you start finding linkages between these and other measures, such as overall customer experience. After all, what drives a customer's willingness to refer your company to others? Yep, you guessed it: a great customer experience.

What we've found, almost without fail, is a strong positive correlation between a customer's overall experience and how highly she scores an organization on these three key metrics. Put another way, if you improve customer experience, you also improve likelihood to recommend and likelihood to repurchase, and you diminish the likelihood to switch to a competitor.

This is a big deal. Why? Because this is the kind of information that can grab the attention of your CFO and CEO. After all, they know in dollars and cents what it means for a customer to refer your company to a friend, to *not* switch to your competitor, and to purchase from you again — *without* the expense of additional marketing dollars.

Analyze This: Using Correlation Analysis

Naturally, you, your CFO, and your CEO are probably wondering just how much you have to improve your customer experience score to move the three key metrics discussed in the previous section. To figure this out, you need to perform correlation analysis.

Correlation is simply the relationship or connection between two things. For us, chocolate and a happy life are highly correlated. The more chocolate we eat, the happier we are. Mushrooms and a happy life are also highly correlated, but in an inverse manner. The more mushrooms we are forced to eat (or look at or be in the same room as), the unhappier we become. Both of these examples have what data geeks call a "strong correlation."

When correlations are calculated mathematically, the result is a correlation coefficient. A *correlation coefficient* is a number between –1 and +1 that measures the degree of association, connectedness, or linkage between the two variables. Correlations above 0.7 or below –0.7 are considered to be strong. We'd calculate our aforementioned chocolate/happiness correlation at +0.9999 — in other words, strong on the positive side. Our mushroom/happiness correlation, however, would be a solid –1.0 — strong on the negative side.

In recent years, researchers have proven a strong correlation between various elements of customer experience and the three key metrics discussed in the previous section — recommend, switch, and repurchase. While correlation does not mean causation, it does mean that with robust data about your customer's experience, you can begin to make logical connections between experience and financial results.

The question becomes, which activities and initiatives will have the biggest impact on customer experience — and by extension, on the aforementioned key metrics? To answer this, you must test, test, and test some more. Start by looking at all the different correlations between your various experience metrics and financial metrics. Which experiences move which financial metrics?

During this process, you want to meet with the strongest analytics people in your organization. Ask them questions like, "What is the repurchase behavior for customers who score an 85 percent in overall customer experience/satisfaction compared to those who score an 86 percent in overall customer experience/satisfaction?" Answering this question enables you to calculate the financial payoff (in terms of repurchase) for each percentage point of improvement in overall customer experience. This should in turn help you determine which customer experience initiatives you may want to tackle first. For example, suppose you have two different initiatives, each of which costs the same amount of money, but you can fund only one of them at a time. Initiative A may lead to a three-point increase in customer experience, but Initiative B will lead to a five-point increase. In this scenario, we'd advise you to pursue Initiative B and execute like crazy in the hopes you'll see the additional boost.

Here's another question you should ask: If you can move the overall customer engagement score by 1, 2, 5, or 10 percent, what happens to customers' price sensitivity? If you can prove that happier, more engaged customers are less sensitive to price increases (which they often are), we practically guarantee your CFO will take you out to lunch. And maybe even pay.

When you get in the habit of probing for the correlations across various metrics, you begin to legitimize your organization's investment in customer experience. Be curious. Ask "dumb" questions; don't be afraid to test all sorts of variables to see which ones yield the best results. What you're looking to find out is what happens to each of your financial metrics when you modify their inputs.

For an example, see Figure 2-2. Here, it's been determined that touchpoints #1, #3, and #5 are the most influential in driving a customer's intent to repurchase. (A *touchpoint* is any point where the customer and company interact.) If the organization wants to improve this repurchase metric, then it would likely be smart to focus its redesign efforts on these most impactful touchpoints, placing less impactful touchpoints lower down the list. Similar analysis could be conducted to determine which touchpoints are most influential in the "intent to refer" and "reduce likelihood to switch" metrics.

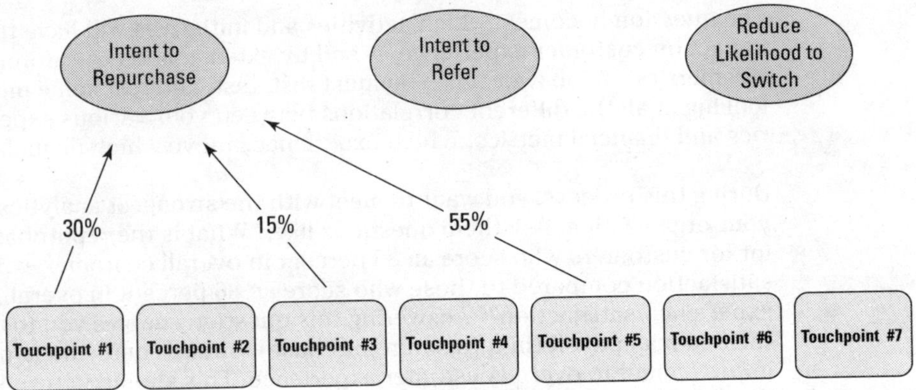

Figure 2-2: Touchpoints #1, #3, and #5 have the most impact on the "intent to repurchase" metric.

Illustration courtesy of Roy Barnes.

Sheer Perfection: Using Customer Experience to Mold the "Perfect Customer"

Yes, we know. Nobody's perfect. But some customers come pretty darned close. These so-called "perfect customers" behave in ways that save your company money. For example, suppose you work for a utility company. In that case, your "perfect customer" might behave as follows:

- **He'd never contact the call center.** For some companies, the cost of running a call center can run $12 to $15 per call! If your organization fields thousands or millions of calls a year, even a modest decrease in the number of customers calling in can save *beaucoup* bucks.
- **He'd use self-service options whenever possible.** Self-service options enable customers to find information and solve problems without the help of a human — and therefore at no (or low) cost to the utility.
- **He'd set up his checking account for automatic withdrawals to pay his bill.** No more late payments! This helps cash flow immeasurably.
- **He'd elect to receive bills electronically.** Sending out thousands of bills each month via U.S. Mail can cost a pretty penny! Having customers switch to e-billing saves the sample utility company a ton of cash.
- **He'd use seasonal billing.** This would allow for a predictable monthly bill throughout the year. If customers start their seasonal billing during a month when they don't use much energy, they may pay more than normal for a couple of months until higher-usage months start. This can help the overall cash flow.

- **He'd allow the installation of load-balancing equipment at his home or business.** Where we live in Florida, the utility company asked if it could install load-balancing equipment on my hot water heater, air conditioning units, and pool pumps. This equipment allows the utility to "brown out" my electrical needs during times of higher demand. In this way, the utility can serve more customers, more effectively, even at times of peak usage. Although I don't *have* to have this equipment in my home, I let the utility company install it because it saves me a few dollars and I like to help out. So yes, I'm a "perfect" customer!
- **He'd welcome new technologies, like smart metering.** In many cases, in order for a utility company to install new technologies at its customers' homes and businesses, it needs permission from the customer. Getting permission means having a good relationship. And having a good relationship necessitates that a good experience has been previously provided!
- **He'd upgrade inefficient equipment.** It sounds crazy, but many utilities don't want their customers to use more energy. Perhaps those companies can't or don't want to build more capacity. These companies must prod their customers to save energy and be as efficient as possible.

If you could persuade more of your customers to exhibit even one of these "perfect" behaviors — for example, using e-billing rather than opting to receive a paper bill — the results could be significant! For example, suppose that only 16 percent of current customers use e-billing, while the current best-in-class for similar-sized utilities is 84 percent. Suppose further that for each customer who uses e-billing, your company saves $11 per year. If your company were to move from 16 percent to 84 percent e-billing, it would save a whopping $3,470,000! Of course, immediately achieving best-in-class results is probably unrealistic. Nonetheless, getting even halfway there would represent a significant cost savings. And if you were able to persuade customers to display *all* the aforementioned behaviors? Your organization might well save tens of millions of dollars, depending on its size!

So how do you change these behaviors? Simple. If you improve customer experience, then you will improve the quality and strength of your relationship with the customer. And if you do that, then you can begin to modify customer behavior in directions that make the company more money. Oh, and one more thing: Research shows that customers who exhibit a greater number of "perfect" behaviors also tend to have significantly higher overall customer satisfaction scores. This makes sense at an intuitive level. After all, if you involve the customer in more things your organization does, her engagement scores will increase. Figure 2.3 shows how all this works.

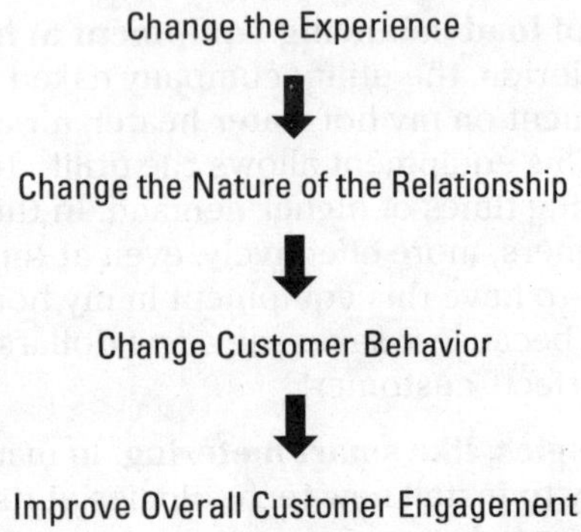

Figure 2-3: Building the "perfect customer."

Illustration courtesy of Roy Barnes.

Obviously, unless you work for a utility company, your "perfect customer" will display a different set of behaviors than the ones discussed in this section. To pinpoint what those behaviors are, gather a group of relatively senior people from a broad cross-section of your company and ask them this question:

> If we could get our customers to behave in ways that would make our company more money (either because customers would be cheaper to serve or because they would spend more), what would we like them to do or not do?

Recently, we posed this question to senior employees at a telecommunications client and unearthed more than 45 different "perfect customer" behaviors. When the cost of each of these behaviors was then determined, the client discovered an additional $8 million in recoverable cost dollars. Needless to say, the CFO was very happy!

REMEMBER: A sound customer-experience strategy yields positive benefits on both sides of the profit and loss statement. On the one side, engaged and happy customers are more likely to buy more and refer others to you, and are less likely to switch to a competitor. On the other hand, thoughtful experience design, done with the goal of modifying customer behaviors, can help you lower operational costs in customer-facing processes.

That'll Cost You: The High Price of Poor Customer Experience

If you can't persuade your CFO and other senior leaders of the value of great customer experience, then scare tactics may be your only option. In other words, you'll have to show them how poor customer experience can hurt your bottom line — and help that of your competitors. Here are some handy statistics:

- Studies suggest that failing to deliver a high-quality customer experience can result in an erosion of your company's customer base by as much as 50 percent over a five-year period.
- After enduring a poor customer experience, 88 percent of consumers do business with a competitor.
- Poor customer experience has caused 78 percent of consumers to bail on a transaction.
- Given the opportunity, 60 percent of Americans would try a new brand for a better service experience.
- Dissatisfied customers are mouthy. Witness: Some 13 percent of dissatisfied customers tell more than 20 people of their bad experience, while 61 percent tell between 5 and 7.

Chapter 3

Identifying Customer Experience Killers

In This Chapter

- Identifying three common problems that kill customer experience
- Understanding the danger of an inside-out perspective
- Thinking about industry perception
- Keeping pace with customer expectations

Sometimes, to really wrap your mind around something like great customer experience, it helps to identify what it *isn't*. For example, great customer experience isn't inconsistent. It isn't transactional. It isn't emotionless or boring. It isn't unplanned or random.

"Great!" you're thinking. "All we have to do is *not* be those things, and we'll be fine!" Well, yes. The problem is, the way many organizations are structured stands in opposition to creating a great customer experience. But that's not the only roadblock. This chapter discusses some of the things that get in the way of delivering a great experience. Some are easy to recognize, but most require some work to fix. Some are your own organization's fault, but others you can justifiably blame on your competitors. Regardless, before you continue on your journey to improve your organization's customer experience, you need to confront some of these foundational problems.

Three Universal Actions That Kill Customer Experience

Do your customers view their experience with your company the same way the American public views Congress — with disdain? If so, it's likely due to one of three experience-killing actions. These culprits are as follows:

- The know-nothing ninja
- The shuffling assassin
- The ownership killer

We give you the lowdown on each of these experience killers in the following sections.

The know-nothing ninja

This killer quietly appears when an organization can't step into its customers' lives and understand their real needs — to walk a mile in their shoes, so to speak. The truth is, many companies suffer from the inability to get out of their own heads and put themselves in the customers' mindset.

Too often, like ships passing in the night, what companies think is important to their customers isn't. So, while you should have two entities (customer and company) that understand each other perfectly, in many cases both parties are making incorrect assumptions about each other. Several years ago, a client's quality of service survey brought this sad reality to light. The survey asked customers to choose which attributes of this particular company were most important to them: responsiveness, product and service expertise, or personalization.

The customers' answer? Responsiveness — that is, they wanted the company to respond quickly and appropriately to their needs. But when the leaders of the same company were asked what attribute their customers would pick, their overwhelming response was product and service expertise. This company and its customers were on paths that didn't intersect.

We're not saying that all customers in every industry would choose responsiveness as their favorite attribute. For some industries, timeliness or personalization might be more important. The point is that too many companies don't dig deep enough to recognize what their customers want most from them, resulting in an experience miss. And that missed opportunity represents an experience killer.

It's easier said than done, but with practice, understanding your customers' needs can become second nature. As a first step, imagine that *you* are the customer, and you're interacting with the company at its various touchpoints. Become the customer. Do what he does, see what he sees, and hear what he hears.

A know-nothing case study

I (coauthor Roy) experienced an experience miss during a recent business trip. After a long day working with my client, I was heading back to my hotel when suddenly, hunger hit. I wanted some dinner, pronto! I spotted a steakhouse in a strip mall and pulled in.

When I got inside, I made for the bar. The bartender came right up. I told him I was in a bit of a rush, so he quickly took my order: a New York strip steak, cooked medium; a baked potato, loaded; and a beer, cold. Moments later, the beer arrived. It was so cold that it was as if it had been brewed in the Arctic. Fifteen minutes later, the food arrived. The baked potato was steaming like a volcano — butter, sour cream, chives, and bacon, all melting into a little puddle of goodness. The steak looked great — thick and juicy. My mouth watering, I cut off a piece and popped it into my mouth . . . only to find that it was cold in the middle. Now, although it wasn't so cold that I wouldn't have finished it, it certainly wasn't what I had expected.

Noticing the frown on my face, Eric, the bartender, asked what was wrong. "The potato is wonderful, and the beer is ice cold, but the steak's a bit chilly in the middle." Looking appropriately concerned, Eric replied, "We're a steakhouse; the steak should be perfect. Let's put another one on the grill for you." But by then it was 7:45, and I was ravenous. "No," I said. "That's okay. I'll just eat it as it is."

Eric wouldn't take no for an answer. "Really," he said. "Let me put another one on the grill for you. It'll just take a minute."

"No need," I said. "It's fine. Besides, it'll take longer than a minute, I'm in a rush, and I'm really hungry."

But Eric was insistent. "I want you to be happy," he said. "I'm going to have them put another steak on the grill for you, and as soon as it's ready, I'll bring it out."

At this point, I realized that Eric wasn't really listening to me. He had been taught his canned response — what he was supposed to do if a customer had a problem with his steak. Exasperated, I said, "Eric, I'm going to eat this one. Let's just leave it at that."

Two minutes later, I felt a light tap on my shoulder. I swiveled around to find a young woman standing there, dressed all in black, like a ninja assassin. Presumably, this was the restaurant manager. "Hi," she said in a very pleasant tone. "I'm Katie. I understand you're not happy with your steak. We're going to put another one on the grill for you."

Despite my best efforts to enlighten them — "No, really, the one I have is fine" — they were pretty certain they knew how to solve my problem. Clearly, I just needed to have a new steak put on the grill! Did they make any effort to understand my concerns? No. Did they put themselves in my shoes to understand what I needed from them? Nope. What did I need? An apology would have sufficed. You might be thinking, "It's the thought that counts, right?" Wrong. Listening is what counts. Paying attention to your customers' real needs is what counts. Prepackaged solutions are nice, but they don't really cut it.

Before you start, determine the following:

- As the customer, what is your issue?
- What are you trying to accomplish?
- As the customer, what is your emotional state of mind/your mood?

Then interact with each of your company's touchpoints, one by one. This may include visiting your company's website, stopping by one of its brick-and-mortar sites, and contacting its call center.

Visiting your company's website

As the customer, when you visit your company's website, ask yourself the following questions:

- **Can you navigate around with ease?** You should never have to wonder where to find something. It should be obvious. Is the next step self-evident?
- **Can you follow a path of inquiry and see where it leads?** Don't let customers get lost on your website. Make sure it's easy to get back where they were.
- **Do the embedded links go where they're supposed to go?** It's amazing how often you find dead links — that is, links that don't lead anywhere. You should keep links fresh.
- **Does anything confuse you?** If your goal is for visitors to stick around for a while, you want to make sure they don't get confused. Confusion leads to frustration, and frustration leads to that user looking to your competitors to find what she needs!
- **Can you find the information you're looking for?** Your site should be well organized, with the information presented in an obvious, logical way. Information should also be searchable.
- **Are items up-to-date?** Every so often, we stumble on a site that apparently was last updated during the Flintstone era. When items are obviously out-of-date, your whole operation looks unprofessional! Better to have no website at all than one that's not kept up-to-date.
- **Do videos and pages load quickly and work correctly?** Your website should be optimized such that everything loads quickly and works correctly. Otherwise, expect to see a lot of customers lose patience and go elsewhere.

TIP

If you sell anything through your company's website, also make a point of stepping through the order process. How is that experience? Here are some really basic things to look for:

- Can you see what's in your cart without having to start the checkout process?
- After putting an item in your cart, can you continue shopping with ease? Or are you essentially forced to check out?
- Are you asked for very detailed information before being allowed to browse products and prices? This type of data-gathering can really turn off potential buyers. Purchasing should be easy, not an inquisition!

Stopping by a brick-and-mortar location

If your company has brick-and-mortar locations that accommodate customers — for example, a store, a service center, or what have you — then make it a point to stop by. When you do, ask yourself the following questions:

- **How does your signage look?** Is it clear and fresh looking? Does it work properly? It's amazing how many lit signs are missing bulbs or flickering. Does no one who works there notice?
- **What does the landscaping look like?** Make sure it's neat, attractive, and welcoming.
- **Is it obvious where to park?** No one wants to waste time driving around trying to figure out where to park. The customer may decide it's easier to just go elsewhere.
- **What is the very first thing you notice when you arrive?** Make sure things are orderly and "ready for business."
- **What's your first impression on entering?** What do you see? What do you smell? What do you hear? Is this what you expected? Does it deliver your experience intent?
- **Is the facility dirty or untidy?** You'd be amazed how many employees become blind to grime and clutter in the workplace.
- **Are you greeted?** By whom? What is that person's attitude?
- **Are the employees dressed appropriately?** Employees should be aware of your company's dress code and abide by it.
- **Are the employees wearing name tags?** Customers should be able to readily identify employees by name.

Contacting your call center

Many large organizations have call centers. If yours is one such organization, call into it to assess how effectively it operates from the customer's point of view. When you do, ask yourself these questions:

- Was it easy to find the call center's phone number?
- How long was it before the phone was answered?
- Were you placed on hold?
- Were you transferred? How many times?
- How much noise was there in the background? What was the quality of the phone line?
- What was the on-hold music like?
- How was the demeanor of the various representatives with whom you spoke? Pleasant? Helpful? Rude? Hurried?

Assessing your company's reputation online

These days, loads of people use the Internet to gather information about a product or service before making a purchase. Often, this means visiting peer-review websites such as Yelp (`www.yelp.com`), TripAdvisor (`www.tripadvisor.com`), and Angie's List (`www.angieslist.com`). It also means asking their friends and followers on social media sites such as Facebook (`www.facebook.com`) and Twitter (`www.twitter.com`). To get a sense of how your company stacks up, do the following:

- Pull up your web browser and type the following: *your company/product name* and *reviews*. This will likely lead you to loads of links to reviews of your company or product. (Brace yourself. Odds are, they aren't all glowing.)
- Read customer comments on your organization's social media channels (Twitter, Facebook, and so on).
- Visit chat rooms and discussion boards where your organization may be discussed and read what people are saying about you, your products and services, your reputation, and so on.

TIP

Customers aren't the only ones who are talking about you online. Your employees are doing it, too. Be sure to search for comments about your company on employer-review sites such as Glassdoor (`www.glassdoor.com`), Rate My Employer (`www.ratemyemployer.ca`), Job Advisor (`www.jobadvisor.com.au`), JobeeHive (`www.jobeehive.com`), and others.

General questions

Regardless of which touchpoint you're assessing, you'll also want to ask yourself the following questions, as if you were the customer, during each interaction:

- Why am I at this point of interaction with the company?
- What am I trying to accomplish with this interaction?
- What will happen to me if I don't accomplish this?

- What interaction did I just complete?
- What will happen to me next?
- How did I feel during this interaction?

To prevent a needs disconnect in your business, you must see, feel, and interact with your company from the customer's perspective. Forget about everything behind the scenes; just be the customer and experience the interaction. We guarantee you'll never look at your business the same way again!

The shuffling assassin

What do customers want? Lots of things. But at the top of the list is for it to be easy to do business with you. Unfortunately, however, this wish doesn't always come true, particularly if the customer runs into a problem. Often, something that seems like it should be very simple to fix winds up taking hours, days, or even weeks because organizations end up shuffling their customers around.

More often than not, this is a result of companies having an inside-out view. (More on that in the later section "Battling the Inside-Out Perspective.")

Sometimes, business processes that work just fine from an internal perspective are a nightmare for customers to navigate. And herein lies the root of the shuffling assassin experience killer.

What causes this kind of experience killer? Nine times out of ten, it's due to how most companies are structured organizationally. Typically, the bigger and more complex an organization is, the more likely it is for parts of the company to specialize in certain technical functions. This compartmentalization may lead to enhanced technical proficiency but it often results in the creation of isolated functional silos — what we call a *castle mentality.*

What do we mean by this? The way we see it, many mid-size to large organizations operate more like a group of individual castles dotting the landscape than as an integrated whole, working together to serve the needs of their customers. Worse, the inhabitants of each castle don't particularly like those other employees who live in the other castles. Yes, they work for the same company but they are not "their people"; they are "others."

To see what we mean, think of what a castle looks like. What's the first thing you notice? Yes, there are thick stone walls with towers along the top. Good for self-defense around budget time. And yes, the windows are probably pretty small — the better to shoot arrows from without exposing oneself to danger. But the feature we're thinking of is the moat.

In most cases, the inhabitants of a castle, like the members of an organizational department, don't really want outside visitors. After all, if you're happily ensconced in your Operations Castle, do you really want someone from the HR Castle dropping in to visit? No. How about IT? Nope. Folks from the Legal Castle . . . heaven forbid! That's what the moat is for: to keep people out. But the moat also keeps people in. Thanks to the moat, what happens in the castle *stays* in the castle, and each castle ends up creating its own mini-culture within the broader organization.

So where is the customer in all this? Odds are, he's stuck being shuffled from castle to castle — that is, between different departments, agents, or levels of support — in an attempt to resolve his problem. Nothing kills customer experience quite like getting shuffled! This seemingly endless shuffling is a major experience killer.

Imagine this scenario: You experience a problem with a product or service, so you contact the provider's call center for help. You explain your problem to the individual who answers the phone. She in turn asks you several questions to assess your needs. She then determines who in her organization can help you, and transfers you to that person.

Now, depending on what type of organization you're dealing with, you'll get either a warm transfer or a cold transfer. With a *warm transfer,* the person with whom you were speaking introduces you to the person you'll talk to next. That's the nicest option. More likely, you'll be cold transferred. With a *cold transfer,* the person you're talking to says something along the lines of, "I can't help you. You'll need to talk to someone in another department. Let me transfer you." Then you hear a click followed by silence. Assuming you haven't been hung up on by accident, you'll eventually be connected with the next agent, at which point you'll have to explain your problem all over again. This may happen any number of times.

You can be shuffled for all sorts of reasons. Typically, however, it's because of the way in which a particular company has decided to segment its customer response, using a system of escalation parameters to connect you and your problem to the person who can solve it. The result? A lousy customer experience.

To beat the shuffling problem, you need to think about all the different kinds of customer support you offer. Then decide how many transfers are acceptable for a customer to get her problem solved. Here are some quick tips:

- Make it easy for customers (and prospective customers) to contact you in the way that works best for them. You want to be able to address most common customer concerns with one click, text, call, or email.

- Take a hard look at your integrated voice response (IVR) system to make sure it isn't unnecessarily convoluted. Better yet, have an actual living human answer the phones. Many of our clients have restructured or completely eliminated their IVRs, while cutting average customer response time in half.
- Have the employee who first connects with a customer stay with that customer all the way through the resolution of his problem.
- Make sure information about your products and services is updated, accurate, and easy to access.
- Make it easy for customers to determine which product or service is the best fit. That means enabling customers to easily compare your offerings (and those of your competitors). Be sure your product and service specifications are standard within both your organization and your industry.

A shuffling assassin case study

One weekend, my family and I (coauthor Roy) were watching TV when, all of a sudden, the cable connection quit. In an attempt to fix it, I did everything I knew to do in an attempt to restore service, including the standard "turn off the router for the requisite 10 seconds and turn it back on" routine to reset the cable box. No dice.

I called the cable company and explained my problem to the call center representative. "Okay," she said. "I'm going to need you to try resetting the cable box."

"I've already done that," I replied.

"Yes," she said. "But I need you to try it again." I was frustrated, but I obliged — after which she said, "I'm going to need to transfer you to technical support." She then put me on hold, where I remained for several minutes until a technical support representative came on the line.

"Technical support," he said. "Can I help you?"

"Yes," I answered, and explained my problem yet again.

"Okay," the technician said. "I'm going to have you reset your router."

"I've already reset my router. Twice."

"I understand," he said. "But I need to have you do it one more time for me."

Needless to say, he couldn't help. And I bet you can guess what happened next: I got transferred — this time to "scheduling," where I was on hold for 11 minutes. When an employee in that department finally answered the phone, she began with a pleasant "Hello. How can I help you?"

You get the picture. I was being shuffled. The funny thing about it was, all of this was going on right in the middle of a heavy marking blitz by the cable provider, which was in the process of rebranding its entire organization. Its new tagline was "Hello Friend." But would a "friend" shuffle you from person to person like that? I don't think so.

The ownership killer

Many companies simply don't see the importance of the ongoing customer experience over time as it relates to their product or service. Too many organizational leaders are myopically focused on one thing and one thing only: the product. How much does it cost to produce it? Is the product meeting our quality standards? On and on it goes. And while a good — even great — product might be produced, if the customer's experience of learning about the product, buying it, and setting it up and maintaining it is difficult, it doesn't really matter. If the ongoing ownership and use of a product or service is nothing but trouble, customers will leave you and never come back.

Customers are fickle, flighty, and downright picky about every aspect of the ownership experience (not just the product) — and rightfully so. Need an example? Consider Toyota. For years, Toyota had a reputation for extraordinary product quality. But the experience of going to a Toyota dealership for service after purchase was abysmal. Indeed, the ongoing ownership experience was so bad, it led many customers to not buy in the first place. The experience of Toyota's physical product was entirely disconnected from the reality of ongoing ownership.

All parts of the experience need to be integrated. And together, they must tell a coherent and consistent story of who you are as an organization.

As you try to assess whether your organization faces an ownership experience killer, ask yourself two really tough questions:

- What is it that is uniquely different about what you are offering?
- What is your customer's experience using your products and services?

Your answers to these questions will help you determine whether you are creating an experience disconnect with your policies, procedures, and methods. If you are, you're not alone — the reality is, most companies are. It's hard not to when an organization is castled or siloed, acting as a group of independent entities rather than as a cohesive whole.

We live in a global economic marketplace where most products and services can be copied with ease and at frightening speeds. In the old days, it was months or even years after a company released some new, innovative product before competitors were able to copy its creations. Now, it happens in a matter of weeks or even days. How do you stay in business when someone can replicate your product or service in less time than it takes to hatch a colony of sea monkeys? The only long-term sustainable differentiator is to purposefully design and consistently execute an extraordinarily thoughtful customer experience. It's very difficult to copy authentic care, honest-to-goodness customer service, and engagement. That's why it's so powerful.

An ownership experience case study

I (coauthor Roy) travel a lot. As a result, I used to miss the occasional bill. Often, a bill would arrive in the mail while I was away, and I wouldn't get to it in time. I was delighted when, several years ago, auto bill-pay came along. I set it up for all my bills. When the due date came, the funds were automatically withdrawn from my checking account and sent to the creditor. It saved me loads of late fees!

Recently, I received a new credit card to replace one I had lost in my travels, but I forgot to update the auto-pay for the new card. When the bill came due, my auto-pay attempted to pay it. However, because I hadn't updated the credit card number in the auto-pay settings, the attempt failed. The bank notified me of this via email, but the message wound up in my email program's junk folder and I never saw it.

A couple months later, the bank called me to tell me my credit card account was past due. I immediately went online to make a payment, but was locked out of the system. "Okay," I thought. "I'll just go to my local branch to straighten this out."

Mind you, I had banked with this company for more than 17 years. I had five accounts there — three personal accounts and two business accounts. But over the course of the next 45 minutes, the not-so-helpful cashier, policy-bound bank manager, and intransigent vice president maintained that due to my two missed payments, they had no choice but to withhold from me the privilege of online banking for one year. As for waiving any of the late fees, forget it. Oh, and the $17,500 travel reimbursement check I had brought to deposit? I'd have to wait ten days to obtain the funds — despite it being issued by one of the five largest companies in the world through the third largest bank in North America.

What did I do? I collected my things and marched right into the bank across the street. They helped me move all my accounts over and cashed my check in 15 minutes. I've been very happy there ever since.

Even though my original bank had better products, more branches, a wider network of ATMs, and fees that were a bit lower than its competitors, it wasn't enough to overcome exploitive policies, insensitive attitudes, and a basic lack of care for the ongoing ownership experience of being their customer. That's what drove me away.

Battling an Inside-Out Perspective

Pop quiz: Who in your organization really sees the entirety of your customers' experience?

a) The people in customer service

b) The folks in billing

c) The individuals in marketing

d) None of the above

If you answered d, none of the above, you win! But you also lose. Odds are, *nobody* in your organization sees the entirety of your customers' experience.

Everyone in your employ is like a horse racing with blinders on. His field of view is limited to what is in front of him. "Race your own race!" people say. "Don't worry about what anyone else is doing!" While that advice might apply if you're running the Kentucky Derby, it's terrible for someone in business trying to holistically manage customer experience.

These blinders explain why, when we ask employees at the front line how well they deliver customer experience, we often get an answer that goes something like this: "My part of the process is fantastic. It's like Christmas morning over here!" Okay, maybe we're exaggerating. But generally speaking, people think they're doing pretty well in the experience-delivery department. And yet, when we ask their customers the same question, we get a completely different answer. One aspect of the experience may indeed be fantastic, but others may well be miserable.

Why this difference in opinion? Simple. Most employees just don't have a broad view of customer experience. They can't see how their work contributes to the overall experience of the customer, either directly or indirectly. They see themselves merely as part of a small team, department, or functional area (remember those castles we talked about earlier?) rather than as part of a larger, enterprise-wide process. (See Figure 3-1.) In other words, they have an inside-out view rather than an outside-in perspective.

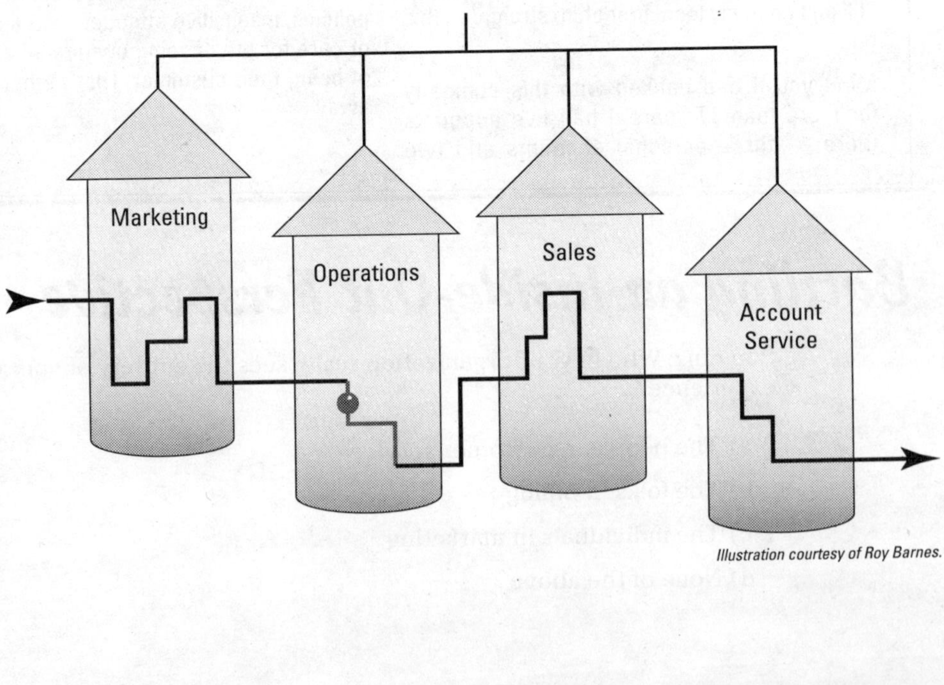

Figure 3-1: Do your teams see themselves as just part of a small team, department, or functional area? Or as part of a larger, enterprise-wide process?

Illustration courtesy of Roy Barnes.

An *inside-out* perspective focuses on an organization's own internal functions — its efficiency, processes, and so on. While all that is important, organizations must temper this internal, inside-out view with an external, outside-in one. Organizations that take an *outside-in* perspective seek to grow and nurture their customer base by providing an excellent customer experience. They put themselves in their customers' shoes and view everything from their perspective. (See Figure 3-2.)

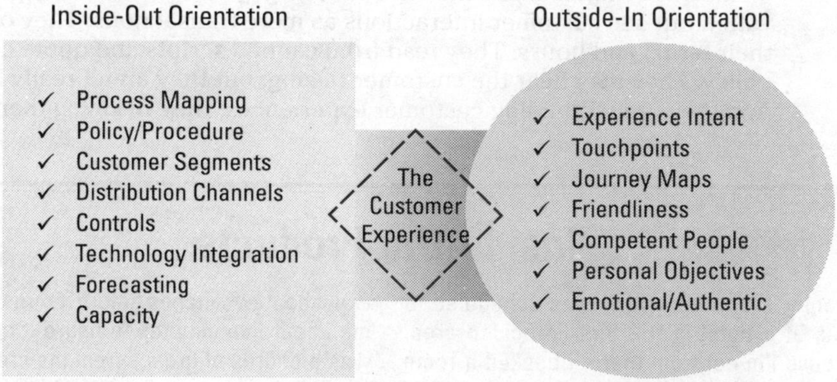

Figure 3-2: Balancing an inside-out view with an outside-in perspective.

Illustration courtesy of Roy Barnes.

Take Blockbuster. Blockbuster didn't go under because its stores operated poorly. Blockbuster went under because it failed to recognize that a different method of distribution — the delivery of DVDs via the U.S. Postal Service, as offered by Netflix, rather than a physical storefront — could provide a superior customer experience. In other words, it was doomed by an inside-out view. For its part, Netflix was more nimble. Thanks to its outside-in perspective, it soon recognized that streaming video content over the Internet offered an even better customer experience than mail delivery and adapted accordingly.

There is a big difference between the traditional inside-out view prevalent in most organizations and a customer-experience, outside-in perspective. The former view has traditionally focused on driving greater and greater efficiency, while the latter is about thoughtful, integrated, and impactful experiences. A lot of people's working hours are spent refining services, products, or processes, stripping away absolutely everything that is deemed unnecessary in order to improve efficiency and reduce cost. This inside-out approach is a sneaky trap, however. In their attempt to improve efficiency, they sometimes eradicate those parts of their business that appeal to their customers' human side — the things that interest, surprise, delight, and engage them. And this could cost the business in terms of customer experience, loyalty, and repeat business. In the end, you must foster an appropriate balance between designing transactions that are efficient and effective and retaining humanity.

In the past, product-focused companies viewed their customer-service function as a secondary, inconvenient expense. Taking care of customers was just a cost of doing business. These days, customer experience has emerged as one of the few sustainable competitive differentiators in business. Organizations that deliver an excellent customer experience are thriving. It's no coincidence that industry leaders such as Zappos, Nordstrom, and Southwest Airlines are also leaders in customer experience! It's easy to spot organizations whose perspectives haven't evolved with the times. These inside-out companies are the ones that go gaga over their latest product innovation but see customer interactions as mere transactions. They operate on their terms and hours. They read from canned scripts and quote company policy. They may hear the customer talking, but they aren't really listening. And they aren't building customer experiences; they're killing them.

Inside-Out Products

Recently, I (coauthor Roy) was scheduled to speak at a hotel in the San Francisco area. Because I'm not from there, I booked a room in the same facility. On the morning of my presentation, I reached into the shower and turned the faucet, only to discover there was no water. Not no water pressure . . . *no water.* In a panic, I spun the faucet this way and that. Suddenly, a tiny flow of water dripped from the shower head. It wasn't much more than a drizzle, but it was something — enough for me to make myself presentable. Still, I was going to need a working shower during my stay, so I called the hotel engineering staff on my way out of the room and asked them to fix the problem while I was gone.

During my presentation, I couldn't resist asking whether anyone else had had a problem with their shower that morning. To my surprise, about half the hands in the room — there were several hundred attendees — went up. Something strange seemed afoot! Then, someone in the back of the room spoke up: "You have to pull the whole faucet straight out from the wall about two inches before it turns on. It took me about five minutes to figure it out." There was a chorus of groans from the crowd as we (well, half of us) realized we hadn't used the shower faucet correctly.

After my session, I returned to my room to find nothing had changed — except that there was a laminated sign stuck to the shower wall above the faucet that said, "pull out." I examined the shower faucet more closely. It was a nice, heavy chrome thing — very attractive. It felt substantial and was obviously of excellent quality. The problem? Half the people who tried to use it couldn't figure out how to operate it.

Look, beyond regulating the temperature of the water, a shower faucet has exactly one function: to turn the water on and off. Performing this task should be intuitive. It should just *work.* It absolutely, positively shouldn't require laminated operating instructions. What was the company that made it thinking? Where was the customer experience in their thought process? Nowhere, that's where.

"They're All Crooks!" Overcoming Negative Perceptions of Your Industry

You can be the greatest company on Earth, providing a tremendous work environment and excellent wages, offering a top-of-the-line product, and backing it up with an out-of-this-world customer experience. But that doesn't mean you won't find yourself in consumers' crosshairs. Why? Because companies aren't held accountable for just their own actions. Your organization may well be punished by consumers for the actions of a competitor. If someone in your industry does something bad, dangerous, or just plain silly, odds are consumers will tar everyone in your sector with the same brush. As far as they're concerned, you're *all* guilty.

Don't believe us? Here are a few examples of companies whose individual failures caused pain for their entire industry:

- **JetBlue:** In 2007, JetBlue Airways experienced what is now referred to as the "Valentine's Day debacle," in which thousands of passengers were stranded for hours on runways at New York's JFK airport. It started innocently enough: The weather forecast called for icy conditions that would soon turn to rain. So in an attempt to stay on schedule, JetBlue employees continued to load flights and allow them to taxi to the runway. But like many weather forecasts, this one was wrong. Conditions didn't change as expected. As a result, several JetBlue planes full of travelers were marooned on the airstrip — some for as long as six hours. This single incident created an enormous brand image problem for JetBlue. Its reputation as a customer-friendly airline was tarnished. But that's not all. Due to JetBlue's mishandling of the crisis, it and every other airline is now responsible for meeting new regulations governing the treatment of passengers on delayed airplanes. The moral of the story: You don't have to be the one who screws up to feel the sting of a customer backlash!
- **Pacific Gas and Electric Utility (PG&E):** In 2010, aging infrastructure in San Bruno, California, caused a 30-inch natural gas transmission pipeline to explode. The resulting wall of fire reached more than 1,000 feet high, killing eight people and causing a devastating fire that leveled 35 houses. Obviously, the impact on the people affected by the fire was tremendous, their loss indescribable. But as you might expect, PG&E's reputation also took a hit. The company's shares fell 8 percent the following day, reducing its market capital by more than $1.5 billion. Moreover, when the California Public Utilities Commission discovered that PG&E had lacked a legally required procedure for monitoring its gas-transmission pipelines for more than 40 years, it levied a $2.5 billion fine. And, as a result of PG&E's failures, utilities in many other parts of the world faced additional scrutiny and new regulation.

- **Firestone:** In the late 1990s, Firestone famously manufactured a "self-shredding" tire. The result was numerous rollover accidents, causing the deaths of more than 250 people. Obviously, Firestone's brand took a huge hit. But it wasn't the only one. In the immediate wake of the Firestone problem, all passenger-car tire sales fell to their lowest levels in decades.

The bottom line? If you — or one of your competitors — blows it, you'll all pay the price. The Internet brings greater exposure to markets in general and to companies, brands, products, and services in particular. Everything your organization and industry does — both good and bad — is now front and center for the world to see.

Adapting to Changing Consumer Expectations

Customers. They're as picky as Gorden Ramsay. One day, they're totally satisfied with your product line and customer service. The next? They're ditching you for someone new. Their expectations change, seemingly every day! Unless your goal is to kill customer experience, you need to keep up with these changing — or, more precisely, rising — expectations.

Why the rise in expectations? Thanks to the Internet, consumers are simply more savvy than they used to be. In the past, your customers may have been willing to just "buy your product and like it." Most likely, they weren't aware that there might be a better option! But these days, customers demand more. As they spend more and more time online, their exposure to different levels of customer service and experience increases dramatically.

Eleven key customer expectations

So what *do* customers expect? Here are just a few examples of customer expectations — at least, for now. (These expectations are discussed in more detail throughout the book.)

- **Speed:** Most customers don't want to take a ton of time deciding what to buy. They check with their friends and followers on social media and maybe do research on a few review websites to make their decision. And once their decision is made, they want to be able to pull the trigger . . . quickly. Don't introduce any impediments in your buying experience!

- **Authenticity:** Customers want no games, no gimmicks, and no fine print. They want straight talk — no bait and switch. That means all your touchpoints (website, stores, and so on) need to be using the same real-time information. Oh — and don't configure your default settings to cheat the consumer. And don't lie to them, because they'll find out.
- **Care:** If customers merely want a transaction, they'll buy online. For anything else, they probably prefer to be treated like human beings. Like you, consumers have feelings, emotions, and dreams. Don't turn them into a persona or a segment. Don't target or quantify them.
- **Knowledge:** If someone's been a customer of yours for years, you should know that. You should know what she's bought from you and remember it when she calls in with a question or for service. Her loyalty to you is worth at least some acknowledgement. Do your customers matter to you? If so, know them and show them.
- **Availability:** Customers will contact you — whether via text, phone, mail, email, tweet, Facebook message, or in person — when it's convenient for *them,* not for you. They don't care about your operating hours. They expect you to be always on and listening. Don't expect to limit your hours of availability from 9 a.m. to 4 p.m. when your customers work from 8 a.m. to 5 p.m.!
- **Ease of use:** People don't like to follow directions. If you want customers to do something, make the process so easy, so obvious, so intuitively clear that they will be able to follow the path you've laid out as easily as water finds the valley floor. Don't expect consumers to think!
- **Immediacy:** Customers want it now, unless they want it later, in which case they want it at a specific time, in a specific location, with a call to verify exactly when so they don't forget.
- **Reception:** Shhhh. Stop talking. Be quiet and listen. Then *do something* with what your customers tell you. If you must ask questions, listen to their response. And don't ask too many questions all at once. Customers don't like being interrogated. Finally, be clear about what you're going to do with the information you collect. Your customers' default position is that you'll misuse their information. Convince them otherwise.
- **One-stop shopping:** Don't shuffle customers around from department to department. They don't care about your organizational structure, your politics, or who has the real clout in the company. They care about getting their questions answered and their concerns addressed — preferably by the first person they talk to, not the fifth.
- **Good design:** Customers appreciate beautiful design, even if they never say so. Nobody wants to buy something that doesn't work well.
- **Problem solving:** If something does go wrong, customers need it fixed, fixed properly, and fixed now.

Comparing experience and expectations across industries

REMEMBER

You can't just measure your organization's customer experience against that of other companies in your industry. You have to compare it across industry types and markets — just like your customers do. Allow us to illustrate by telling you a tale of two customer experiences.

Experience 1: The other night, I (coauthor Roy) found myself having to call the NYPD — you know, New York Pizza Delivery. They make a great pizza, and I use them all the time. Here's how they answered the phone: "Hey Roy! Do you want to order the Queens Deluxe again?" I mean, the fact that they knew my name is no big deal, right? They have caller ID, so obviously they could see who was calling. But how did they remember what I ordered? The person went on to say with a laugh, "Or are you ordering 18 different pizzas, like last time, when your son's soccer team was over?" Wow! I was floored. "Just the one," I replied, smiling. "Same credit card as always?" he asked. "Yep," I said. "Great. Your pizza will be there in 29 minutes." Look, I don't know what your expectations of your local pizza joint are, but to be honest, mine aren't very high. I was positively blown away by the NYPD customer experience!

Experience 2: As I believe I've mentioned, I (coauthor Roy) travel a lot for business. One of my clients is in Spokane, Washington. When I visit this client, I typically stay in a certain hotel downtown. It's nice and has a good reputation. In the last two years, I've probably stayed there 60+ nights. For a recent stay, I arrived at the hotel around 11:30 p.m., my usual time. I dragged my luggage through the sliding front doors to the front desk to check in. I recognized the clerk, having seen him many, *many* times before. But did I get even a glimmer of recognition from him? Nope. Nada. Zip. I'm not saying I want a brass band and rose petals at my feet (although I wouldn't turn them down), but shouldn't I at least be acknowledged as a frequent repeat guest?

The local pizza company, with whom I have roughly 15 interactions per year and spend about $200, knows me better and gives me a more engaging and welcoming experience than the four-star hotel where I spend 60+ nights and spend more than $20,000 per year. Should I compare the two? Is that fair? Yes.

The reality is, every consumer makes that comparison. Customers transfer their experience expectations across transactions. It's not unreasonable to think that if the pizza company can make me feel welcome and valued for being a repeat customer, the hotel should be able to not only match that experience, but exceed it.

Chapter 4

Is There a Doctor in the House? Diagnosing Your Customer Experience Ailments

In This Chapter

- Looking at how good customer relationships go bad
- Identifying behaviors that send customers packing
- Asking five "why" questions to determine where problems lie
- Prioritizing problem-solving with Pareto analysis
- Creating and conducting your own customer experience diagnostic

Human relationships — whether a marriage between two people or the relationship between a customer and a business — constantly change and evolve. No one person is the same as she was yesterday, and neither is any one relationship. There is no neutral; things are either getting better or they're getting worse. Unless you work tirelessly to stay current with your customers — to be aware of their level of engagement with you, your products, your services, and your brand — you'll find that the relationship will change for the worse, right under your feet.

This chapter pinpoints the problems that commonly plague relationships between customers and businesses. People sometimes refer to these problems as "low-hanging fruit." They're typically not difficult to solve; they just require someone to commit to fixing them.

Strike Three: The Three Main Reasons Good Customer Relationships Go Bad

Your relationship with a customer is a little like a marriage. Keeping it on track requires hard work and focus. Sometimes, these relationships run like well-oiled machines. Other times, dirt, grit, and plain old neglect begin to gum up the works. And on occasion, the machine breaks down altogether. The relationship ends, and you're left wondering, "What the heck just happened?"

In our experience, customer relationships end for the following three reasons:

- **Inflicting one too many minor wounds:** More often than not, a customer ends his relationship with a company not because of one big failure on the company's part, but rather because of the slow, cumulative effect of several tiny mishaps. Take flying. When you fly, you expect the airline to run on time, the staff to be friendly, and the in-flight Internet to be operational. If any one of these expectations occasionally isn't met, you probably aren't too upset. But when failures in these areas begin to stack up, it puts your relationship with the airline at risk. For more information about the types of "wounds" that cause customers to flee, see the next section.
- **Failing to acknowledge and take responsibility for mistakes:** Everyone screws up. It's not a matter of if, it's a matter of when. But the real failure is acting as though nothing has happened. When you make a mistake, no matter how small, 'fess up and take immediate steps to rectify it. Your customers will appreciate it!
- **Failing to communicate when things go bad:** Everybody knows that things sometimes go wrong. But when they do, it's up to you to immediately communicate that with your customers. Unlike fruit, problems don't improve with ripening. They get worse — *a lot* worse. Just ask executives at Target Corp., who, after suffering a data breach in late 2013, waited close to three weeks to alert some 40 million consumers to the problem. Needless to say, customers weren't happy about the lag time — and still aren't.

REAL WORLD EXAMPLE

Years ago, the company Roy worked for discovered that it had lost track of a backup data tape containing information — including credit card numbers and Social Security numbers — about thousands of its customers. The company was fairly sure the data tape hadn't been stolen, but it was missing nonetheless. The company quickly informed its customers of the problem, enlisted a credit-monitoring service to help the customers, and kept everyone up-to-date on our efforts to find the missing tape. Although the company never did locate it, it scored major points with its customers (and with federal government oversight agencies) for its quick response.

Avoiding Behaviors that Send Customers Running

In the preceding section, we warn of inflicting one too many minor wounds, or "death by a thousand cuts" — the slow, cumulative effect of several tiny mishaps. Often, these tiny cuts are the result of five bad behaviors:

- Being rude
- Having negative phone manners
- Ignoring complaints and inquiries
- Failing to listen
- Shuffling customers

Odds are, you've experienced these behaviors firsthand or, heaven forbid, you've displayed them with your customers. The following sections offer tips on solving these problems.

Being rude

Maybe you are seriously understaffed. Maybe your legacy technology infrastructure doesn't transmit appropriate customer data from one customer service agent to another. Or, on the flip side, maybe your customer-facing processes are so highly efficient that customer empathy has been engineered right out of the workflow. Regardless, there is absolutely no excuse — zero, zilch, nada — for a customer service rep to be rude to a customer or a potential customer.

Comcast recently learned this lesson when an overzealous customer retention specialist simply refused to allow a customer to cancel service with the company. The phone call, which went viral on the Internet, went on for what seem liked hours as the customer repeatedly asked to cancel and the phone rep kept refusing to acknowledge the request.

REMEMBER

Rude employees are rude for a reason: You allow them to be. It's not their fault — it's yours. You hired wrong, you trained wrong, or you coached wrong. Just as you must kill an aggressive cancer by nuking it with chemotherapy, you must eradicate rudeness by displaying a zero-tolerance attitude. We don't care if an employee "makes his numbers" or excels at some other aspect of his job. If he's rude, he has to go. Fire him and, for good measure, encourage him to work for a competitor.

Having negative phone manners

In many organizations, employees must interface with customers via phone. Often, however, customers are left feeling frustrated by these exchanges (or lack thereof). Following are some tips for easing their irritation.

Answer calls quickly

We're often asked to provide the definitive answer to the question, "When answering a call, what is the optimal wait time?" The definitive answer is, there is no definitive answer. It's industry- and customer-dependent. If you're calling 911, you want zero wait time. If you're calling for tickets for your favorite rock band, you're probably willing to wait a little longer (although not much).

Generally speaking, most call centers shoot for a wait time between 20 and 50 seconds, but you need to do the math to see what makes the most financial sense for you. Remember: Every call operator you add to answer phones costs money — as does every call you lose. It's a balancing act.

If you have a more sophisticated call center or an automatic call distribution (ACD) software package, you want to look at abandonment rates by hold-time interval. For example, look at how many customers drop off (that is, stop waiting for you to pick up) after 10, 20, 30, 60, 90, and 120 seconds. By analyzing this information, you'll quickly see how long your customers are willing to wait. As a very first step, you can then attempt to answer each call in the last few seconds before the majority of your customers hang up.

All that being said, it doesn't make financial sense to staff your call center to answer the phones more quickly than the customer expects. Roy had one client who insisted that his call center phones be answered after the first ring. That was totally unnecessary and very costly.

TIP

Many call-center systems and some voice-mail systems offer a feature that enables callers to elect to be called back automatically as soon as the next call-center representative is free rather than being put on hold. See whether your system has this capability (or other capabilities that may be more user-friendly)!

Test your own interactive voice response system

Don't delegate this task — try it yourself. Call into your company's interactive voice response (IVR) system and perform some common task. Try to pay a bill or get a question answered. See how easy it is — or isn't — to get these simple things done. While you're at it, listen to the greeting and the on-hold music and determine whether it gives the right impression. We bet it doesn't!

Return calls

If you can't always answer the phone right away, make the process of leaving a message unbelievably easy, and be sure to state exactly when the customer can expect to hear back from you. Don't say, "Please leave a message and we will get back to you as soon as possible." That's too blah — not to mention completely unhelpful. Instead, try something like this: "Thanks for calling the ABC company. We're sorry we can't answer your call right now. Please leave your name, number, and a few helpful details, and you'll hear back from us within four hours." Customers like specificity, especially when their immediate needs aren't being met. Tell them what to expect with as much precision as possible — but don't make any promises you can't keep.

TIP

In a similar vein, set a clear and inviolate standard for when a response must be made to a customer inquiry and publicize it well throughout your organization. Your policy may call for response within ten minutes or on the same business day. (Waiting much longer than a day may lead customers to conclude that you're not that interested in their business.) The right response time frame depends upon your customer's expectations.

Ignoring complaints and inquiries

Consider the following experience, related by Roy: Recently, I was on a flight on an airline with whom I've maintained the highest-level frequent-flier status for several years. Normally, I'm able to upgrade to a first-class seat, but this flight was packed. As a result, I found myself sitting in a middle seat at the very back of the plane, resigned to my fate and more than a little irritated that my upgrade request hadn't been fulfilled.

About 20 minutes into the flight, a flight attendant approached my row, leaned over, and said, "Hi Mr. Barnes. I'm so sorry we weren't able to accommodate your request to upgrade to first class on this flight, but I don't want you to think for a minute that we don't appreciate your business. Thank you so much for flying with us." Nice, huh? I mean, not as nice as a first-class seat, but still. I appreciated the flight attendant's acknowledgment of my request and her apology for the airline's inability to accommodate it.

It's a fact: Customers hate to be ignored. And yet, companies do it all the time. This situation is made worse by the fact that customers now have a seemingly infinite number of channels to contact companies. They call, they text, they email, they snail mail, they post, they tweet, they blog — you name it. Your job is to respond quickly, regardless of which method they use to contact you.

Social media — Facebook, Twitter, and the like — is of particular note here. These days, more than a billion consumers use social media, and that number is only going to grow. Neglecting to communicate using this channel may soon be more harmful to your company's reputation than ignoring phone calls and emails is today.

Just as you should set a clear and inviolate standard for when a response must be made to a customer inquiry via phone, you should do so for messages received through social media as well. Be aware, however, that customers who communicate with you via social media likely have very high expectations. A recent study by Edison Research revealed that a third of customers who contacted a company through social media channels expected a response within 30 minutes.

TIP

For best results, put a specific person or dedicated team in charge of responding to feedback received via social media. This person or team needs to have the authority to decide whether feedback is relevant and deserves a response, and if so, to immediately manage that response until the interaction is complete.

TIP

If you receive an inflammatory message, it's usually best to respond offline if possible. In addition, the resolution of specific problems should definitely be handled offline, out of the public view. When you take a customer concern offline, your response feels more personal to the complaining customer. Even better, it stops the "airing of dirty laundry" for everyone in the online world to see.

Failing to listen

Listen up! Listening is important. These days, customers expect organizations — including yours — to act and communicate like people (and nice people at that). They expect to conduct conversations with you and for you to hang on their every word. That means you must watch and listen in on what's happening at all your touchpoints.

In addition, you must "listen" by asking your customers lots of questions and paying very close attention to their answers. The best way to achieve this is to conduct short, highly targeted surveys. (We're talking one or two questions here.)

Smart organizations make it a point to constantly gather this type of feedback from customers and really take that feedback to heart. That's great! Unfortunately, however, too often companies conduct these surveys so infrequently that the process is completely ineffective.

You may think that conducting the occasional survey is better than doing nothing, but it isn't. It's *worse*. Here's why: Suppose your customer experiences a failure in customer service in February, but you don't conduct your annual survey until November. That means you've given the customer eight months to find another supplier to meet her needs. Then, after that eight months, you've reminded her all over again how disappointed in you she was back in February. Not good!

Conducting the occasional customer satisfaction survey is like asking your husband, wife, or partner how the relationship is going only once every few years. No relationship is going to withstand that low a level of feedback, care, and response! Heck, even the Mars Rover gets more communication that that! Imagine if it didn't:

> "Uh, Houston, we have a problem . . . "
>
> . . . silence . . .
>
> . . . six more months of silence . . .
>
> Then, at last, crackling through the quiet of space: "Thank you for taking our annual satisfaction survey. On a scale of 5 to 1, with 5 being 'out of this world' and 1 being 'not so much,' please rate your overall satisfaction with Houston Control."

Ridiculous, right? But this pokey survey mentality happens all the time. Just recently, Roy received an invitation from the Orange County Sheriff's Department to take a customer service survey for an interaction that occurred more than nine months ago. (If you must know, he got a traffic ticket.) Why wait almost a year to survey him about his experience? He barely remembers what he did yesterday, let alone what happened nine months ago!

So, what should you do? Follow these steps:

1. **Perform a quick inventory of every customer survey that your company is currently fielding.**
2. **Start reading the survey responses — particularly any written comments that customers have shared with you.**

   Written comments are gold.
3. **Figure out how you're going to respond to those customers who complained or who requested that you follow up with them.**

   When you first start this work, you may very likely find months-old surveys that contain comments and complaints that were never addressed.

4. **Call those customers, apologize profusely (and mean it! — don't just give them the textbook apology), listen to their concerns, and, if possible, fix their problems.**

5. **Take a hard look at your organization to make sure the problems those customers experienced aren't still happening to others.**

Listen and follow up. Listen and follow up. Listen and follow up. That's your new mantra.

Shuffling customers

At the root of most frustrating customer experiences is decentralized, uncoordinated service. Exhausting cycles of telephone tag, endless explanations to countless service representatives, and circular referrals to rude, faceless, and uninformed customer-facing employees are all sure-fire ways for a customer to lose patience — and for your company to lose customers.

The solution? One-stop customer service and problem resolution. The benefits are twofold:

- Your customer can complete her business with your company with a single point of contact.
- Your company can better allocate resources, increase operational efficiency, and simultaneously improve customer experience and satisfaction.

So how do you achieve this? Here are a few broad suggestions:

- Attempt to resolve your customer's problem in a single phone call or email exchange. Don't shuffle her from one representative to another.
- If your customer is visiting you in person, have all the necessary information, approvals, products, and services available to you at that location. Always think one-stop shopping!
- Have a customer deal with one staff member or, at a minimum, one team of representatives who are dedicated to satisfying her needs. If you go with the team approach, make sure the team can maintain a continuous dialogue with the customer. That is, have each team member take notes and develop next steps as they work with the customer, and have them pass that information on to other team members. Your goal? To ensure there are no gaps in the conversation and that the customer is never asked the same question twice.

One company that has adopted the one-stop customer service approach is the Ritz Carleton. At the Ritz Carleton, any employee who receives a complaint from an unhappy customer "owns" that complaint. Even if she can't fix the problem directly, she assumes responsibility for the complaint and works rapidly behind the scenes to resolve it. She is the one who then responds to the customer and ensures that the problem is resolved to the customer's complete satisfaction.

Why Ask Why? Diagnosing Customer Service Problems with the Five Whys

If you ever spent time with a young child, you probably noticed the frequency with which said child used the word "why." "Why is the sky blue?" "Why are there bugs?" "Why don't fish walk?" "Why can't I draw on the wallpaper?" "Why are you crying?" "Why are you taking antidepressants?"

All those "whys" probably drove you insane. Nonetheless, the question "why?" is a good one to ask when you're trying to diagnose the root cause of customer service problems in your organization — hence this discussion of the *Five Whys technique.* This technique, often used in the "analyze" phase of the Six Sigma methodology, is easy to use, doesn't require deep research or lots of quantitative data gathering, and best of all, is kind of fun.

With this technique, you simply ask "Why?" over and over again — five times, or even more — until you unearth the root cause, or the *real* reason a customer problem has occurred. It's a little like peeling an onion, with the answer to each successive "why" revealing yet another layer until you reach the root cause.

To use the Five Whys technique, follow these steps:

1. **Gather some smart people who know a bit about the problem together in a room.**
2. **Write down the problem on a flip chart or whiteboard.**
3. **Ask for agreement from the group that this is, in fact, the problem.**
4. **Ask why the problem occurs.**

   Write down all the answers you get from the group.
5. **For each of the answers that you write down, ask "why" again.**

6. **After several rounds of this, ask the group whether they think that they have identified the root cause of the problem.**

   If so, write it down.

For example, consider the following problem:

> Customers are unhappy because your organization is taking too long to pay its warranty claims.

Now ask "why":

- **Why does it take so long to pay warranty claims?** Because customers often fill out the claim forms incorrectly. Claims supervisors can't quickly process claim forms with errors, which delays the processing of *all* claim forms.
- **Why are the forms filled out incorrectly?** Because they are confusing to customers.
- **Why are customers confused by the claim forms?** Because the language used to describe products under warranty no longer matches the new product lines. We haven't updated the claim forms since we updated the offerings list.
- **Why haven't we updated the claim forms?** Because the new product development team isn't aware of the need to update the claim forms.
- **Why isn't the new product development team aware of the need to update the claim forms?** Because the person who was responsible for communicating with the claims team was laid off.

In this case, just five "whys" were needed to reveal that the problem was not that customers were making careless mistakes when filling out claim forms, but rather that the claim forms were populated with dated information. The answer to the last "why" leads us to the root cause of the problem. You must act to fix this root cause. Sure, you can also work to address any other causes or symptoms, but doing so in isolation and not addressing the root cause only leads to a temporary fix. Soon, problems will resurface. It's critical that you keep pushing your team to find the root cause and to act on it.

You can ask "why" five times, ten times, twenty times, or more. It doesn't matter how many times you ask, as long as you get to the root cause of the problem. That being said, we've found that asking "why" fewer than five times may not cut the mustard. Odds are, doing so will reveal symptoms, but not the root cause. Asking "why" is a little like mining for gold. You must keep digging and digging until you find the source. Don't give up too early; the problem quite often lies where you wouldn't have expected it!

You Say Tomato, I Say Pareto: Using Pareto Analysis

If you use the Five Whys technique (see the preceding section for details), you may find some of your customer service problems are the result of several root causes. In that case, you must decide which root cause you should tackle first. To do so, you can use Pareto analysis.

Pareto analysis follows the Pareto principle. In basic terms, this principle states that in all situations, 80 percent of problems come from 20 percent of causes. Conversely, and more importantly for our purposes, 80 percent of a problem's resolution comes from 20 percent of the fixes. The challenge is to determine which fixes fall in that 20 percent.

Although there are several different ways to conduct a Pareto analysis, all involve the following steps. (You completed the first two when you used the Five Whys technique.)

1. **Identify and list problems.**

   Write down a list of all the customer problems that you need to solve.

2. **Identify the root causes.**

   For each problem, identify its root cause.

3. **Score the problems and root causes in terms of the level of their impact.**

   The scoring parameters to use depend on the sorts of problems you have. For example, you may score each problem based on its financial impact, its financial cost, its impact on customer engagement scores, or some other measure. Use a simple three-point scale to prevent analysis paralysis, where 3 = high, 2 = medium, and 1 = low. This approach works just fine in most cases.

4. **Compare the scores for each problem.**

   The problem or root cause with the top score should be your highest priority. Fixing this problem will yield the most benefit. In contrast, the problem with the lowest score should be the lowest priority.

5. **Take action.**

   Start tackling the causes of the problems. Deal with the top-priority problem (or group of problems) first.

Here's an example of how this might work. Suppose you want to improve the customer experience at your call center. Your first task is to identify the problems at the call center — for example, by conducting a customer survey. Say the survey unearths two main problems: customers being frequently disconnected or unable to get through, and customers perceiving agents as being rude.

Next, you use the Five Whys technique to identify the root causes for each problem. For the first problem, these might include such causes as "too long to answer," "confusing IVR menu," and "too many transfers." For the second problem, the root causes might be "unfriendly employee" and "employee wants to end call." Then you should score each of these root causes in terms of its relative impact to your organization.

Finally, you add up the number of complaints in each category and then calculate each category as a percentage of the whole. (See Figure 4-1.) Pretty quickly, you're able to deduce that "too long to answer" and "unfriendly employee" are the cause of more than 78 percent of all complaints. With just this simple exercise, you can see where you should be focusing your problem-resolution efforts.

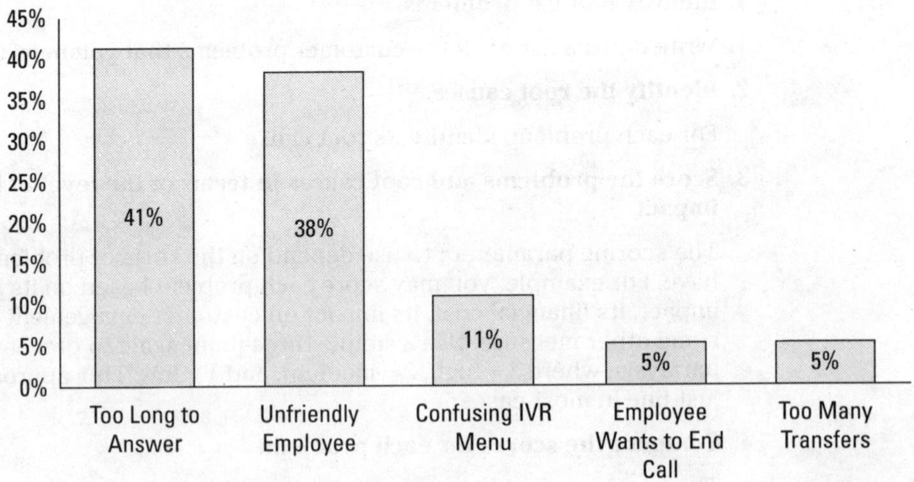

Figure 4-1: Customer issues.

Illustration courtesy of Roy Barnes.

Self-Diagnosing Your Company's Customer Experience Problems

Perhaps author Edward Hodnett said it best: "If you don't ask the right questions, you don't get the right answers. Only the inquiring mind solves problems." In this section, you discover the right questions to ask to diagnose your organization's customer experience woes.

We've found that the majority of customer experience problems arise in one of the four following areas:

- Personnel
- Processes and technology
- Customers
- Financials

For this reason, we've categorized these questions accordingly.

We encourage you to gather together a group of customer experience co-conspirators to review these questions. Discard the questions that don't quite apply to your situation, and add ones that do. Then take your best shot at answering the questions. When you do, consider using a three-point scale, where 1 correlates to "not doing this," 2 equals "partially doing this," and 3 equals "yes, doing this." If you identify areas where you're not quite making the grade, use the information in this book to improve. Then come back in six months and answer the questions again.

REMEMBER

Execution is everything!

Questions about personnel

Following are several questions pertaining to personnel:

- Have you clearly articulated the experience you want your customers to receive, in a way that all employees can understand?
- Are you hiring for the best basic customer service traits, such as warmth, empathy, optimism, detail-orientation, and teamwork?
- Are you recruiting new customer-facing employees with the skills and abilities to deliver the customer experience you want?

- Have you profiled your existing successful customer-facing employees to identify traits that work in your organization?
- Do you use an on-the-job "trial" period to determine the customer-centricity of a potential employee?
- Does your new-employee onboarding process support your organization's customer experience mindset?
- Are your customer-facing new hires creative problem-solvers? Do they have unusual and unpredictable solutions to common customer issues?
- If you owned a small customer service firm that had only one customer service rep, would you hire each of your existing employees for that role?
- How do you recognize and reward employees who deliver an outstanding customer experience?
- Do you have the same customer experience delivery expectation for your "internal" (that is, those departments that don't serve external customers but serve other internal areas instead) customer delivery support teams?
- Have you reviewed your policies and standard operating procedures (SOPs) to identify those that prevent your employees from delivering an awesome customer experience?
- If given the choice to steal something from your organization, would your competitors choose your people?

Questions about processes and technology

Here are some questions you should ask about processes and technology:

- Do you give employees enough time to listen to, diagnose, and solve individual customer problems?
- Is it extremely easy for your customers to find one telephone number or email address to contact you about a service issue?
- Does your IVR menu have an appropriately limited number of selections?
- Can a customer press zero at any time within your IVR system to talk to a customer service representative? (Watch out: How many customer service representatives are you willing to employ to deal with questions?)

- Do your customer-facing systems pass the necessary customer information and data from touchpoint to touchpoint so that an ongoing customer dialogue can be maintained throughout the customer journey?
- Do you have a good selection of leading and lagging customer-performance metrics regarding the use of your process and technology?
- Are all your key customer-facing processes optimized and mobile enabled?

Questions about customers

Following are several questions pertaining to customers:

- Do you know what your customers' expectations are of your service, product, and brand?
- Do you proactively solicit customer feedback at your key customer touchpoints?
- Do you immediately respond to customer complaints and concerns, no matter what channel is used to communicate with you?
- Do you actively promote your brand, products, and services on all appropriate social media outlets?
- Do you proactively manage customer complaints and dialogues on all social media outlets?
- Have you mapped all your customer touchpoints?
- Do you know who "owns" each customer touchpoint within your organization — that is, who is accountable and responsible for improving it?

Questions about financials

Here are some key questions related to financials. (Note that some of these are of the "yes/no" variety. The three-point scale we mentioned earlier may not apply here.)

- Have you created a list of "perfect" customer behaviors? (Chapter 2 discusses "perfect" customer behaviors.)
- Have you worked with your CFO or financial team to identify some elements of your return on customer experience (ROCE) model?
- Are your products and services commodities?

- Is customer experience a competitive differentiator in your industry?
- Do you know all the costs associated with poor service in your organization — for example, customer defection, churn, buy-backs, cancellations, nonrenewals?
- Have you calculated the costs to acquire a new customer versus the costs to retain an existing one?
- Have you determined what percentage of customer defection is for price-related issues versus service-related issues?

Part II

Creating Awesome Customer Experience

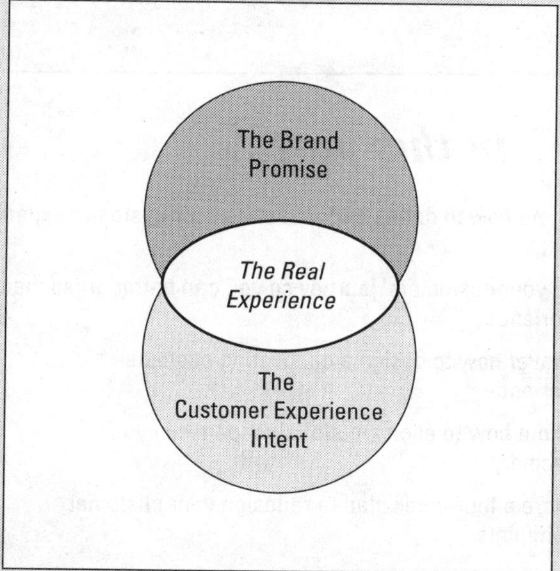

Learn how to manage large-scale touchpoint redesign efforts in a free article at www.dummies.com/extras/customerexperience.

In this part...

- Find out how to define and articulate your customer experience intent.
- Map your customers' journey so you can better grasp their experience.
- Discover how to design a captivating customer experience.
- Find out how to elicit emotional response in your customers.
- Explore a four-week plan to redesign your customer touchpoints.

Chapter 5

The Anger Games: Dealing with an Angry Customer

In This Chapter

- Finding the best tactic for dealing with angry customers
- Developing and practicing effective resolution methods
- Applying the RESOLVED approach to dealing with angry customers
- Knowing what to do when a confrontation escalates
- Understanding that the customer is *not* always right

Ideally, every one of your customers will walk away from your establishment or organization completely satisfied. His every need will have been met and every interaction with members of your staff will have been pleasant.

In reality, that often won't be the case. Sometimes, despite all your best efforts, things just go wrong. You mix up a customer's order. You drop a drink on her lap. You misplace his luggage. Her package gets lost in the mail. Whatever the reason, it's an unfortunate fact that, on occasion, you'll be faced with a customer who is upset, angry, or even irate.

First, it's very helpful to recognize that customer complaints are often opportunities in disguise. In other words, if you effectively solve a customer's problem, that customer's level of satisfaction, engagement, and loyalty will often go up — so much so that it often winds up higher than that of customers who never had a problem in the first place. (Now, that doesn't mean you should double-down your efforts to tick off as many customers as possible in the hopes of turning them into adoring fans afterward.)

Second, you should take immediate steps to resolve the situation. Remember: You're in charge of customer experience. That means it falls to you to wrestle the customer's bad attitude to the ground. You have to "run at the bear," so to speak — keeping in mind, of course, that thoughtful personal interactions can do absolute wonders in turning around a seemingly intractable situation! For more specific direction on dealing with a displeased customer, read on.

Avoiding Angry Customers from the Get-Go

Not to be cute, but the very best tactic for dealing with angry customers is to do whatever you can do to avoid upsetting them in the first place. The reality is that a lot of angry customers are angry because of your actions (or those of your organization), whether intentional or not. Preventing that scenario from unfolding is key.

So what should you do? B. Joseph Pine II and James H. Gilmore, authors of *The Experience Economy: Work Is Theater & Every Business a Stage* (published by Harvard Business Review Press), have an interesting approach. To understand their view, first imagine a theater where plays are performed. There's the stage, where actors and actresses do their thing in front of an audience. And then there's the back-of-the-house area offstage — those chaotic quarters where props, set pieces, equipment, and other necessary items are kept.

According to Pine and Gilmore, your interactions with customers are onstage activities. Your customers should be like the audience in a theater — aware only of the magic on the stage, oblivious to the chaos offstage. All too often, however, companies allow onstage and offstage activities to blur together. The result? Frustrated customers.

Thoughtful organizations realize that by better managing the environments of their onstage touchpoints, they can avoid situations where customers are more likely to be frustrated, temperamental, or angry. Often, the behavior of a single customer-facing individual can make all the difference!

A Tale of Three Airlines

Can a single individual really foster an environment that minimizes customer frustration and eliminates problems? You bet. To illustrate, we examine the actions of three different flight attendants, on three separate flights, on three different airlines.

If you've been a passenger on a commercial airliner in the last, oh, forever, you will likely agree: Flying ain't what it used to be. Frankly, it stinks. Unless you fly first class, the legroom is nonexistent and the seats are cramped, to say the least. (Claustrophobia, anyone?) Add to that the astronomical and seemingly indiscriminate fees. Ouch! But perhaps worst of all is being at the mercy of a thoughtless and uncaring flight crew — something that, unfortunately, seems to occur with great frequency. It's hell on Earth (or, more precisely, hell in the air)!

Often, the flight crew's bad attitude is evident from the moment you step on the plane. In an attempt to get all passengers on board and in their seats, many flight attendants take a cattle-car approach. To be fair, these flight attendants are under great pressure to ensure an on-time departure. This metric is among the most critical to airlines, and there are serious consequences for nonperformance. Nevertheless, it's our view that individual employees can create environments where passengers are treated like human beings — and *still* push back from the gate on time!

Witness the following experiences related by coauthor Roy and how they affect customer experience.

Ramping up

Last month, I flew from Philadelphia to New York City on an airline that shall go nameless. As I waited on the jetway to board the plane, I heard a flight attendant's voice over the plane's loudspeaker. Speaking in a very stern tone, this is what she said:

> "Sit down!"
>
> "If you are standing in the aisle, you need to sit down!"
>
> "If you notice people bunched up behind you in the aisle while you arrange your belongings in the overhead compartment, you are blocking their way. You are keeping them from sitting down!"
>
> "Please sit down immediately!"
>
> "We cannot leave until you sit down!"

Needless to say, the 150 people on the plane, as well as those of us about to board, were instantly transported back to kindergarten — and not in a "play all day and take a nice nap" kind of way. It was more like an "I'm being yelled at by a bitter schoolmarm" scenario.

When a harried, metric-driven flight attendant castigates her already anxious customers as they frantically attempt to claim their fair share of precious overhead space, there's going to be trouble. Within minutes, the cabin was positively reeking with frustration, anxiety, and anger — and the flight attendant was the cause. Let's just say these were *not* the friendly skies!

Sadly, this flight attendant failed to recognize that it's bad enough that passengers are being packed into uncomfortable seats with insufficient legroom, no work space, and no amenities. Worse, she believed her job was to prod the cattle (read: passengers) into their pens and quiet them down. That's an offstage concern (see the preceding section for a discussion of onstage versus offstage). In actual fact, her job should have been more like that of the hostess of a well-thought-out dinner party: to graciously greet arriving guests and to set the environment, mood, and tone for the party . . . er, flight. Apparently, she didn't realize that everything she said and did set the tone for how the next few hours were going to go. (Hint: They went badly.) Although she was onstage, she was not prepared for her real role.

Lightening up

A few weeks after my cattle-drive experience, I found myself flying out of Baltimore, Maryland, on a different airline. And once again, I found myself standing on the jetway, waiting to board the plane. This time, however, the flight attendant's voice on the loudspeaker was a bit different. This is what I heard, in a humorous tone:

> "Hello everybody, and welcome aboard!"
>
> "We are awfully glad you're with us today. I think you probably know by now that we cannot leave if we're all standing and milling around. This isn't cocktail hour, you know — although I'm sure several of us wish it were!"
>
> "In order for us to leave on time, you will need to find your seats. Visiting hours are over. Let the other patients get their rest. The sooner you take your seat, the sooner we can beat feet and leave."
>
> "But, if you're not interested in leaving, that would be just fine with us. Because, you see, we are a Baltimore-based flight crew. We really don't want to leave home today. We actually like our spouses and children. If you all want to stay here, that's perfectly okay with us. In fact, we know the people who run the concessions at the loading gate. If you want, we'll just let them know that you really would rather have a cocktail hour. We will even buy the snacks."

After a brief pause in her welcome-aboard routine, she continued:

> "For those of you just coming on board, please poke your head into the cockpit and say congratulations to the pilot. Today is his 105th birthday!"

By that time, the plane was full of laughter. The passengers were happy. And more importantly, they were *sitting down.* What an incredible difference one individual — someone who understood what it meant to be onstage — can make! The legroom on this flight was not significantly different from that on other flights. The drinks and snacks were the same. And yet, what a difference being on this flight compared to the previous one!

On which airline would you rather fly? For which airline would you rather work? For the first airline, where creating misery appeared to be the principal corporate value? Or for the second one, which appeared to recognize the importance of humor and fun? Which airline do you suppose has the least amount of employee turnover? Which airline do you suppose has lower recruiting costs?

Calming down

Here's another example of a flight attendant who handled his duties with grace and aplomb. In this case, I was flying on yet another airline from my hometown, Orlando, Florida, to Spokane, Washington — and things weren't off to a good start. As I boarded the plane, the sky over the airport darkened. Soon thereafter, the heavens opened up and thunder began. Ground operations at the Orlando airport were suspended due to hail and multiple lightning strikes.

The lead flight attendant, a gentleman named Alan, informed those of us on the plane that boarding had been suspended due to the weather. He also turned on the in-flight entertainment system so that those already onboard would have a way to pass the time during the delay. As the storm raged, he served beverages and chatted with passengers throughout the cabin.

After the storm passed, boarding resumed. But instead of barking at passengers to take their seats as quickly as possible, Alan used the public address system to apologize for the delay and welcome everyone aboard. Then he used a tactic that I'd never encountered before in all my 985,000+ miles as a commercial airline passenger. In a calm, friendly voice, he said the following:

> "Hello everyone! There are some planes out on the tarmac that landed quite awhile ago but haven't been able to unload their passengers because there were no gates available. Those poor people have been

> flying all day, and now they're stuck out there. The quicker we can get everyone seated, the quicker we can push off from our gate, and the quicker one of those planes can come in. Can you please help get those people home to their families by finding your seat as quickly as possible?"

There was an immediate and noticeable shift in the attitude of the plane's passengers. As Alan had so graciously expressed, speeding up the boarding process wasn't about us. It was about other passengers waiting for our gate — about human beings who just wanted to be *home.* Quickly and quietly, my fellow passengers sat down. Purposeful and relaxed, they moved with a clear intent to get our plane going and out of the way.

REMEMBER

Those few moments of customer experience didn't cost this airline a dime. They required no capital budget and no deep customer relationship management system. All it took was the right kind of person doing what we all want others to do: care about us and others.

Planning for Effective Resolution

We admit it: We've had our faces ripped off (figuratively, of course) by countless angry customers over the course of our careers. So we know from experience that the most important tool for anyone in a customer-facing role is a plan for resolving these types of conflicts. Believe us: When you're dealing with an irate customer, winging it is not the way to go!

Of course, it's not enough to develop a plan. You must also practice using it. Think of a football player — say a wide receiver. There's no way he'd expect to win a game if he'd never bothered to practice running the preplanned routes. Along these same lines, you should never go *mano y mano* with an incensed customer (or force your employees to) if you haven't practiced your plan. Otherwise, you'll find there's just too much going on in the heat of the moment to respond smoothly and appropriately. Your problem reaction process should be ingrained.

REMEMBER

Repeat after us: You must develop and practice your customer resolution plan before you find yourself dealing with a specific customer's specific problem.

Ritz-Carlton, the legendary hotel chain, uses a 21-day certification process to ensure employees understand not only the company's customer service values but also how to perform the technical aspects of their jobs — including dealing with unhappy customers. Read: Ritz-Carlton *never* puts brand-new employees in the position of interacting with guests on their first few days on the job.

Ritz-Carlton understands that the stakes are just too high to risk a disenchanted customer dealing with an ill-prepared employee! Yet, all too often, companies push new hires to interface with customers very early on — sometimes even on their very first day of work. If your goal is to deliver a great customer experience, this is a no-no.

Taking the RESOLVED Approach

So you know you need a plan for dealing with unhappy customers. But what should that plan entail? To help you remember what you should do when you're staring into the bulging red eyes of an infuriated customer, we've developed a handy acronym: RUN. Just kidding! Actually, the acronym is RESOLVED. It stands for the following:

- **R:** Respond to the person who is upset
- **E:** Empathize and apologize
- **S:** Seek to solve the problem
- **O:** Open your mind to the customer's proposed solution
- **L:** Listen intently
- **V:** Verify the solution
- **E:** Execute the solution
- **D:** Document the problem

Respond to the person who is upset

People need to be heard. They need attention. They get cranky when they feel disrespected, rushed, or processed. They don't like to be put aside, treated like a number, or otherwise handled roughly. If you're dealing with an upset customer, it's imperative that you respond to him in such a way that he feels heard, attended to, and respected. Take care of the person first and the problem second.

If you can't remember any other step of the RESOLVED process, remember this one. It's a slight modification of the Golden Rule:

> Treat others as you would like to be treated — only just a little better.

So what does this mean in practical terms? Here are a few points to keep in mind:

- **Personalize the interaction:** This makes the customer feel important and lets her know that you are intent on fixing the problem. To personalize the interaction, ask for and use the customer's first and last name. (Note that this is true in written communication as well, in part to convey to the customer that she's not receiving a computerized response.) If the customer is older than you or it seems appropriate, don't hesitate to use the more formal salutation of Mr. or Ms. Customer.
- **View each customer's situation as unique:** Even if the problem is one you've seen before, remember: It's new to the customer. That means your responses can't be canned.
- **Make the customer feel important:** How? By listening a lot more than you talk (unless you're asking questions). Maintain eye contact. Smile (and mean it!). Respond with nonverbal actions. Don't do anything but pay 100 percent attention. No multi-tasking!
- **Show concern for the customer's situation:** Don't paste a plastic smile on your face. It's fake. You know it, and the customer knows it. If the customer is upset, look appropriately concerned. Ask her exactly what transpired and listen to her complete answer. Ask probing questions without making the customer feel like she is being interrogated.
- **Tailor the solution:** Have you ever been offered a solution to a problem that had nothing whatsoever to do with the issue you raised? If so, you were probably pretty frustrated. That's because being offered a nonsensical solution indicates that the organization doesn't care much about addressing your actual concern. Rather, it's more interested in getting you out of its face so it can move on. The bottom line? It doesn't feel good to be on the receiving end of a generic response. Make an effort to ensure that your proposed solution fits the situation at hand.
- REMEMBER **Note the specific areas of concern the customer mentions:** More than anything else, humans like, want, and need to be heard. The best way to transmit a sense of genuine caring is by reflecting back specific references to what the customer just raised.

Empathize and apologize

When faced with an upset customer, you must stop whatever you're doing and put yourself firmly in his shoes. Just be one-on-one with the customer in that moment. Job #1 is to empathize. To *empathize* means to focus on someone else's emotional state — in this case, your customer's. Relate to the feelings the customer is expressing. Dignity and genuine concern are the watchwords here. If it helps, imagine the person you're dealing with is a beloved grandparent.

Using a calm, interested, and reassuring voice, say something understanding, to the point, and affirming. Then apologize. Take responsibility for any errors made and say you're sorry for the inconvenience, frustration, or other negative result. When a customer is upset, odds are he wants someone to own the mistake. So own it, even if it's not actually your fault. It's no skin off your back. To quote the great and prolific Anonymous: "Apologizing doesn't always mean you are wrong and the other person is right. It just means you value the relationship more than your ego."

REMEMBER

A sincere apology delivered with genuine care is a powerful thing. It can melt people's anger, shift conversations, and prepare the way for reconciliation. But merely thinking it doesn't work. You have to *say* it . . . and say it correctly. Don't just toss off a one-size-fits-all apology. That's likely to tick off your customer even more. Rather, start with the two magic words — "I'm sorry" — and recount as specifically as possible the customer's complaint. For example, "I'm sorry your package didn't arrive on time. We made an error, and I apologize." Simple!

REMEMBER

Now, a wee bit of advice: When apologizing, leave your customer's feelings out of it. In other words, don't say something like "I'm sorry you're upset" or "I'm sorry you were confused." Why? Because these types of apologies shift the blame from you to the customer. Even if you don't intend it, the customer may perceive you as failing to own the mistake. The idea is to communicate that you care, and you want to resolve the problem.

How often should you apologize to an upset customer? When we pose this question to groups we're training, we often hear answers like "Just once. Any more than that and they'll just take advantage of you." Or, "I'll apologize twice and that's it." These kinds of answers typically come from people who shouldn't be in a customer-facing role. The fact is, there is no "right" number of times to apologize. Or, more precisely, the "right" number is however many apologies it takes for the customer to feel heard and for the situation to be resolved. It may take just one apology, or it may take a dozen or more.

Seek to solve the problem

First, the bad news: Problems, obstacles, setbacks, and service failures are bound to happen. They're to be expected. Now the good news: Most problems are solvable!

When dealing with an upset customer, working to solve the problem is critical. First and foremost, that means cleansing your speech of the phrase "It's our policy." If a customer is unhappy, she doesn't give a badger's behind what your "policy" is. Besides, she probably recognizes that you saying "It's our policy" is in fact just a shorthand way of saying "I'm not interested in working with you to find a solution to your problem."

Second, be aware that the customer probably doesn't care what caused her problem. Was it a cumbersome internal process? Is your organization in the midst of a major overhaul? Are you short-staffed? Frankly, it doesn't matter. All the customer wants to know is what you're going to do about it. So take a page from the great Henry Ford's playbook: "Don't find fault; find a remedy."

If you can, take your time developing a solution. A number of studies have suggested that often, the second or third solution you come to is best. When possible, suggest multiple solutions to the customer, saving the one you think will work best for last.

Open your mind to the customer's proposed solution

Often, the best solutions come from the customers themselves. They'll frequently devise solutions and alternatives that you never would have considered. Even better, their solutions are commonly less costly than your solution may have been. Don't be afraid to ask what would make the customer happy. Only rarely will customers suggest something truly outlandish.

Listen intently

As the great Greek philosopher Epictetus once said, "We have two ears and one mouth so that we can listen twice as much as we speak." Put more bluntly, when dealing with an upset customer, your best bet is to shut up and listen. If you fail to listen, you can rest assured that you will make the situation worse.

What do we mean by listen? Well, we *don't* mean "I'm just waiting for my turn to speak" listening. We're talking about full-tilt-boogie listening, 100-proof listening, listening with generosity, listening to learn . . . the list goes on. This type of listening is hard. Doing it well requires a deep well of focus and patience. It means suspending your prejudgments and prejudices. To listen in this way, you must be okay with paradox and ambiguity.

To listen intently, you must practice what counselors and therapists call *active listening*. With active listening, you must concentrate deeply on what is being said, giving your undivided attention. It's not enough to simply hear the message; active listening requires you to pay attention with all of your senses. When you listen in this way, upset customers will recognize it and begin to calm down.

Active listening requires patience. Give your customer time to say everything he needs to say. Even if the customer pauses, don't interject. However tempting it may be to jump in when you hear a lull, don't. Hear him out until he is drained. Don't make judgments about the customer's situation until you have listened to everything he has to say.

Here are some tips to help you with active listening:

- **Maintain eye contact:** This can be tricky, because patterns of eye contact vary significantly from culture to culture. Some Americans may feel uncomfortable with the long gaze that is often associated with Middle Eastern communication; it comes across as too intense. Yet too *little* eye contact may also be viewed negatively, because it conveys a lack of interest, inattention, or even lack of trust.
- **Nod your head:** Don't come across like one of the expressionless stone heads on Easter Island! Practice nonverbal communication, like nodding. You want to look like you're interested and convey that you understand what the customer is saying.
- **Communicate your understanding verbally:** Using a calm voice, say "yes" or "I understand" to convey your understanding of the situation. Try mirroring back what the customer has said. If you need clarification or more information, try saying "Tell me more about that."
- **Practice:** Try active listening with your spouse, a coworker, or a friend. That way, it will come more naturally when you are faced with an unhappy customer.

By giving both verbal and nonverbal clues that you are listening, you encourage the customer to fully express the reasons for his frustration.

Verify the solution

When you have a proposed solution — whether it comes from you or the customer — take a moment to verify that it's what the customer wants. Say something like, "Thank you for the opportunity to speak with you about your concerns. If we do X, Y, and Z, will that satisfy you?" This shows the customer that you won't move forward unless you're both in agreement that the situation has been resolved to his satisfaction.

If, when you ask this question, you find the customer is *not* in agreement, it's likely that you rushed one or more of the previous steps in the RESOLVED process. Do not despair! This gives you an opportunity to further analyze the problem, which will yield a better solution for the long term. Simply go back and redo the steps.

Execute the solution

When you and the customer agree on the solution, you must act immediately. Don't let anything get in the way of immediately executing the resolution you've reached. If you can text or email the customer a few minutes after your conversation to update her on your progress, then so much the better. Show her that you are completely on top of things!

If you can't solve the problem straightaway, keep the customer constantly informed of the progress you're making (even if there is no good news to report). Bad news is better than no news.

Document the problem

Great! Now that you've solved your customer's problem, it's time to take steps to prevent that problem from ever happening again. That means documenting the customer's complaint. This step enables you to track the complaint, maintain a history of it, learn from it, and identify and eliminate preventable problems. It's imperative that you (and your organization) have the discipline to record customer concerns each and every time one occurs.

Documenting a problem can be as simple as jotting down notes about your conversation or entering them into a more formal customer database. Either way, you want to provide adequate information about the complaint to the part of the organization that can fix the underlying cause of the customer's problem. Thorough documentation of the problem conveys that this is a credible concern, not just some passing observation that the organization can ignore.

Handling an Escalated Confrontation

Sometimes, interactions with unhappy customers go beyond run-of-the-mill exchanges, ratcheting up to something more extreme. Even relatively benign customer conflicts can escalate quickly. When that happens, it's up to you to take specific and focused action to prevent the situation from escalating even further. Fortunately, doing so isn't difficult. It simply requires your total focus. And if it feels overwhelming at first, fear not; it gets easier with practice. Following are the five key steps to managing an escalated conflict.

Step 1: Let go of your ego

Rest assured: No matter how angry a customer may be, it probably isn't personal. That is, the person isn't angry with you; more than likely, she's angry with your organization or one of its policies.

It's critical, then, that you maintain a certain emotional distance during the interaction. Don't let your ego enter the equation. Otherwise, the conflict *will* become personal — and you don't want that.

One way to keep your ego in check is to avoid spontaneous responses during your conversation with the customer. These types of responses are often driven by anger or fear — two emotions that are toxic to any interaction, especially one that's already escalated. Instead, you must make a conscious effort to control your responses. Manage them carefully. Be cautious with your words and tone, as well as with your body language. In this way, you can ensure you behave with the utmost professionalism.

Step 2: Decide to defuse

New parents are advised against ramping up their own emotional states by matching the emotional distress of their upset child. According to some, the secret to dealing with a screaming child is to stop, get down on his level, look him straight in the eye, take a breath, smile, and . . . wait for it . . . whisper. Easier said than done, we know, but changing the emotional environment is a potent way to defuse the situation.

Now, we're not suggesting that you start whispering the next time you're faced with an irate customer. Unless you work the birthday shift at Chuck E. Cheese, this tactic will likely prove unsuccessful. But we *are* suggesting that you consciously work hard to defuse the situation. After all, you're the one who's thinking clearly, right? That means you have to take 100 percent responsibility for managing things. It's a little like being a lifeguard. When rescuing someone who is drowning, lifeguards are taught to remain in charge, no matter what the other person does.

Here are a few quick tips that you can use to help defuse:

- Remember that when dealing with an escalated problem, it's often more about understanding and managing emotion than dealing with facts.
- Manage the conversation cadence. If the customer is shouting, speak softly. If he is talking very quickly, speak slowly.
- Ask for and use the customer's name.
- Introduce yourself by name.
- Ask the customer to explain what happened so you know the *real* problem. Actively listen.
- Agree that there is a problem. Don't defend, deny, or explain why the problem happened — it'll just sound like you're making excuses. Besides, those are all offstage issues that the customer doesn't really care about.
- Apologize . . . several times, if need be.
- Tell the customer that you're going to act immediately to fix the problem.

Step 3: Understand the problem

To make progress with an enraged customer, you must work to understand the problem. What is he *really* upset about? What is the root cause of his anger?

As you work to understand the customer's problem, avoid these three common errors:

- **Focusing on the facts:** Often, employees attempting to understand a customer's problem wrongly assume that their goal is to unearth facts. But understanding a problem is as much about understanding and acknowledging the emotions that have resulted from the problem as it is about understanding the cold, hard facts of the situation.
- **Assuming your view of the situation is correct:** Often, customer service personnel assume their view of the problem is correct. They may agree with the customer about the facts of the case but differ in their interpretation of those facts and whether they are relevant. This is a mistake! You must at least consider the possibility that the customer's view is, in fact, the correct one.

- **Playing the blame game:** Often, customers — and even customer service personnel — get bogged down in assigning blame for the problem. Avoid this by apologizing, taking ownership of the problem, and then moving to understand the real issues.

Step 4: Allow time for venting

Let the customer speak. Give him a chance to vent — that is, to safely discharge his anger and/or frustration. Don't rush him, and don't jump in to defend yourself. Be patient.

Venting serves one important purpose: to blow off steam. Usually, when someone vents, it lasts only a minute or so. Unless the customer's physical state is chemically altered by drugs (which does sometimes happen), most people simple cannot rant and rave forever. If you provide an open environment to let the customer vent, his anger will decrease simply because he has been given a chance to express it.

Three active listening tips really help here:

- Let the customer know that you understand that he is upset or distressed.
- Indicate with verbal or nonverbal cues that you understand what the customer is saying and how he is feeling. Don't stand there stone-faced or remain silent (especially if you're on the phone). Nod, smile sympathetically, murmur politely — do *something* to acknowledge that you are listening.
- Ask one or two reflective questions about what the customer has told you. (*Reflective questions* are simply questions that you formulate based on what the customer has expressed.) When you ask these types of relevant follow-up questions, it shows that you are listening and enables you to regain control of the conversation and situation. For example:

  Customer: I've tried three different times to call your call center and each and every time I was put on hold for at least half an hour.

  You: I'm so sorry that happened to you. We've obviously done something wrong. Can you tell me the times you called so that I can understand exactly when this was happening?

Often, listening and asking reflective questions gives the customer time to slow down and consider the situation more carefully and rationally.

Step 5: Get to common ground

As noted by authors Roger Fisher, William Ury, and Bruce Patton in their book *Getting to Yes: Negotiating Agreement Without Giving In* (published by Penguin Books), most major negotiations are merely a series of small sub-agreements and even smaller yeses. When interacting with an incensed customer — or when engaged in any high-stakes conversation — your job is to listen for any small "yes" that can move the conversation forward. The idea is to quickly reach some small agreements.

REMEMBER

Why is this important? Because in this way, you can turn a conflict into a productive conversation — one that seeks a mutually beneficial solution. By reaching common ground, you reduce the distance and difference between you and your customer. Establishing this type of rapport signals that you are ready to connect on a human level and that you're open and ready to work together to resolve the problem. Be aware, however, that this rapport can't be faked. If you act as if you have reached common ground but you haven't, you will quickly receive a negative response, and you'll have to start the de-escalation process all over again. Take your time.

Realizing that the Customer Isn't Always Right

Don't get us wrong: Pioneering retailers like Harry Gordon Selfridge, John Wanamaker, and Marshall Field, who popularized the saying "The customer is always right," were no dummies. Their business holdings — Selfridges, Wanamaker's, and Marshall Field, respectively — were each empires in their own right. Nevertheless, in this one case, they were wrong. That is, contrary to popular belief, the customer is *not* always right.

I (coauthor Roy) learned this surprising fact from one of my bosses, a very senior-level executive at Marriott International, one of the world's leaders in delivering consistently high-quality customer experience. One day, as I sat in his corner office at Marriott Corporate headquarters in Bethesda, Maryland, an irate customer phoned him. During the conversation, my boss, using a clear, calm, and caring voice, called the guest by his name, actively listened, empathized with the man's situation, and attempted to solve his problem. But the customer was so angry and upset, he could not stop swearing. My boss asked him politely to curb his language so they could find a way to solve the problem together, but the man refused. He kept on with the colorful language. My boss asked him to stop swearing a second time, explaining that if the man could not control himself, he would hang up. Again, the man kept swearing . . . so down the phone went, into its cradle.

I was dumbfounded. A senior executive at Marriott had hung up on a guest! That was not in any employee handbook I had read. Noting my slack-jawed expression, my boss said with a smile, "He'll call back." Sure enough, two minutes later, his phone rang again. Needless to say, it was the same guy — and he was even more upset. With perfect clarity, I could hear him shouting and swearing over the phone. Once again, my boss asked him to stop swearing and explained that he would hang up if he did not — to no avail. So once again, my boss hung up. "He'll call back," my boss repeated, "but maybe not this afternoon."

About 45 minutes later, the phone rang again. My boss answered in the same clear, calm, and caring tone as before. Not surprisingly, it was the same guest. By that time, he had calmed down. He apologized for his behavior, and the two of them proceeded to work out a satisfactory resolution in about ten minutes. "They're not always right," my boss said to me afterward. "At least, not in the beginning. By the end though, they should always *feel* right."

It was a great lesson, and one I never forgot. I subsequently taught that concept to every customer-facing employee who ever worked for me. Sometimes, customers are just plain wrong — sometimes staggeringly, diabolically, purposefully, obnoxiously wrong. The challenge for those in the business of creating awesome customer experience is to turn these customers around. Make lemonade out of lemons, as the expression goes.

Yes, the world would be a better place if nasty, complaining customers just went away. But unfortunately, that won't happen. Besides, the reality is that most customers who are unhappy feel that way for a pretty good reason. Fortunately, you now have the tools to turn their frowns upside down.

I was [illegible] lesson, and one I never forgot: [illegible] good for every customer (or employee). [illegible] for me is that customers are not always wrong — sometimes strategically and situationally, they are just plain wrong. The challenge for those in the business of creating awesome customer experience is to turn those customers around. Make them feel as if the company is on their side.

Chapter 6

Good Intentions: Identifying Your Customer Experience Intent

In This Chapter

- Grasping the power of intent
- Deciding who should determine your customer experience intent
- Checking out the characteristics of a customer experience intent statement
- Looking at sample customer experience intent statements
- Making sure that your intent statement lines up with your brand
- Dealing with dissenters

In the course of our consulting work, we've helped hundreds of companies. With each new client, we often start by asking one simple question:

> "What do you want your customers to feel and experience when they are interacting with you?"

Seems easy enough to answer, right? Perhaps — but here's the catch: We ask people to limit their answer to three words. No paragraphs, no sentences . . . just three measly words.

Invariably, people respond with wildly different answers. In fact, for every ten people — regardless of how long they've worked with the company, what area of the organization they're in, or what role they play — we may hear only one or two words that match. That translates to an alignment rate of around 7 percent. Yikes! Would you trust a dentist who pulled the right tooth just 7 percent of the time? Would you choose to fly with an airline that safely landed the plane in the right city only 7 percent of the time? Of course not.

According to Martha Rogers, a thought leader in customer relationship management, "Customer experience shouldn't be random." And yet, because so many companies fail to identify their customer intent, too many customer experiences are just that — random. If your organization employs 100 people, then depending on the person with whom your customer interacts, she could have 100 different experiences!

Job #1, then, is for your organization to identify exactly what you want your customers to feel and experience at every point of interaction with your organization — what we call your *customer experience intent.*

In this chapter, you find out how to identify and articulate your customer experience intent in easy-to-understand, easy-to-communicate, easy-to-interpret language. The result of your efforts will be your *customer experience intent statement,* which serves as the basis of everything you will create, build, and execute for your customers going forward. Your customer experience intent statement is the foundation upon which your customer experience will be built. You'll be amazed by what happens when you identify — and declare — what you really want!

For All Intents and Purposes: The Power of Intent

French chemist Michel-Eugène Chevreul (1786–1889) was best known for his research on animal fats, which led to improvements in the manufacturing of soap and candles. But he also spent considerable time studying what is now called the *ideomotor effect,* which deals with the power of intent.

Chevreul discovered that if someone imagines something intensely, that person's body will behave as if that thing has already come to pass. Chevreul went on to prove that the subconscious can affect physical movements not under the obvious control of the conscious mind. He also observed that these actions can be sustained by the subconscious without the interference of the conscious mind. Finally, he showed that the subconscious mind can be trained by repetition.

Uh, what? The subconscious can be trained? Yes indeed. If you're familiar with the work of the very popular speaker and life coach Tony Robbins, you've seen this idea in action. The effects of clearly articulated intention are at the center of Robbins' philosophy and are described in his many tapes, books, and seminars. Indeed, tennis great Andre Agassi credits Robbins' ideas for helping to pull him out of one of the deepest slumps of his professional sports career. The best-selling book *The Secret* also discusses the power of intention vis à vis personal success and achievement.

Imagine That: Olympians and Visualization

Have you ever watched competitive ski racers waiting for their turn to start? In the minutes leading up to their race, you'll often spot these athletes standing in a quiet spot, eyes closed, heads and bodies swaying. No, they're not possessed; they're visualizing — skiing down the course in their head. They're imagining every gate, every turn, every bump, and every jump. Why? Because visualizing has been proven to improve performance. Essentially, by imagining themselves skiing the course perfectly, they are identifying their intent. That's something you and your employees can do, too. Imagine what you could achieve if, consciously and subconsciously, every single one of your employees had the same customer experience intent firmly in her mind!

REMEMBER

Yes, it sounds like something straight out of Hogwarts. But the clear articulation of intention turns out to be surprisingly powerful! It can spur serious change in the people and organizations that use it. So how can you use this bit of brain science to your best advantage? By clearly identifying and articulating what you want.

Teaming Up: Assembling Your Customer Intent Team

REMEMBER

Your goal is to identify exactly what you want your customers to feel and experience at every point of interaction with your organization. We call this your customer experience intent. Then you need to write it down. This becomes your customer experience intent statement.

Your customer experience intent statement should resonate with all the different parts of your business. That means you want very knowledgeable people from every corner of your organization to participate in the intent statement's development. The people in this diverse group should have a clear understanding of how customers interact with their particular part of the business, as well as how customers interact with other parts of the organization.

As you choose your team, keep these points in mind:

- **Representation:** Ensure that every group (department or functional area) that interacts with the customer inside your organization is represented on the customer experience intent statement team.

In particular, invite someone from your company's marketing arm or brand team (if your organization has one) to participate.

- **Assertiveness:** Select employees who have a strong opinion but are also collaborative in nature to participate on the team. This isn't a job for shy, shrinking violets. You need strong, informed voices at the table!
- **Influence:** If possible, include some influential individuals on your team to help with efforts to persuade the organization to adopt the proposed customer experience intent statement when the time comes.
- **Experience:** Be sure to include seasoned veterans who have a substantial history in your organization. At the same time, don't overlook younger, less-experienced workers. Include your next-generation leaders. These employees have a personal and professional stake in how the business will operate over the next five to ten years. If you're prescient enough to know who your CEO will be in the coming years, get her on the team.

After you've pinpointed who should develop the intent statement, assemble the group for a one-day meeting. Its mission? To answer the same question we posed earlier: "What do we want our customers to feel and experience when they are interacting with us?"

This time, however, the group can — and should — use more than three words to answer the question. The idea here is to come up with a paragraph or two that will serve as the customer experience intent statement. You want this group to struggle over the words, parse their exact meaning, and fight over the nuances until they develop a statement that's right for your organization.

For more on the particulars of that statement, read on!

I Declare! Developing Your Customer Experience Intent Statement

Your customer experience intent team is charged with developing your organization's customer experience intent statement. This statement — typically no more than a paragraph or two — should convey the experiential and emotional elements you want to deliver in a way that is inspiring, measurable, and easy to understand.

REMEMBER

Your customer experience intent statement should be built to last. It should be part of your organization for a long time. You and your team must commit to it in a serious way!

The customer experience intent statement should have depth, character, and emotion. Vagueness is a no-go. Think of the intent statement as a set of engineering specifications. It's a blueprint of the experience you want to create for your customers.

In addition to being clear, your customer experience intent statement should be aspirational. There's enough mediocrity in the world; don't add to the problem! Reach a little higher than you may normally think possible. Don't merely strive for your customers to feel satisfied. If you want to stay in business, you need customers who are pleased, happy, delighted, or even thrilled!

Your customer experience intent statement should be a stretch. It should be something that seems just outside the arc of what's reasonable. Take a risk with your customer experience intent statement! If you're a little nervous about whether your statement is achievable, you're probably right on target.

That being said, if your customer experience intent statement is completely at odds with the operating reality of your business — if the words in your statement are not true today and will never realistically be true in the future — then you need to step back and start over. Otherwise, your organization's employees will summarily dismiss it. They must see the customer experience intent statement as attainable. It can be difficult and challenging, sure, but it must ultimately be doable.

One resource you *shouldn't* mine for guidance in developing your customer experience intent statement is your company's mission or vision statement. Why? Because many of these statements are sweet-sounding gobbledygook that don't reference the customer experience in the actual day-to-day operating reality.

Keeping It All Inside: Where to Communicate the Customer Experience Intent Statement

Yes, we know. We outline a scenario in which a customer reads your customer experience intent statement. In reality, however, this statement is *not* for customer consumption. It isn't a slogan, a catch phrase, or a buzzword, and it shouldn't be advertised or marketed.

Your customer experience intent statement is for you and your organization only. It represents your company's end game with respect to what must be delivered. Don't open your yap and start reciting your intent statement to your customers! Customers should discover your intent by experiencing it. Period.

Also, you must avoid developing a customer experience intent statement that focuses on your organization's processes, goals, and so on. The customer experience intent statement isn't about *you;* it's about *them.* An effective customer experience intent statement focuses on the customer — on what she will experience at your various points of interaction, or *touchpoints.* If a customer were to read your statement, would she think "Hey! This is about your internal stuff. It doesn't really talk about *me*"? If so, you've missed the mark. The response you're going for is, "Wow. If you guys really did this, I would be amazed!"

Checking Out Some Customer Experience Intent Statement Examples

In this section, we give you several examples of real-life customer experience intent statements from a variety of industries and sectors. These include retail, education, financial services, manufacturing, hospitality, and regulated utility. Even if your industry isn't represented here, the sample statements shown here can help you find your footing as you develop your own statement.

The idea here is not for you to cut and paste these sample statements into your own intent statement. (Trust us, it won't work. Each industry and organization is different.) Rather, it's to help you get a sense of what a good customer experience intent statement looks like.

Note that although most of these customer experience intent statements are written from the organization's point of view, the last one is written as if the customers themselves were saying the words. Either perspective works, but we find that it's often more impactful to write the statement from the customer's slant.

Retail

Here's an example of a customer experience intent statement for an organization in the retail sector:

> We will be renowned for our reliable service. Our people will be knowledgeable and respond to and resolve all customer questions promptly, making customers feel assured. This service will be delivered in an enjoyable and caring way that will ultimately make our customers feel special and valued. Our customers will trust us and believe we provide value for the money they spend with us.

Education

Following is an intent statement for an educational organization:

> At each point of interaction with us, our students will feel that they are treated as individuals and that we have invested the time to understand, remember, and meet their unique needs, wants, and personal expectations.
>
> Each of our team members will always shows attentive and engaging care. We will be known as both supportive educators and trusted advisors who identify and eliminate barriers to our students' success. The educational environment we create will be innovative, challenging, and fun, supporting and encouraging a lifelong desire to learn.

Financial services

This customer experience intent statement is written for "internal" customers — that is, the organization's business partners.

> Our intention is that each and every interaction with our business partners mirrors and measurably exhibits the following ideals:
>
> - We honor them and their mission, and serve as the dedicated financial enabler and steward of their success.
> - While executing our fiduciary responsibility, we act in a way that respects and values the business partnership between us.
> - We provide honest, efficient, caring interactions, as well as professional advice and counsel.
> - We are seen as proactive, approachable, rapidly responsive, and easy to do business with.
> - We skillfully sustain the balance of regulator and trusted partner.

Manufacturing

Here's a customer experience intent statement for a medical products manufacturer:

> Every interaction with our customers will create experiences that
>
> - Build confidence and assurance
> - Communicate individual care

- Show sincere appreciation
- Strengthen the relationship

Following is another example of an intent statement for an organization in the manufacturing sector:

> We want our consumers to be proactive advocates of our products, service, and care. At every point of interaction with us, we want consumers to feel that we are easy to do business with and that our products and services are understandable and straightforward. We want to build or reinforce a sense of confidence, assurance, and empowerment. Our consumers should have a sense of protection and that we are always looking out for their best interests and security. They should feel a pride of ownership knowing that our product matters and that they have made the right and best choice by choosing us.

Hospitality

This example of a customer experience intent statement is from an organization in the hospitality industry:

> Our hotel is a place where the genuine care and comfort of our guests is our highest mission. We pledge to provide the finest personal service and facilities for our guests, who will always enjoy a warm, relaxed, yet refined ambience. Our experience will enliven the senses, instill well-being, and fulfill even the unexpressed wishes and needs of our guests.

Regulated utility

The following customer experience intent statement is for a regulated utility, written from the customer's point of view:

> In every interaction with [insert company name], I feel like I'm dealing with people who genuinely care about my home, my business, and me. They make the effort to understand and anticipate my needs. They proactively communicate. When there are problems, they are creative in resolving them quickly. I feel like they view my time as being as valuable as theirs. They're easy to do business with, any way I choose. It's seamless and

effortless, and I never feel taken for granted. They are my trusted energy advisor, active and visible contributors to the well-being of our community. They're the first to help when I need them. They're my neighbors.

Aligning the Customer Experience with Branding

The line between customer experience and company branding can be as thin as a supermodel. Even so, there are some important distinctions to consider.

A company's *brand* is an easy-to-grasp identifier that enables customers to quickly understand what products and services the company offers, as well as who the company *is.* The brand clearly conveys the organization's attributes. In contrast, customer experience refers to a customer's actual interactions with a company, regardless of whether they match the company's brand, or declared attributes. One — the brand — is a promise. The other — the customer experience — is the truth.

It doesn't really matter which comes first, the brand or the customer experience. What *does* matter is that an organization's branding works synergistically with the customer experience. The two must overlap. (See Figure 6-1.) If, after reviewing your customer experience intent statement, you find that it's out of sync with your company's brand positioning, consider it a red flag.

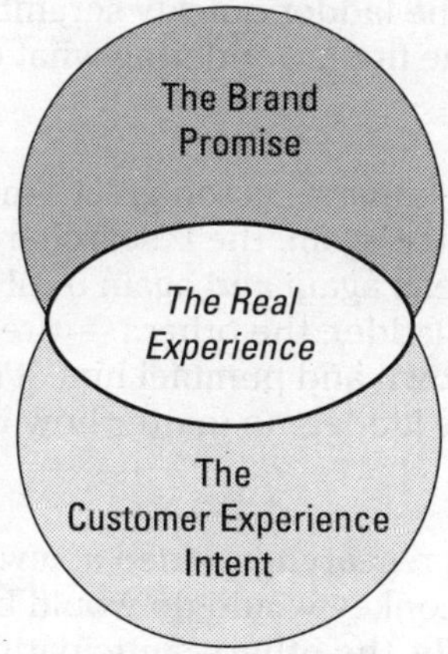

Figure 6-1: The brand and the customer experience should overlap.

Illustration courtesy of Roy Barnes.

Dissents and Sensibility: Overcoming Dissenters

Okay, it's time for some straight talk. Odds are that some people in your organization have no enthusiasm, no energy, and no real interest in improving your customers' experience. Some of these miscreants may even be pretty senior leaders. So as you work to develop your customer experience intent statement, expect to meet some resistance. Be aware, too, that said resistance may come from some unexpected people.

Your organization's culture and its views of the customer are products of time, history, and tradition. If that tradition is good, then great! That's something to celebrate and take pride in. But if it's *not* so good . . . well, watch out. You're going to have a fight on your hands. (To be clear, this fight won't be a physical brawl. The resistance you'll meet will be of the passive-aggressive variety.)

Here's a story to prepare you for what you may encounter as you develop your customer experience intent statement. Imagine a scientist who is studying the group dynamics of monkeys. She places five monkeys in a large room. Hanging from the ceiling is a bunch of ripe bananas, and underneath the bananas is a stepladder.

Naturally, the monkeys immediately spot the bananas, and one of them begins to climb the ladder. As he does, however, the researcher, who is hidden from view, sprays the remaining four monkeys with extremely cold water. Chaos ensues, and the monkey on the ladder quickly scrambles down in the confusion. All five monkeys sit on the floor, wondering what on Earth just happened.

Soon, however, the sweet smell of the ripe bananas is too great. Another monkey begins to climb the ladder. And once again, the researcher sprays the remaining monkeys with water. This happens again and again until finally, the next time a monkey attempts to climb the ladder, the others — tired of being sprayed with ice-cold water — drag him down and pummel him. It's not long before none of the monkeys dare climb the ladder, no matter how hungry they are.

What do you suppose would happen if the researcher added a new monkey to the mix? Naturally, the first thing that monkey would do would be to climb the ladder to get the bananas. And naturally, the others, anticipating that cold shower, would immediately drag him down and pummel him — even if the researcher *didn't* turn on the hose. After a few rounds of this, you can be sure the new monkey would learn never to climb that ladder again, although he would never know *why.*

Now imagine that the researcher replaced *all* the monkeys in the room, one by one. As each new monkey was introduced, there would be a strong likelihood that the monkeys already in the room would beat him up for climbing the ladder, even if they themselves had never experienced the frigid spray from the hose. Why? If you were to ask the monkeys (and, further, if monkeys could speak), the smartest one would likely reply, "We've always done it that way!"

Here's the point: Repeated behaviors eventually build your organization's culture. In fact, repeated behaviors are all culture really is. Frequently, habits become processes, which later become policies, hardening into accepted "fact" over time. Odds are, no one knows the reason for the existing behavior anymore, but everyone mimics it to try to fit in. So your organization's current attitude about customer experience (and everything else) is likely the result of years and years of habit, myth, and unchallenged assumptions.

Here's the deal: You're going to have to challenge what is considered normal and acceptable behavior. Why? Because your customer experience intent statement is going to dismantle, change, batter, and/or reform something that has been accepted in your organization for quite some time. Resistance is natural. So watch your back, watch your front, and step up to make this change.

Now is the time to put an end to the business-as-usual customer experience. Developing your intent statement is the first step. Although history and tradition are very good things, they don't necessarily have a place in your customer experience intent statement. You want to acknowledge and respect the past, but not be bound by it.

As you develop your customer experience intent statement, expect to feel a little like one of those monkeys on the ladder. There's a good chance you'll be pummeled for your efforts. Don't give up! Become a strong, vocal advocate for improving the customer experience in your organization — even if some other monkeys don't like it.

the researcher would turn on the hose. After a few rounds of this, you can bet the new monkey would learn never to climb the ladder again, although he would never know why.

Now imagine that the researcher replaced all the monkeys in the room, one by one. As each new monkey was introduced, there would be a strong likelihood that the monkeys already in the room would beat him up for climbing the ladder, even if they themselves had never experienced the frigid spray from the hose. Why? If you were to ask the monkeys (and, if the monkeys could speak), the smartest one would likely reply, "We've always done it that way."

Here's the point: Repeated behaviors eventually build your organization's culture. In fact, repeated behaviors are all culture really is. Frequently habits become processes, which later become policies, hardening into concepts that, over time, folks are no longer [illegible] the reason for the existing behavior anymore, but everyone is doing it [illegible] it's sure that, [illegible] customer experience (and everything else) is likely the result of years and years of habits, myths, and unchallenged assumptions.

Here's the deal: You're going to have to challenge what was considered normal and acceptable behavior. Why? Because your customer experience intent statement is going to dismantle, change, alter, and/or retool something that has been accepted in your organization for quite some time. Resistance is natural, so watch your back, watch your front, and step up to make this change.

Now is the time to put an end to the business-as-usual customer experience development. Your intent statement is the first step. Although history and tradition are very good things, they don't necessarily have a place in your customer experience intent statement. You want to acknowledge and respect the past, but not be bound by it.

As you develop your customer experience intent statement, expect to feel a little like one of those monkeys on the ladder. There's a good chance you'll be pummeled for your efforts. Don't give up. Become a strong, vocal advocate for improving the customer experience of your organization — even if some other monkeys don't like it.

Chapter 7

Channeling Your Inner Magellan: Mapping Your Customer's Journey

In This Chapter

- Seeing why you should map your customer's journey
- Taking a closer look at the term "touchpoint"
- Working through the charting process
- Viewing examples of journey maps

Every year, in every corner of the business world, companies spend millions of dollars in an attempt to improve customer experience. That money may go toward designing new products, developing new services, opening new call centers, or creating new channels for customers to interact with. Or it may be shelled out to build new stores, design new websites, or develop and distribute new marketing collateral. And yet, for the most part, customers don't even notice — and if they do, they aren't always that impressed.

The fact is, customers are under constant bombardment from your "New This!" and your "Improved That!" But this "shock and awe" approach simply doesn't work. Providing an excellent customer experience requires a deep understanding of how your customers interact with your business — at each of your individual touchpoints as well as across your entire organization.

A key first step in this effort is to map your customer's journey and touchpoints. Doing so enables you to view your organization from the customer's perspective. In this chapter, you learn what journey mapping is, why it's a good idea, and what steps are involved in the journey-mapping process.

What Is Journey Mapping?

Mapping your customer's journey can provide you with a clearer understanding of his experience with your organization. Essentially, you produce a visual representation or "story" of the customer's interactions with your company. Journey mapping yields the following benefits:

- It enables you to identify whether (and where) you may be confusing customers.
- It provides an understanding of what information you are transmitting to customers at their various points of interaction.
- It uncovers stress and failure points on the customer's typical path.
- It reveals where customer information is siloed by your legacy information systems.
- It exposes touchpoints whose internal management and ownership are unclear.
- It enables you to target limited resources for maximum effect by avoiding duplication and possibly even reducing the amount of time spent interacting with customers.
- It helps you create the foundation upon which to deliver an integrated and seamless experience across all the different functional areas of your organization.
- It may lead people within different functional areas to actually communicate with each other about what they are delivering to the customer.

Remember, though, that mapping your customer's journey isn't an end in itself. It's the starting point to realizing your customer experience intent.

There's a Map for That: Why Map Your Customer's Journey?

In the spirit of Socrates, we answer this question by posing a few others:

- Do you have a complete understanding of how your customers interact with your organization?
- Do each of your employees have a view of what happens to customers upstream and downstream from their particular points of interaction?

- Is there an existing understanding of the different emotions that your customers may be experiencing as they interact with various parts of your company?
- Do you understand what data and information systems the customer interacts with across your enterprise? Do these systems transfer the appropriate quality and quantity of data from one touchpoint to the next?
- Do you understand who "owns" each customer touchpoint internally? In other words, do you know who is responsible for each specific touchpoint's performance?
- Do you know which of your touchpoints have the biggest impact on your overall customer experience (both positively and negatively)?

If you answered "no" to any of these questions, don't worry. You're not alone. Most organizations (and the people who work for them) have very little idea how their companies look from the outside in. They're paid to see what's happening in their own little work silo. But this isn't what the customer experiences. To get a clear understanding of how your organization really works from the outside in, the best place to start is with a journey map!

Understanding What Constitutes a Touchpoint

Touchpoint. We've used that word a few times already. But what does it mean? Simply put, *touchpoints* are all the ways in which your customer interacts with your organization. Each of these interactions takes place at a particular point in time, in a certain context, and with the goal of meeting a specific customer need or want.

REMEMBER

Customer experience begins to be manifested in one place, and one place only: at each of your touchpoints.

Of course, part of understanding what something *is* is identifying what it is *not*. In the case of a touchpoint, it is not an internal process, visible only to your company. That is, touchpoints are not your marketing processes, your IT processes, your sales processes, your operating processes, your finance processes, your customer research processes, and so on. Touchpoints are not what happens behind the scenes.

Nor are touchpoints activities undertaken by customers *before* they interact with your company, activities that are visible only to them. That is, touchpoints are not in play when the customer is understanding his needs, identifying alternatives, and so on. Yes, your advertising and marketing messages, which *are* touchpoints, may influence your customer's thinking, but the thinking itself is not a touchpoint.

REMEMBER

Essentially, touchpoints are those processes and activities that are visible both to your company and to the customer. Examples of touchpoints include the following:

- Advertisements
- Websites
- Emails
- Direct mail
- Phone calls
- Text messages
- Point-of-purchase displays
- Signage
- Physical storefronts
- Vehicles
- Contracts

There's a lot going on at these touchpoints — more than you may think. At almost every touchpoint, one or more of the following may occur:

- Some task, transaction, or process is executed.
- Some customer need, want, or desire is uncovered.
- Customer expectations are set.
- Promises are made, met, or broken.
- Customer emotions — be they good, bad, or ugly — are created, cemented, or ignored.
- Employees behave or misbehave.
- Customer data is used (remembered) or abused (forgotten).
- Additional customer information is gathered, stored, and passed on (or not) to the next point of customer interaction.
- Marketing collateral is distributed and (hopefully) used.

- Performance measures are recorded and captured.
- Standard operating procedures are ignored, executed brilliantly, or perhaps rammed down customers' throats. ("Sorry, that's our policy.")
- The cash register rings.

Figure 7-1 illustrates what are — and aren't — touchpoints. As you can see, it shows three different views: activities visible only to the company (along the top), activities visible only to the customer (along the bottom), and activities visible to both (in the middle). Those activities in the middle should be your focus.

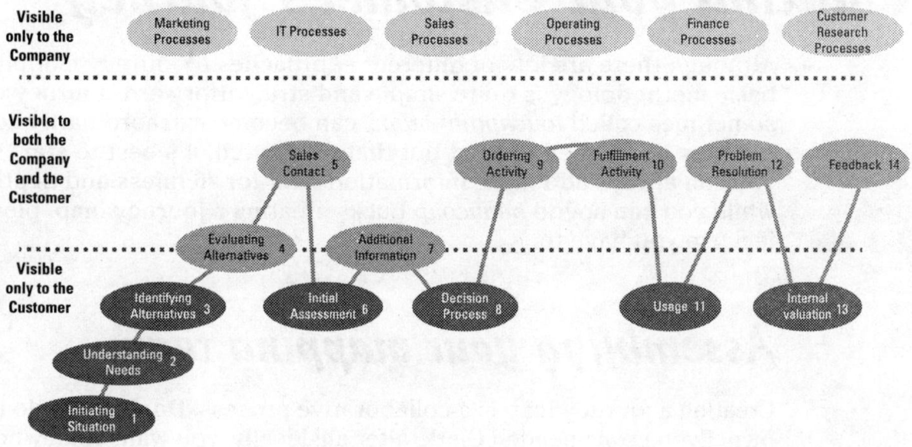

Figure 7-1: What is — and isn't — a touchpoint.

Illustration courtesy of Roy Barnes.

Not sure what you're looking at here? Maybe an example will help. Imagine you're driving down the highway and you run over a piece of debris, shredding your tire. That's your "initiating situation" (labeled "1" in the bottom group of activities). After you've removed the damaged tire, mounted your spare, and gotten back on the road, you ruminate about what you need to do next — namely, replace the shredded tire (2). Having pinpointed your need, you begin to identify your options. For example, you could buy a new tire or a used one. You could purchase a tire from Michelin, Firestone, Goodyear, or some other manufacturer (3).

At this point, however, no tire manufacturer, seller, or supplier is aware of your need. Your thoughts and actions are thus far unknowable. In other words, there have been no touchpoints. But as soon as you begin evaluating your alternatives — for example, by visiting a tire store or looking online, both of which are touchpoints (4) — you become visible. Your actions can be seen. From here on, you will likely alternate between being visible and invisible to various tire suppliers (in other words, you'll alternate between being at a touchpoint and not being at a touchpoint). This process may involve talking to a sales representative (5), retreating to assess your budget and your options (6), seeking additional information (7), and making your decision (8).

As you embark on mapping your customer's journey, only the touchpoints are what you want to chart — not all the rest of the activity that you can't directly affect.

Charting Your Customer's Journey

Although there are lots of different approaches to journey mapping, the basic methodology is quite simple and straightforward. Journey maps, sometimes called *touchpoint maps,* can become extraordinarily complex, but they don't need to start out that way. Often, it's best to start simple; you can always add more information later for richness and depth. And while you can spend *beaucoup* bucks creating a journey map, please don't feel like you have to.

Assembling your mapping team

Creating a journey map is a collaborative process. Don't try to do it on your own. Even Lewis needed Clark, after all! Ideally, you want somewhere in the neighborhood of 10 to 18 smart, opinionated people. (If you opt for more, just remember that managing a large group can get a little unwieldy.)

Whom should you include? Here are a few suggestions:

- **A cross-section of subject matter experts from every customer-facing part of your business:** Not only does this help you identify the touchpoints you need to map, but the very process of creating the map fosters greater connectedness among this broad group, which helps to improve customer experience overall.
- **Front-line, customer-facing staff and support function folk:** These guys likely know the details about all the nitty-gritty points of the contact.
- **Some marketing and brand types, as well as a strategic planner:** You want to include some people who have a broader, company-wide view of the organization. They think differently about the whole enterprise versus the pieces.

- **Some process owners and operators:** These are the factory owners who churn out the products and services that customers actually buy. They have insight into what lies behind the scenes for some of the touchpoints you unearth.
- **Someone who is kept abreast of customer surveys and other similar research conducted by your company:** These data wonks often have great insight into where customers are interacting with the organization, and they have the quantitative information to prove it. (***Remember:*** Surveys and research are touchpoints, too!)
- **Some creative types, such as design experts:** They think differently than the rest of us — thank goodness! These people can be particularly helpful in laying out the journey map in a way that is engaging and easily understood.

The "Spider Web of Experience" exercise

After you've assembled your team, you might want to kick off the mapping process by conducting the "Spider Web of Experience" exercise, designed to illustrate the interconnected nature of customer experience. This fun exercise, which takes only 15 or 20 minutes to complete, reveals the sometimes confounding path that many customers are forced to travel when they interact with a business or other organization.

To conduct this exercise, you need the following:

- An open area with enough space for your journey-mapping team to gather in a circle.
- 150 feet of mason's line (or some other easy-to-unroll, lightweight string). Mason's line works well because it comes on a handy roller. It's available at most big-box hardware stores.
- A sample customer experience to use as your "story." This can be from your own company, or you can use any other example you can think of. In this example, we use a customer experience from an automobile insurance company.

To conduct the exercise, follow these steps:

1. **Ask the members of your group to gather around you in a circle.**
2. **Inquire who among them has had the most automobile accidents.**

Invariably, someone will have had three or four. (It doesn't matter whether they caused these accidents. Everyone denies being the cause of accidents anyway.)

3. **Bring the person who has had the most accidents into the center of the circle with you.**

   You can call him the "accident victim." Ask the group to pretend that he's just had an accident and has totaled his car. (This is your "story.")

4. **Hand the end of the roll of mason's line to the accident victim.**

   Tell him to hold on tight for the duration of the exercise.

5. **Ask the group to identify each of the steps the accident victim has to take in order to obtain reimbursement for his insurance claim.**

   These should be in chronological order. Some of these steps involve touchpoints with the insurer, while others don't. The steps might include the following:

   - Getting information from the other person involved in the accident
   - Getting a police report
   - Talking to the insurance agent
   - Talking to a tow truck driver
   - Talking to a taxi driver
   - Talking to the insurance adjuster
   - Talking to the insurance appraiser
   - Talking to a rental car agency to get a replacement car
   - Talking to the insurance company's accounting/finance group

   As participants identify the steps taken, assess whether they are indeed touchpoints or whether they're invisible to either the company or the customer.

6. **When someone correctly identifies the first touchpoint — in this case, talking to the insurance agent — walk the roll of mason's line to that person and tell him to hang on to the string; then return the roll to the accident victim at the center of the circle.**

7. **Repeat Steps 5 and 6 for each subsequent touchpoint.**

   Keep asking, "What happens next?" Soon, you'll have a veritable web of string, with the accident victim at the center.

8. **Optionally, you can run a separate string between the various "behind the scenes" or "customer only" steps.**

(Although this does result in a more complex web, it's not strictly necessary.)

9. **Ask the accident victim to describe what it feels like to be in the middle of this web.**

   Is it pleasant? Confining? Overwhelming?

10. **Ask the group what will happen if someone on the other end of one of the strings doesn't respond to the accident victim in a reasonable time frame.**

    How will this affect the customer?

Most employees — including senior leaders — have never seen the experience that their customers have when interacting with their organization. This exercise makes visible something that normally isn't seen by those inside a company, but is seen and felt by almost all of its customers. Figure 7-2 illustrates the result of this exercise.

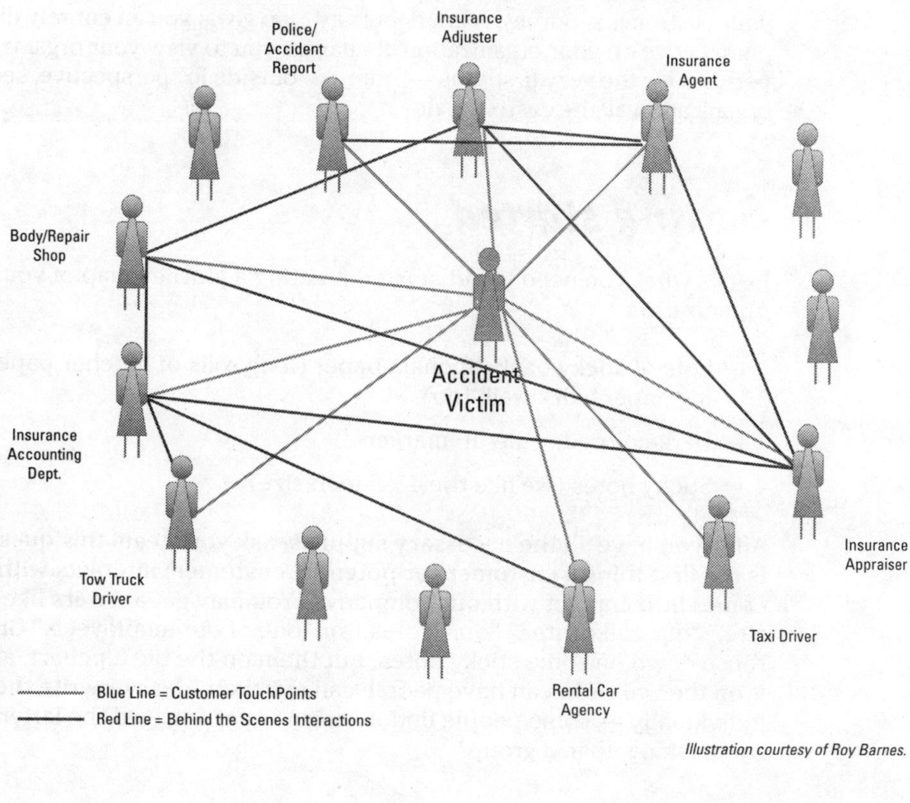

Figure 7-2: The "Spider Web of Experience."

Illustration courtesy of Roy Barnes.

A word to the wise

As you begin creating your organization's journey map, don't get carried away. Yes, you could start to include an almost limitless variety of information on your map — different customer personas, emotion mapping, deep analytical insights on each touchpoint, and so on. But if you do, you'll find that your map will soon spiral into a level of complexity that only Stephen Hawking could unravel. Resist the temptation to include every piece of data. Instead, for now, keep things simple. Journey mapping is merely a tool to assist you and your organization in better understanding your customer and her needs. If it's too complicated to explain to your grandmother, then it's too complicated, period.

Creating a journey map

Now that you've seen how complex a customer's path can be, it's time to map your customer's journey. A good journey map gives you an entirely different perspective on your organization. It enables you to view your organization — perhaps for the very first time — from an "outside in" perspective, seeing your organization as the customer does.

Getting started

Here's what you need to get started creating a journey map of your own organization:

- Lots of sticky-back flipchart paper (long rolls of butcher paper or packing paper work well, too)
- Dark-colored, wide-tip markers
- Sticky notes (we like the 4-x-6-inch size)

After you have all the necessary supplies, ask your team this question: "What is the first thing a customer (or potential customer) interacts with when she comes into contact with our company?" You may get answers like "our website," "our call center," "our stores," or "one of our employees." Great! Write those down on some sticky notes, put them on the big flipchart, and post it on the wall. You can have people call out their ideas or write them down individually — some people find it easier to get engaged the latter way than by speaking up in a group.

Next, ask this question: "What is the next thing a customer will do, and with whom or what will she interact?" In this case, you may get answers like "she'll look for a specific product on our website" or "she'll interact with our call center's integrated voice response (IVR) system." Fantastic! Again, write those answers down on some sticky notes and put them on the big flipchart. You're starting to identify the customer's path.

Continue asking "What happens next?" and posting your answers on the wall. Within a half hour or so, you should have a pretty clear picture of the main points of interaction between your customers and your company. Then, group these activities into broader categories that describe the customer's typical path. For an example of the "right" level of detail, see Figure 7-3. It shows a high-level list of customer interactions generated by one of our recent clients, a technical college.

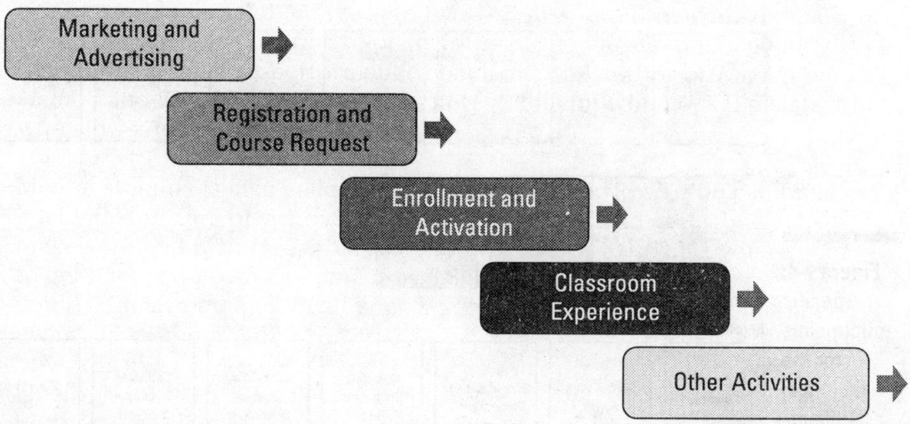

Figure 7-3: High-level journey map experience categories for a technical college.

Illustration courtesy of Roy Barnes.

Digging deeper

Now it's time to dig a little deeper into each of your broad categories. To achieve this, break your team into groups and assign each group a category. The goal is for each group to outline what specific steps the customer will take in each area. Using sticky notes and flipcharts to record their answers, groups should ask the following questions:

- What does the customer want to accomplish?
- What actions will the customer take to satisfy her needs?

- What does the customer do first?
- What comes next?
- What happens after that? (And so on and so forth.)

TIP

To answer these questions, your team may need to look at outside sources of information. Yes, you should leverage the knowledge you have in the room, but don't be afraid to pick up the phone and call a subject matter expert who may not be present!

After each group has completed its work, try to consolidate it into one top-level view, like the one in Figure 7-4. (Note that most organizations have between 150 and 200 touchpoints. For the sake of simplicity, we've shown significantly fewer here.)

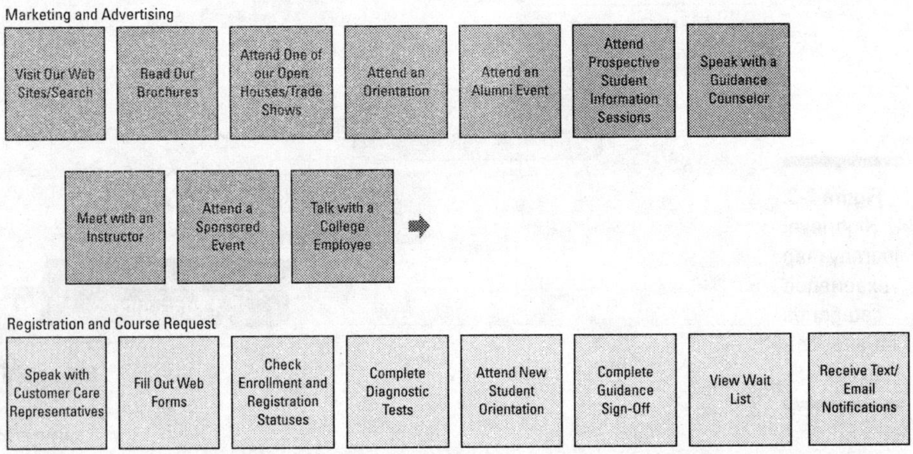

Figure 7-4: Specific touchpoints for the technical college.

Illustration courtesy of Roy Barnes.

TIP

Print your journey map on the largest paper you have available. Many organizations print them on poster-sized plotter paper to improve readability.

Be aware that "walking the customer's journey," as you do during this phase, will undoubtedly reveal both surprises and gaps. Know, too, that for 99 percent of the people in your organization, this will be the very first time that they will have seen the entirety of your customer interactions. This can be both daunting and disappointing. Often, organizations discover that instead of providing a clear path for customers to follow, they in fact are doing nothing more than offering an à la carte menu of services.

The result? Customer confusion and a lousy customer experience. If this happens to you, don't feel too bad. We have yet to work with a client who, upon seeing his organization's journey map, hasn't been at least a little bit distressed over what their customers have been put through!

REMEMBER

One more thing: No organization gets its journey map right the first time. It's an iterative document. As you discover more about how your customers experience your organization, you should adjust and modify your map. It also gives you fantastic insight into very obvious — but then again not so obvious — easy-to-fix problems, which you can tackle straightaway to improve your customer experience.

Mapping nonlinear interactions

At some point during this process, someone in your group might say, "Hey! Not all of our customers go through this process. What about our VIP customers? Or our largest industrial clients?" Great questions!

In many cases, customers don't follow a prescribed path. In fact, there can be dozens of appropriate routes for your customers to follow, and that's fine. Don't get hung up on the idea that there is only one path and all your customers should follow it. In reality, a customer should be able to jump from one touchpoint to another based on her particular needs. She'll interact with some touchpoints and miss others entirely.

Just because some of your customers don't follow the same linear path as others, however, doesn't mean you shouldn't map their journey. We advise our clients to create as many maps as are needed to represent the majority of their customers. If there are common interactions among different customer groups and segments, that's great! But if interaction paths diverge for different types of customers, your journey map should reflect that. Just remember to try to bring the various paths back together on one path whenever possible.

Taking action

After you map your customer touchpoints, it's time to ask a few questions:

- **Who owns each of these touchpoints?**

  That is, who in your organization is responsible for managing the performance of each touchpoint? If you don't know who should be held accountable for improvements in the customer experience at individual touchpoints, it's unrealistic to think things are going to get better.

- **What technology infrastructure supports each of these touchpoints?**

  The idea here is to understand what information systems are in play at each touchpoint. (One client of ours took down one of its IT systems for replacement, unaware of how that system supported one of the organization's customer touchpoints. Chaos ensued.)

- **Does data about the customer flow freely between adjacent touchpoints?**

  That is, do your systems move the right customer information from place to place? Or are there little "black holes" where customer data is sucked in, never to be seen again? Don't force customers to repeatedly enter their information because your systems don't "talk" to each other.

- **Which touchpoints tend to experience the most problems?**
- **Is the path that the customer needs to follow from touchpoint to touchpoint clear and intuitive?**
- **Which touchpoints are most important from your customers' perspective?**

  As you begin the process of redesigning your touchpoints to improve customer experience, you should take into consideration which ones are most important from the customer's perspective.

- **Which of these touchpoints are most important from your organization's perspective?**
- **At which of these touchpoints do you fully deliver the customer experience intent?**

  If your customer experience intent statement outlines, say, six or seven experiential elements that you want to deliver, can you quantitatively measure the degree to which each touchpoint achieves this goal?

- **At which of these touchpoints (if any) does your organization fully utilize all of an individual customer's data to personalize her experience?**
- **At which of these touchpoints (if any) does your organization currently collect customer feedback and survey data?**
- **Can you conduct correlation analysis to determine which customer touchpoints have the greatest impact on overall customer engagement and satisfaction?**

  You need robust customer feedback and survey information at each touchpoint to do correlation analysis. For more information on customer feedback, see Chapter 15.

- **Which touchpoint currently benefits from the most investment spending to improve performance?**
- **Are any of your touchpoints unnecessary or duplicate in nature?**

A journey map helps you think in a different way about what your organization does and can provide new and different paradigms in terms of how you look at your business. These concepts may include the following:

- The relationship between different customer touchpoints
- How various types of customers move through their interactions
- Where additional touchpoints may be needed
- Where you unknowingly require duplication of effort from customers

With regard to the last point, the view provided by your journey map will likely identify areas where you can eliminate non–valued-added work for your customers. If you're looking to improve customer experience, this is a no-brainer!

TIP

Asking a small group of customers to review your journey map can be helpful. Does it reflect their own experiences with your company? Try to engage them in conversation using open-ended inquiries rather than yes-or-no questions. Find out which touchpoints create frustration and which ones might work better.

Taking a Look at Sample Journey Maps

Journey maps come in all sorts of shapes and styles. They can be very basic. Or, with a little bit of creativity and work, you can transform your basic journey map into a more interesting story. Figure 7-5 shows the journey map for a utility company, which depicts its customer interactions in an interesting and compelling visual manner. The company used this map as a communications tool to summarize key points of interaction and to walk through the customer journey with employees at every level in the organization. The style of the map helps to engage employees. Heck, they may even *enjoy* looking at it!

TIP

Want to see more examples? A quick Internet search for "customer journey map" or "customer touchpoint map" will reveal hundreds (if not thousands) of different versions!

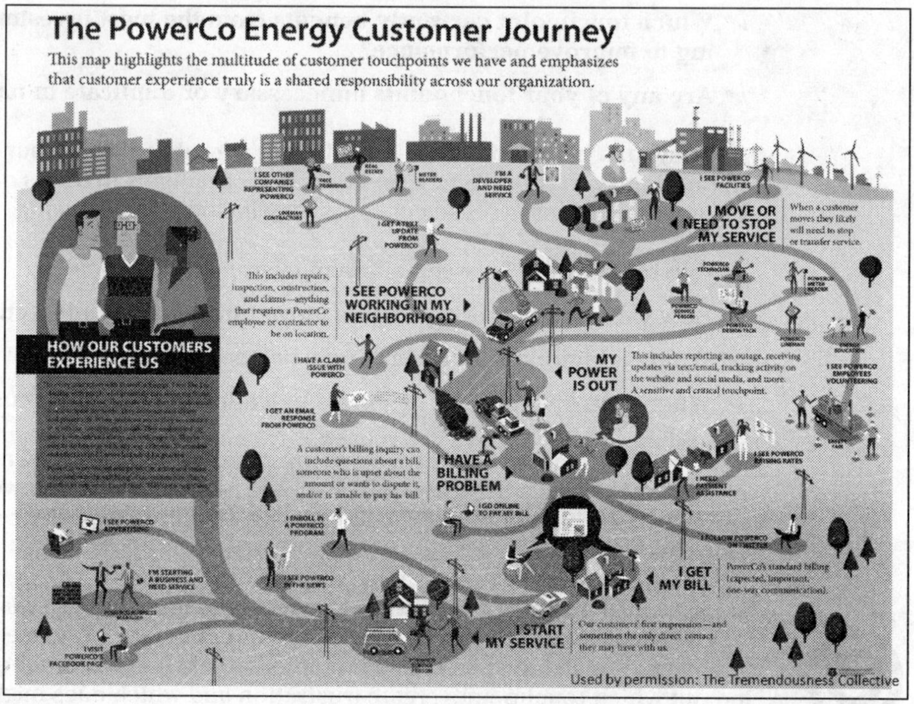

Figure 7-5: This journey map tells a more interesting story.

Illustration courtesy of The Tremendousness Collective.

Chapter 8

Experience by Design: Designing a Captivating Customer Experience

In This Chapter

- Looking at the seven core elements of a great customer experience
- Understanding the five foundations of experience design

What were you doing last Saturday night? Perhaps you, like many others, watched a movie. Now, whether you enjoyed that movie is a different question altogether.

What makes a good movie? What makes a theater full of people sit quietly(ish) in a darkened room for two hours? Well, it's a combination of factors. A good movie has an interesting story. It features actors and actresses who are engaging and believable. A good movie engages the audience's senses and emotions. And unless it's an entry in a Fellini film festival, a good movie makes sense. It's logical.

A good movie doesn't just happen. It takes great effort and extraordinary attention to detail. Take James Cameron's *Avatar,* for example. *Avatar* — the result of work done by thousands of actors, actresses, designers, and technicians from all over the world — took four years to make. And yet, the movie ran just under three hours. In other words, each hour of the movie required 30,000 hours of visioning, designing, and creating. That may seem like a prohibitive amount of work, but consider this: With box office receipts of more than $2.8 billion (that's billion, with a "B") worldwide, *Avatar* became the highest grossing and most watched movie *ever.*

If you were to turn all the experiences that customers have with your organization into a movie, what would it look like? Would it be engaging? Would it make sense? Would your customers know what was happening from one scene to the next, or would they be confused?

REMEMBER

Good customer experience, like a good movie, engages the senses. It captures and transports. It seizes and retains attention. It's seamless. In other words, designing a good customer experience is a lot of work. But the payoff — increased revenue, profitability, and hordes of happy customers — is significant!

And don't worry: As you'll see, you don't have to spend $300 million to achieve engaging customer experience! In this chapter we look at how you can design great customer experience simply and effectively.

7-Up: The Seven Core Elements of a Great Customer Experience

A great customer experience does more than please your customers. It influences them to change their behaviors and do more business with your organization. (That means a great customer experience will ultimately make you more money!)

But how do you offer a great customer experience? We've distilled the answer to that question into seven core elements:

- Offering relevant solutions
- Assuring and protecting trust
- Eliminating the unjust
- Going above and beyond
- Balancing customer experience with business profitability
- Engaging all human facets
- Having a consistent and authentic brand

The following sections discuss each of these core elements in greater detail.

Offering relevant solutions

In dealing with customers, you must leverage your understanding of what your customers are really trying to accomplish — that is, the series of actions they seek to complete — and of how they think about and react to what happens to them along the way. But that's not enough: You must also ferret out ways to solve problems that customers may not be able to articulate or even realize that they have. Take a page from the late Steve Jobs's playbook — not the one that involved relentlessly berating underlings, but the one about anticipating customers' wants, even before the customers themselves do!

Trust #FAIL

A while back, I (Roy) decided I wanted a new plasma flat-screen TV for the living room. I spent three weekends in a row doing all the wiring and setup necessary to install it. Then I went online to look at the inventory of a well-known electronics retailer in my area to see whether they had the unit I wanted. Lo and behold, they did!

I hustled over to the store to purchase my new TV. When I reached the TV department, I was greeted by a sales clerk. I asked him if I could see the model I wanted to buy. "I'm sorry," he said. "We don't have that model in stock and on display."

"Huh," I said. "I checked your website this morning, and it said you had two of the exact model I want."

He shook his head. "Well, sometimes the website isn't accurate."

I found this hard to believe. I mean, what is the point of allowing customers to see your available inventory if the numbers are wrong? To his credit, the sales clerk *did* try to help. He walked me over to the 3D version of the model I wanted. "This 3D model is only $75 more than the model you were looking at, and we do have it in stock and on display," he said.

I wasn't interested in the 3D version, and I didn't really want to spend the extra $75 to get it. But there was something else bothering me: the phrasing used by the clerk — "in stock and on display." Suddenly, I flashed back to 6th-grade English, where I learned about compound sentences — joining two ideas in one sentence. I realized what the salesperson had been saying to me all along.

"Wait," I said. "You said earlier that the TV I wanted was 'not in stock and on display,' right?"

"That's right," he smiled.

So I asked him, "Is the TV on display?"

He shook his head, smiling. "No," he said. "It's not on display."

"But is it in stock?" I asked.

"Well," he said, his smile fading. "Yes, it's in stock."

Dumbfounded, I stared at the clerk. Finally, I shook my head. "How can you stand here and lie to people?"

He tried to explain: "I said we didn't have it in stock *and* on display." Finally, however, he broke. Shoulders slumped, he admitted the truth. "They make us do it. Nobody is buying the 3D sets and we're way overstocked. I get paid a little extra when I offload one."

Does your organization force employees to do anything remotely like this? If so, take steps to stop it. It's not just a game — it's a lie. And by lying to customers, your organization will lose them in the end.

Assuring and protecting trust

Like most people, you've probably known someone who broke your trust. Maybe your brother rolled you over to your parents, and you got in trouble for something *he* did. Maybe your girlfriend told you she was studying when she was *really* out with another guy. Maybe your boss took credit for your great idea when the CEO visited your department. Whatever the circumstances, no doubt you quickly discovered that once your trust is broken, it's very difficult to repair.

The same goes for customers. If your organization violates a customer's trust, it's an experience killer; you can bet that customer will think twice before doing business with you again.

According to Charles Green, the author of *The Trusted Advisor,* earning and retaining trust requires a real and sincere interest in helping your customers. Too often, however, organizations aren't really interested in those whose trust they seek to gain. When you're designing your organization's customer experience, be sure to take this into account!

Eliminating the unjust

Customers often have a surprisingly vehement reaction to things they perceive as unfair. If you include enough of these small, antagonizing pinpricks to their interactions — what coauthor Roy's daughter used to call "unfairies" — you may eventually face a mutiny.

What do we mean by unfairies? They're the nickel-and-diming things some businesses do. Following are some examples of modern-day unfairies:

- Four- or five-star hotels charging $15 or more a day for (very slow) Internet access when budget hotels offer high-speed connections free of charge.
- Hotels charging guests $1.50 to make a local phone call from their room.
- Airlines charging extra baggage fees, carry-on fees, preferred seat fees, please-don't-put-me-between-two-Sumo-wrestler fees, and the like (although we might consider paying for that last one).
- Purposefully deceptive packaging that gives the impression that the product you're purchasing is three or four times larger than it actually is.
- Satellite TV reception that fails every time it rains.

- Anything less than a 30-day return policy. (We're big fans of the Zappos return policy. You have 365 days to return merchandise in its original condition. They'll even pay for the return shipping!)
- Extended warranty plans that cost more than the product you're purchasing. (Does anyone really need a $50 protection plan on a $35 clock radio?)
- Onerous overdraft protection and bank fees. (If more than 60 percent of your entire profit stream depends on sneaky and unreasonable fees, something may be inherently wrong with your business model.)
- Credit recovery "charge cards" with interest rates in excess of 25 percent.
- Gift cards with high usage fees.

REMEMBER

Sure, these types of practices may make you more money on the margins. But they cost you much more in the long term. Just because you *can* charge for something doesn't mean you *should*. Not sure whether one of your policies or fees is an unfairy? Ask yourself, "Would I make my grandmother pay this?" If the answer is no, you're in Unfairy Land.

Going above and beyond

Customer experiences that deliver just a tiny bit more than the customer expects can go further in fostering engagement than you may expect. We're not referring to the "Wow!" moments here; we're talking about small, thoughtful acts of attention.

A lesson in delight

One year, I (Roy) took my kids on a Disney Cruise. As you might expect, the Disney Cruise Line provides exceptional service, outstanding accommodations, and copious distractions. The ship has everything imaginable for kids: huge slides, full musical shows, clubs, decorations, character interactions . . . you name it.

In those days, my daughter liked to travel with her entire stuffed-animal collection. For this trip, however, she had pared down to her five favorites. Late one evening, upon returning to our cabin after a full and fun day, we found that all of her stuffed animals had been tucked into bed, the sheet pulled up to their tiny little necks. Propped up next to one of them was a handwritten note. It read: "Sorry. We tried to stay up but we got sleepy. Goodnight. We love you!"

To this day, when my daughter talks about that Disney Cruise, she doesn't mention the slides or the shows or the clubs. She talks about the note that our cabin attendant took the time to write.

Have you ever trudged into your hotel room after a long day sightseeing with your family only to find that the housekeeper has placed a bath towel folded into the shape of an animal on your bed? We have, and we're here to tell you that it made our day. This doesn't cost the hotel management any extra (well, except 30 to 60 extra seconds per room). But it sure does delight the guests!

Here's another example. While on the Internet, have you ever run into a screen that looks like the one in Figure 8-1? This "404" page is a standard response page that indicates that the hosting computer server couldn't find the page you were looking for. It's efficient and to the point — but pretty impersonal.

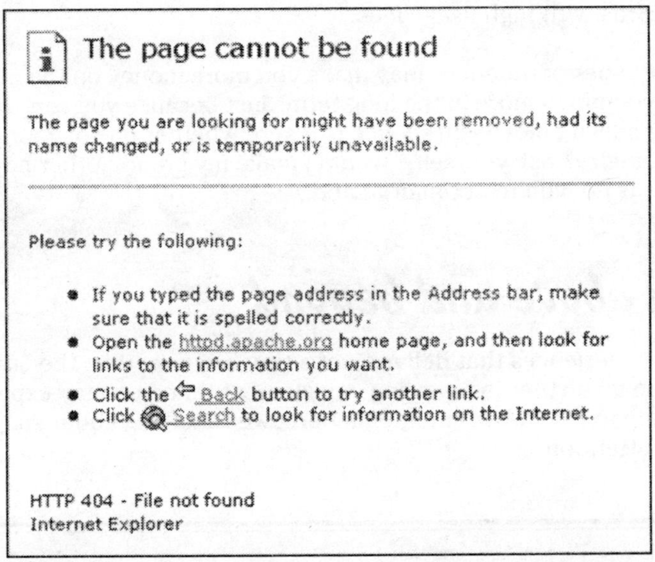

Figure 8-1: A standard "404" page.

Illustration courtesy of Roy Barnes.

Compare that standard "404" page with the page shown in Figure 8-2. What does this attention to detail say about the brand? Sure, it may be that only 1 percent of Heinz's Internet visitors end up on this page by mistake. But when they do, they'll appreciate that Heinz pays attention to the little things in its efforts to engage its customers.

REMEMBER

The bottom line? You don't want to miss any opportunity to go beyond what's expected to engage and delight your customers. Any communication you have with customers is an opportunity to delight them — even something as mundane as a "404" page. It's the little things that demonstrate your organization's real and sincere commitment to its customers!

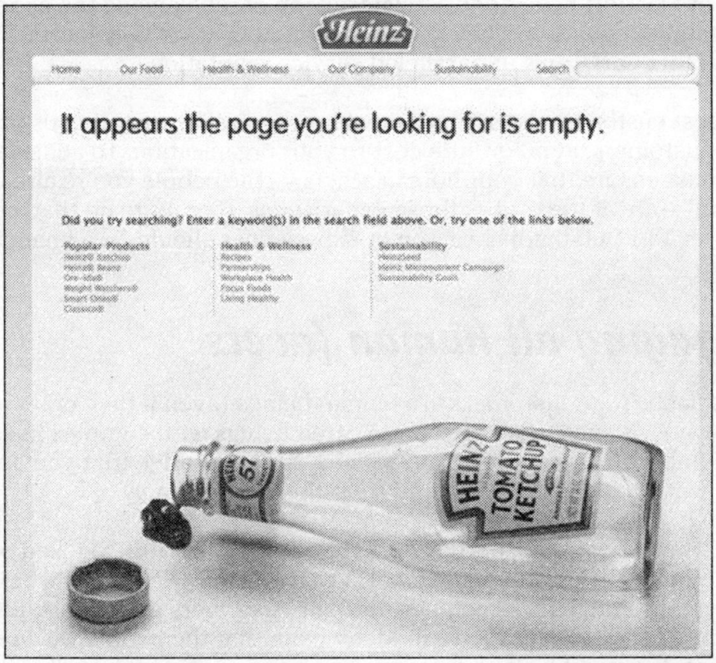

Figure 8-3: Heinz's version of a "404" page. Which one is more engaging?

Illustration courtesy of Roy Barnes.

Balancing customer experience with business profitability

You can buy happiness, just not for long. Creating a great customer experience is easy if you're willing to throw a lot of money at the effort. But unfortunately, no business can sustain that for long.

A few years back, Marriott International acquired the Ritz-Carleton Hotel Company. Executives at Marriott quickly discovered that the customer experience/business profitability equation was out of whack. The service and guest experience was out of this world. Indeed, Ritz-Carleton hotels were recognized worldwide as *the* leaders in delivering an outstanding guest experience. Their reputation for going above and beyond was (and still is) legendary. But the hotel's individual operating profits? Not so much. As one Marriott exec observed, "They lose money on everyone they check in! This is not a problem you fix with more occupancy." Over a period of years, the folks at Marriott have done a masterful job of rebalancing the experience/profitability equation. They restored profitability without sacrificing one iota of Ritz-Carleton's unparalleled service reputation.

REMEMBER

The best customer experiences create recognizable and obvious value for your customers, at no or little cost to your organization. To achieve this, you must ensure that your human assets — the people you're already paying — are at the root of those experiences. (For more on that, see Chapter 13.) Outstanding customer experiences should be a financial win-win!

Engaging all human facets

News flash: Your customers are human beings (even if they don't always act that way). As such, they are complicated beings with complex lives. They're not numbers, nor are they transactions. It's imperative that you and your organization remember this, and treat them accordingly.

Back when I (Roy) was a front desk manager at Marriott, I kicked off each shift by reading the following mantra to my team: "No matter what happens during this shift, let's remember that our customers are people, just like you and me." I then went on to remind my team that the people we would be serving that day might well be experiencing one or more of the following:

- Mourning a recent death in the family
- Coping with a serious physical or mental illness in their family
- Caring for an aging parent
- Worrying about a loved one in the military
- Questioning their self-worth
- Going through divorce
- Caring for a new baby
- Sending a child to college
- Struggling with alcoholism or drug addiction — either in themselves or in their close circle of friends
- Dealing with a business failure (or success)

Providing a great customer experience means addressing all facets of your fellow human beings' physical, intellectual, and emotional needs. In other words, it means treating customers as the unique individuals they are.

Having a consistent and authentic brand

Each and every year, organizations spend hundreds of millions of marketing dollars in branding efforts. That means creating positioning statements, developing logos, and poring over presentation decks, all in an attempt to establish in their customers' minds an idea of who the organization really is.

Note we said "attempt." The reality is, any branding effort will result in a description of who the organization *wants* to be, not what it *is*. What an organization is — what its brand *really* means — is nothing other than the sum total of how its customers perceive it in their minute-by-minute, day-by-day touchpoint interactions.

Often, customers experience a disconnect between marketing dreams and operational reality. Put another way, what's on the box doesn't match what's inside. If the brand you put forth in your marketing efforts doesn't jibe with what your customers experience in real life — if your story isn't backed up by the facts — you're not just wasting your marketing dollars, you're alienating your customers.

Not long ago, a friend and I (Roy) decided to install a zip line for our kids. It would span some 200 feet across Canada's Georgian Bay. On the zip line, the kids would be able to soar from one island to the one adjacent or to plunge 10 feet into cold water at the midpoint.

We bought the parts for the line from a company that specializes in that sort of thing, called Zip Line Gear. As we unpacked the box that contained them, I noticed that the box had bold red printing on one side. It read: *"Caution: Contains Awesomeness."* I smiled, thinking of some Zip Line Gear employee taking the time to design that box to reflect the brand. (Lots of companies do this type of thing with their packaging. Think of Amazon's ubiquitous smile logo, printed on every package it ships, intended to cheer whomever receives it.)

Of course, if the zip line had been a dud, then the printing on the box would have been a joke. But it wasn't. The kids *loved* the zip line. The box was right: It really *did* contain awesomeness. What was on the box matched what was inside!

REMEMBER

Here's the deal: Your customers' actual experiences tell the story of your brand, not the other way around. Those are the experiences that help cement your customers' understanding of where you're coming from, what you stand for, and what makes you special, not some commercial you run or some logo you redesign. This is the real meaning of a brand: a consistent story that is told and retold each and every time the customer interacts with you.

5 Alive: The Five Foundations of Experience Design

Merely knowing the core elements of a great customer experience is not enough. You must take steps to *design* that experience. Following are the five foundations of customer experience design:

- Storyboarding the experience
- Nailing the basics
- Designing for basic human needs
- Owning the complexity
- Testing the customer experience

For more on each of these foundations, read on!

Storyboarding the experience

At the beginning of this chapter, we talk about how designing a great customer experience is a little like making a movie. If you want your customer experience to be as engaging for your customers as *Avatar* was for moviegoers, it all has to make sense.

To help you create a cohesive and engaging customer experience, why not do what Hollywood directors do — namely, create a storyboard? A *storyboard* is an easy-to-understand visual aid that makes it possible to organize, share, and explain your vision. Think of it as a sort of comic-book version of your organization's customer experience. It tells the entire story, but in bite-sized pieces.

To create a customer experience storyboard, follow these steps:

1. **Draw a series of rectangles on a piece of paper.**

   Each rectangle represents a different moment in the customer experience. (If you prefer, you can use a storyboard template; loads of these are available online. Alternatively, you can use ours — see Figure 8-3.)

2. **In each rectangle, draw what will take place in that moment.**

   You can sketch the scenes by hand, draw them using a computer, or even paste in a photo from your phone. Artistry isn't important; you just want to give a sense of what's happening.

3. **Beneath each rectangle, write down what is happening in that scene.**

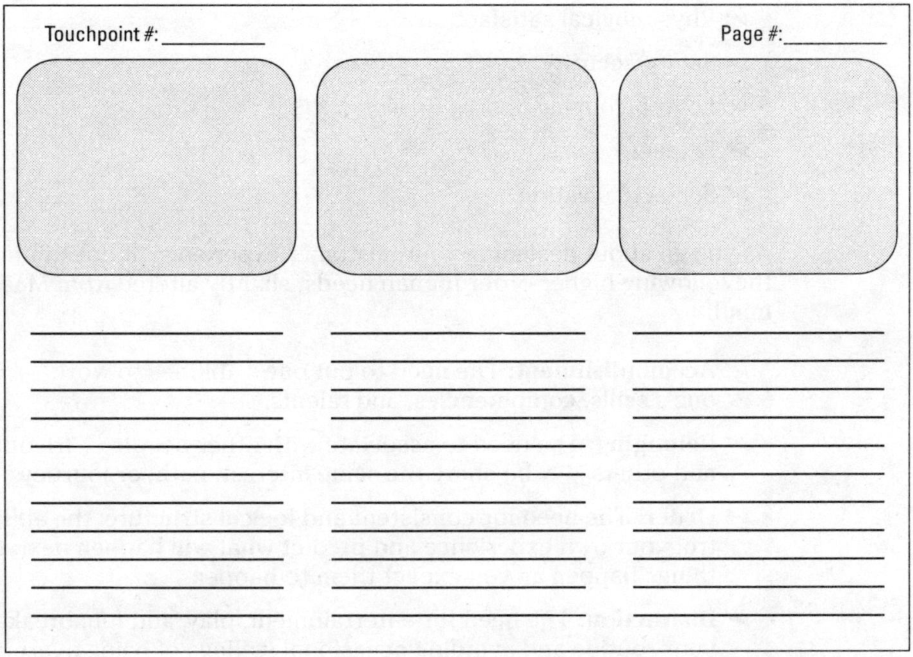

Figure 8-3: Feel free to use this storyboard template as you develop your customer experience storyboard!

Illustration courtesy of Roy Barnes.

Anyone should be able to read your storyboard like a comic book to get a sense of exactly what will happen in the customer experience you're planning.

Nailing the basics

This step assumes you have your customer experience intent statement and touchpoint/journey map nailed down. If not, take a gander at Chapters 6 and 7 to get those sorted out.

With these resources in hand, look at each touchpoint and determine whether it's meeting the basic standards set forth in your customer experience intent statement. If you discover touchpoints that are not meeting these standards (and you will), start there.

Designing for basic human needs

Famed psychologist Abraham Maslow was among the first to identify the most basic human needs. As he saw it, these needs — which he presented in pyramid form, with the first need being the base and each subsequent need representing the next level of the pyramid — were as follows:

- Physiological satisfaction
- Safety/security
- Love/belonging
- Esteem
- Self-actualization

As you go about designing your customer experience, it doesn't hurt to keep the following higher-order human needs, slightly altered from Maslow's, in mind:

- **Accomplishment:** The need to put one's abilities to work — to exercise one's skills, competencies, and talents.
- **Belonging:** The need to associate with other people — friends, family, and others — who share the same interest, path, or journey.
- **Order:** The need for consistent and logical structure; the ability to control your own experience and predict what will happen next; to have things happen as you expect them to happen.
- **Distraction:** The need for entertainment, play, and fun; breaking from your routine and avoiding occasional feelings of being overmanaged, overbooked, and overstressed.
- **Delight:** The need for novelty, for interacting with something new. (The first time we witnessed a *Cirque Du Soleil* performance we were completely and utterly delighted.)
- **Status:** The need for recognition for your efforts, work, commitment, and dedication; being seen as unique. For example, Roy really likes being able to board an airplane first. He knows its elitist, but after more than a million miles in the air he has rationalized his need for status.
- **Safety:** The need for personal security — avoiding dangerous or compromising situations; feeling no immediate threat from harm, and being able to protect yourself, your loved ones, and your friends from danger.
- **Helpfulness:** The need to be of help to others; sharing what you've learned, coaching and counseling others who are on the same path, and assisting them with problem-solving.

Or, just remember this quote from writer Robert Anson Heinlein and design accordingly:

> A human being wants to be able to change a diaper, plan an invasion, butcher a hog, conn a ship, design a building, write a sonnet, balance accounts, build a wall, set a bone, comfort the dying, take orders, give orders, cooperate, act alone, solve equations, analyze a new problem, pitch manure, delight someone, program a computer, cook a tasty meal, fight efficiently, die gallantly.

We're humans, and our customers — well, most of them anyway — are humans too. Maslow pointed out the importance of respecting human needs. You're doing that, right?

Owning the complexity

Larry Tesler, a computer scientist and an expert in the field of human-computer interaction, has worked at such companies as Xerox, Apple, Amazon, and Yahoo!, among others. During his career, Tesler developed something he called The Law of Conservation of Complexity. Also known as Tesler's Law, it suggests that every computer application (and we extend that to most processes, designs, and interactions) has a certain amount of irreducible complexity. The question is, who will own it? The designer or the user? Put another way, whose time is more important — yours or your customer's?

We believe an organization must view its customers' time as more important than its own. It must own the complexity. If something you're working on would be easier for your customer to use if you spent another week or two engineering it, it's our belief that it would be time and money well spent. Otherwise, you'll wind up creating another customer pain point.

To see the negative effects of unnecessary complexity in action, look at Figure 8-4. Without using your finger to point, try counting the circles. You can even use a stopwatch to see how long it takes. Pretty painful, huh?

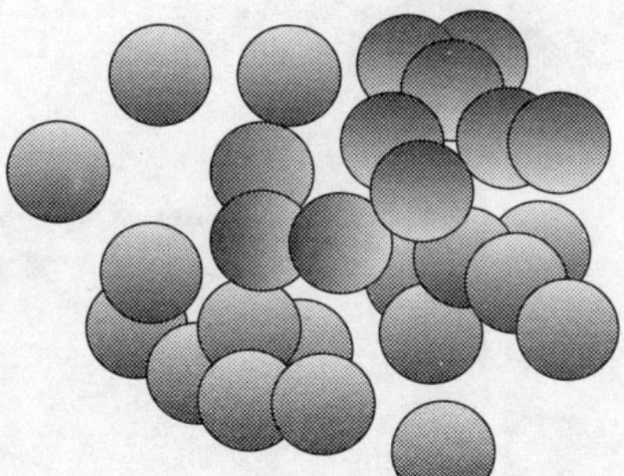

Figure 8-4: Try counting the circles. Don't point; just look and count.

Illustration courtesy of Roy Barnes.

Next, try counting the circles in Figure 8-5, which have been organized into groups. See how much easier it is? If you time yourself, you'll find you can count these circles way faster than the ones in Figure 8-4, even though both figures contain the same number of circles!

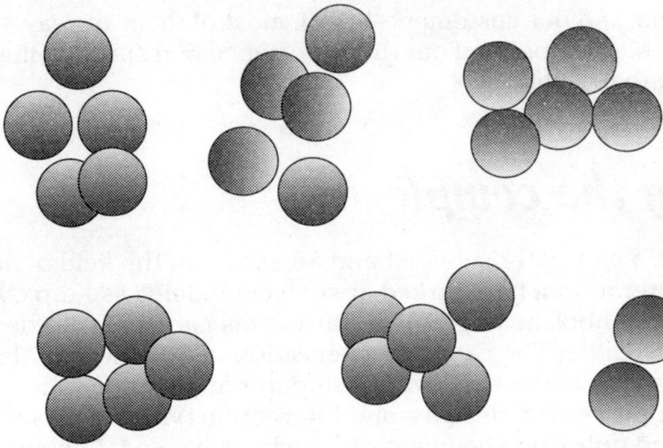

Figure 8-5: Now count these circles. Because they've been organized into groups, these circles are much easier to count!

Illustration courtesy of Roy Barnes.

For a real-world example, take a look at Figure 8-6. The image on the left features the operating manual for a Nest smoke detector. As you can see, it's clean, simple, and easy to understand. The image on the right shows the instructions for a smoke detector offered by a competing brand. Be honest: Which smoke detector would you rather buy, install, and use? The Nest? We thought so. The bottom line? You want your customer experience to be cognitively congenial — in other words, user-friendly.

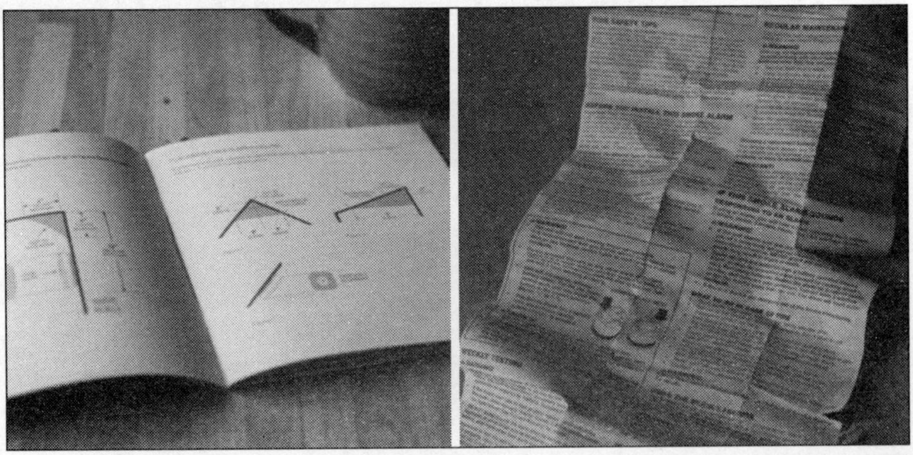

Figure 8-6: As evidenced by the image on the left, the folks at Nest have owned the complexity of their user manual.

Illustrations courtesy of Roy Barnes.

Testing the customer experience

Yes, we know. You're *super smart*. But almost nothing that human beings create works perfectly right out of the box. That's why you must perform usability testing of your customer experience design *before* you release it into the wild. Turn some users loose on your design and see what happens. Then tweak your design based on their feedback.

That being said, don't go *too* crazy with testing. Yes, you must do usability testing. But the amount of testing you need to perform depends on the relative risk of customer frustration and failure. If your customer touchpoint involves a nuclear missile launch control, then yes, you should do lots of testing. But if you just want to know how the customer is going to fill out a web form? Perhaps just a touch less.

Chapter 9

So Emotional: Eliciting an Emotional Response from Your Customers

In This Chapter

- Seeing how the brain processes emotions
- Appealing to the five senses
- Gauging your customers' feelings at each touchpoint

A few years back, a video went viral. It was of an audition by a contestant on *Britain's Got Talent,* a show similar to *American Idol.* The video featured a plain, middle-aged woman with frizzy hair — an unlikely pop sensation, to say the least. In the segment in which she was introduced, it was revealed that she lived alone with her cat; that she had never been married; indeed, that she had never been kissed.

It was clear from the audience's reaction to this woman, whose name was Susan Boyle, that they dismissed her the moment they saw her. When Boyle revealed that it had been her lifelong dream to sing before a large audience, the video cut to a young woman in the crowd, rolling her eyes in derision. Even the panelists were visibly skeptical. In mere moments, Boyle had been typecast — labeled and dismissed.

But then she sang . . . and everything changed.

As Boyle sang the first soaring notes of the beautiful "I Dreamed a Dream" from the musical *Les Miserables,* the audience erupted in cheers — and they continued to cheer, up on their feet, until the last note faded. For their part, the panelists were blown away. Even the irascible Simon Cowell was grinning from ear to ear. (If you've never seen this video, we urge you to watch it. Even if you *have* seen it, you should watch it again! Just enter "Susan Boyle" in your favorite browser.)

Perhaps Lisa Schwarzbaum, a critic for *Entertainment Weekly*, put it best:

> In our pop-minded culture so slavishly obsessed with packaging — the right face, the right clothes, the right attitudes, the right Facebook posts — the unpackaged artistic power of the unstyled, unhip, unkissed Ms. Boyle let me feel, for the duration of one blazing show-stopping ballad, the meaning of human grace. She pierced my defenses. She reordered the measure of beauty. And I had no idea until tears sprang how desperately I need that corrective from time to time.

So what does this have to do with customer experience? Simple. Humans want to feel. We want to have our defenses pierced. We want to make an emotional connection. As you're designing your organization's customer experience, your task is to forge that connection. In this chapter, you discover how to do just that.

Weird Science: Understanding the Human Brain

To be able to make an emotional connection with your customer, it helps to understand how the human brain works. Odds are, you already know that the brain is neatly divided into two hemispheres: left and right. The left brain is good at numbers, reasoning, and written and spoken language. The right brain's specialty is spatial awareness, insight, creativity, and imagination.

What you may not know is that human beings actually have *two* brains. We call them the first brain and the new brain. The *first brain,* which has been around for approximately 300 to 500 million years and is common among most animals, is primitive. It's emotional. It manages your pre-conscious and unconscious thoughts. It's the source of instinctive survival impulses like hunger, thirst, danger, sex, and parental care.

The *new brain* is quite different. It's only 3 or 4 million years old. It is intellectual and advanced, the center of rational and conscious thought. It's your source of memory, language, creativity, planning, and decision making. The new brain is uniquely human. Typically, when people refer to their brain, they're talking about their new brain, not their first brain.

Although it's certainly good to appeal to your customers' new brain, when it comes to forging an emotional connection, it's the first brain that counts. The first brain is concerned with the following positive feelings:

- Joy
- Gratitude

- Serenity
- Amusement
- Inspiration
- Hope
- Pride
- Love
- Belonging
- Safety

It's not all rainbows and kittens in the first brain, however. It's also where these negative feelings are processed:

- Anxiety
- Disgust
- Grief
- Humiliation
- Feeling overwhelmed
- Worthlessness
- Feeling lost
- Feeling unsupported
- Feeling conflicted

You must make sure anything you do, say, or write doesn't tap into these negative emotions. It's your responsibility to create an environment and experience in which your customers have nothing to fear.

Sense and Sensibility: Stimulating the Five Senses

So how do you appeal to the customer's first brain? Recent science suggests that one way is to stimulate the five senses — sight, hearing, smell, taste, and touch. That may explain why the last decade has seen an explosion in research on the integration of the five senses into customer experience. Indeed, whole industries and hundreds of companies are now devoted to helping organizations stimulate their customers' senses. This section covers a few of the tactics you can use.

Sight

Have you ever visited the Bellagio Hotel and Casino in Las Vegas? If so, you probably remember the massive Dale Chihuly glass sculpture that hangs from the ceiling in the hotel lobby. Composed of some 2,000 hand-blown glass flowers weighing more than 40,000 pounds, it's an extraordinary piece of art. But why is it there?

"It's just art," you might think. "It's there for our enjoyment." Well, yes. But more likely, the artwork — said to be worth more than $3 million — is meant to provide an amazing first impression and to elicit certain kinds of emotions. Indeed, the artwork is so magnificent, it's hard to feel anything but amazement when you're standing underneath it. It fills you with a sense of satisfaction and belonging, like you've *arrived.* It makes you feel, well, rich — like you can spend a little more than you had planned. A perfect feeling to have when entering a casino!

REMEMBER

You never get a second chance to make a first impression!

People depend more on sight than on any other of their senses to navigate their environment. Indeed, most impressions they have of their physical environment come from their visual senses. In a single glance, lasting mere fractions of a second, their eyes tell them the size, shape, texture, movement, and speed of objects around them. In a similar vein, according to a Harvard Health Sciences report, people make judgments about other people in three seconds or less — and most of that judgment is based on visual information.

As you design your customer touchpoints, ask these sight-related questions:

- With what visual cues do customers interact at this touchpoint?
- Do these visual cues represent your customer experience intent?
- Is the visual path (sightline) clear and uncluttered at this touchpoint?
- Have you used the clearest possible instructions, diagrams, and representations to ensure that customers experience no confusion as to what actions they should take at this touchpoint?

Hearing

Sound brings the visual world to life. It can induce relaxation, stress, or just about any other kind of emotional state. Sound — particularly music — can bring memories to life.

REMEMBER

Speaking of music, many organizations use it at their touchpoints to create greater definition and dimension for their brand. Indeed, these days, music and sound programming is a critical thread in the fabric of many customer experiences. As but one example, Delta Airlines has recently begun playing Pharrell Williams's popular single "Happy" during boarding and deplaning on many of its routes.

Your touchpoints' soundscape can be as simple or complex as you choose. Some businesses even use different sounds for different areas of their property. Take a hotel, for example. You may hear a chill sound in the lobby, classic rock in the bar, soothing tones in the spa, deeper relaxation sounds in massage areas, and something entirely different for on-hold music.

Your soundscape may vary by time of day, too. For example, music with a higher number of beats per minute (BPM) is often played at theme parks when the facility opens and is changed throughout the day and in different areas to manage the mood. Supermarkets, too, play different types of music at different times of the day to cater to their varying demographics. One of our clients, a chain of grocery stores, discovered that effective music management increased sales by more than 22 percent!

TIP

You don't have to be a DJ or work in an alternative record store to develop a musical soundscape for your touchpoints. You can use any of dozens of apps. Some are very simple, while others are quite sophisticated. Our favorite is Moodagent (`www.moodagent.com`). It analyzes the songs on an iPhone, Android, or other similar device and organizes them by emotion, mood, genre, subgenre, style, tempo, beat, vocals, instruments, and more. You tell the app what mood you're in or what type of music you want to hear, and Moodagent generates a playlist accordingly! That being said, if your organization is particularly large or complex, you may need the help of a sound-management company to develop a complete portfolio of music for you.

Your soundscape may also include spoken audio. For example, many airports feature canned audio to warn visitors about potential safety hazards. Obviously, you want to make sure that the voice used in these types of recordings is pleasant! (Read: Pass on Fran Drescher if she auditions.)

As you design your customer touchpoints, ask these hearing-related questions:

- What sound, music, and/or audio are customers hearing at this touchpoint?
- What would you like customers to feel at this point of interaction? Can music, sound, and/or audio help create that emotion?
- What is your organization's playlist? Why?
- If you wanted to be known for a sound at this point of interaction, what would it be?

Smell

"Wait," you're thinking. "Sight and hearing I get. But my organization has to worry about *smell?*" In a word, yes. Smell is a powerful sense. Most human beings have more than 1,000 smell receptors and can easily identify more than 10,000 individual scents. Scent can

- **Evoke emotion.** Just think about the smell of fresh-baked bread, the aroma of coffee, or the scent of your mother's perfume. It makes you *feel* something, doesn't it?
- **Trigger memories.** Smell is the strongest and most powerful trigger of emotional memory. Don't believe us? Try catching a whiff of Play-Doh. Odds are, you'll be instantly transported to your childhood!
- **Increase sales.** Maybe you have the willpower to walk past the Cinnabon kiosk at your local mall. But for most people, the aroma of those fresh-baked goodies is an irresistible pull!
- **Create a calming effect.** That's why calming scents are often piped into stressful environments — think dentists' offices and hospital waiting areas.
- **Provide mental stimulation.** Certain scent formulas are great for this. Having trouble waking or staying up? Peppermint and lemon can move you into a state of alert productivity. Watch out for jasmine and lavender, though. A couple of whiffs and you'll be off to la-la land.

The feelings scents inspire may explain why the use of perfume dates back some 4,000 years! Nowadays, companies use smells to drive specific emotional responses in customers. Indeed, *scent management* has evolved into a $14 billion global industry! Some companies even develop custom formulas for use at consumer touchpoints.

Whether you're aware of it or not, companies purposefully manage your mood — and, by extension, your customer experience — by way of your nose. Convenience stores, spa and fitness facilities, hotels, cruise ships, retail stores, markets — they all do it.

REMEMBER

If you're looking to incorporate scents into your customer touchpoints, keep the following tips in mind:

- **Scent is subjective.** What smells good to you may not smell the same to everyone else. Be sure you test out any scents before deploying them in your touchpoint! Otherwise, you may actually drive business away.
- **Moderation is key.** As coauthor Roy's mother told him when he bought his first bottle of cologne, limiting the amount of scent you use is essential. Unless you're selling ice cream or candy, you don't want

to overpower your customers with smells. Most touchpoints require a more nuanced approach. (If you've ever been asphyxiated at an Abercrombie and Fitch store, you know what we're talking about!)

- **Context matters.** Smelling baby powder in the men's department is confusing. Smelling popcorn in a dentist's office is just plain mean.
- **Be "scent"sitive.** Some people are sensitive to scents and the chemicals used to disburse them. Be aware of those with allergies and other sensitivities.

As you design your customer touchpoints, ask these smell-related questions:

- What, if anything, does a customer smell at this particular touchpoint?
- Would a particular scent significantly change the customer experience for the better?
- Are unintended odors present at this touchpoint? (As an extreme example, consider the $100 million water park built directly adjacent to a waste-management facility. On hot summer days, waiting your turn for the water slide was unbearable.)
- Could the introduction of a scent help to induce a particular emotional reaction at this touchpoint?

Taste

They say there's no such thing as a free lunch. But if you've ever been to Costco, you know that's just not true. A walk through Costco's aisles means an opportunity to sample any number of food products offered for sale! Costco has offered samples of its food products for years. Indeed, this practice is a cornerstone of Costco's advertising strategy.

Of course, Costco isn't the only company to offer customers free samples of its food products. Odds are, the last time you strolled through the food court at your local mall, you were chased down by a smiling employee from Panda Express or a similar eatery and urged to take a bite-sized portion of their kung-pao chicken. Why? Because food industry research indicates that consumers who taste food being offered are 48 percent more likely to purchase from that vendor. Offering samples is big business and can have a big payoff if you do it well.

Even companies who aren't in the food business can introduce taste into their customer touchpoints in an effort to improve customer experience. One easy way is to simply set out a dish of candy at your checkout counter. One client of ours, an energy company, sends recipes to its clients. (We've tried the apple pie, and it's *dee-lish.*)

As you design your customer touchpoints, ask these taste-related questions:

- Is there a way to introduce taste at any of your touchpoints?
- Would activating this sense make sense (see what we did there?) for your organization?

Touch

Does this sound familiar? After a long day at work, you walk through the front door of your house, take off your shoes, and change into your favorite slippers. Then you put on an old T-shirt, give your cat a quick scratch beneath her chin, make yourself a cup of hot tea, and sink into your favorite recliner. *Aaaaaah.* Finally, you can relax!

In the few minutes that passed from when you first opened the front door to when you sank into your chair, your sense of touch gathered, processed, interpreted, and assimilated gazillions of touch, or *somatic,* inputs. By and large, you experience touch through your skin — mainly through your fingers and hands.

Whether exploratory and inquisitive or intimate and healing, your sense of touch is always "on." Touching, often used to test and verify the quality of an object, is an extraordinarily sensitive and nuanced activity. Merely touching a thing moves it from a representation — an idea — to something substantive and true. When you touch something, it's because you want to understand its deeper characteristics.

Your mind quickly registers feeling and touch in a complex formula of preference. In other words, you choose to use what you enjoy touching. When picking out a new briefcase or suit, the feel of the leather or the fabric between your fingers often dictates which item you buy.

Although our sense of touch is quite extraordinary, it often goes ignored by customer experience designers. That's a mistake! Whether it's the paper on which you print your marketing materials or the finish you use on your product samples, you should take into consideration how they *feel.*

You want to design an environment that promotes touch. People instinctively want to touch things; allowing and encouraging them to do so helps to engage them and fosters a personal connection. How do you promote touch? For one, try displaying your products at hand level. For another, place your products directly in your customers' hands whenever possible.

Of course, if your product is fragile or potentially dangerous, allowing customers to touch it may not be such a great idea. In that case, you need to identify other ways for the consumer to explore the product. Absent the ability to touch, customers need some other way to fill in the blanks about the product.

Plan on adding more oomph to your other sensory experiences. Your best bet is to provide a very creative and engaging online experience.

As you design your customer touchpoints, ask these touch-related questions:

- What things does the customer touch at this touchpoint?
- What do these things feel like?
- Do these things impart the sense of quality that you intend?
- Are there other ways to allow customers to touch that you're not taking advantage of?

There's a Map for That: Emotion-Mapping Your Touchpoints

All customers move through a predictable series of stages in their interactions with your company (see Figure 9-1).

1. **They become aware of your organization through its media, marketing, and branding.**
2. **They find out more about you through your offline and online reputation.**
3. **They consider using your products or services.**
4. **They purchase, use, and — depending on their level of satisfaction — continue to do business with your or seek a different provider.**

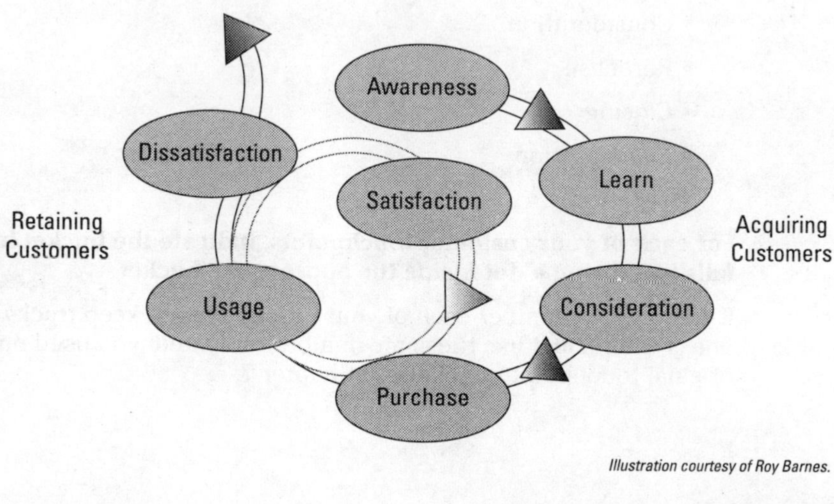

Figure 9-1: The customer relationship/experience cycle.

Illustration courtesy of Roy Barnes.

When you perform emotion-mapping, you gauge the customers' feelings at each stage of this process as they pass through each touchpoint. (Chapter 7 focuses on mapping your organization's touchpoints. If you haven't read Chapter 7 or created your touchpoint map, we recommend you do so now.)

If the emotion map you create reflects your intentions with regard to customer experience, great! Mission accomplished. If, however, you had *no idea* of the emotional path your customers were on until you saw this map, you'll want to use it to redesign your customer experience so it aligns more fully with your customer experience intent statement. (For more on developing your customer experience intent statement, refer to Chapter 6.)

An emotion-mapping example

To give you a sense of how this works, consider this example: Suppose you're in the time-share business. You want to map how your customers are feeling at each stage of their relationship with you. Follow these steps:

1. **Using the customer relationship/experience cycle outlined in Figure 9-1 as your guide, create a diagram that outlines your major clusters of interaction, in order.**

   Use whatever descriptors work best for your industry.

   As shown in Figure 9-2, these clusters of interaction — we call them *buckets* — are as follows. (Notice that these align closely with the phases outlined in Figure 9-1, with "Plan Vacation" and "Vacation" being employed instead of the more general "Usage.")

   - Awareness
   - Knowledge
   - Consideration
   - Purchase
   - Closing
   - Plan vacation
   - Vacation

2. **For each of your customer touchpoints, indicate the bucket in which it falls by placing a dot inside the appropriate bucket.**

   If you want to number each of your touchpoints to keep track of which one is where, just use the same numbering system you used on your original touchpoint map back in Chapter 7.

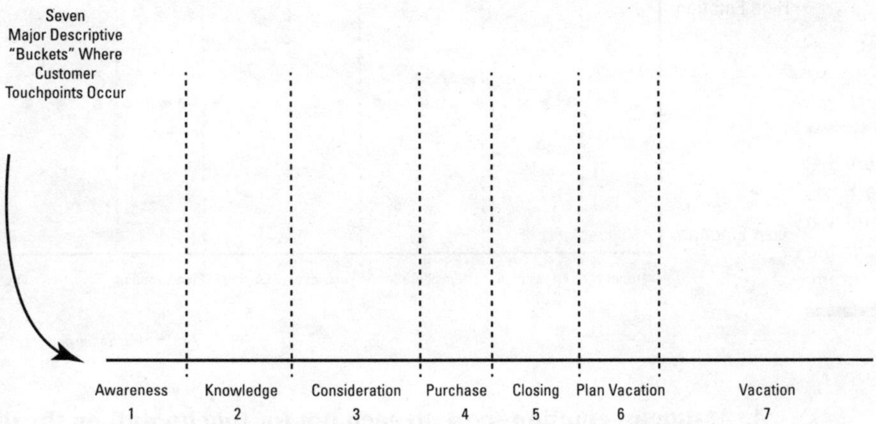

Figure 9-2: Major clusters of interaction for the time-share industry.

Illustration courtesy of Roy Barnes.

In Figure 9-3, each of the dots on the horizontal line represents a touchpoint. As you can see, the placement of each dot reflects the bucket with which it is associated.

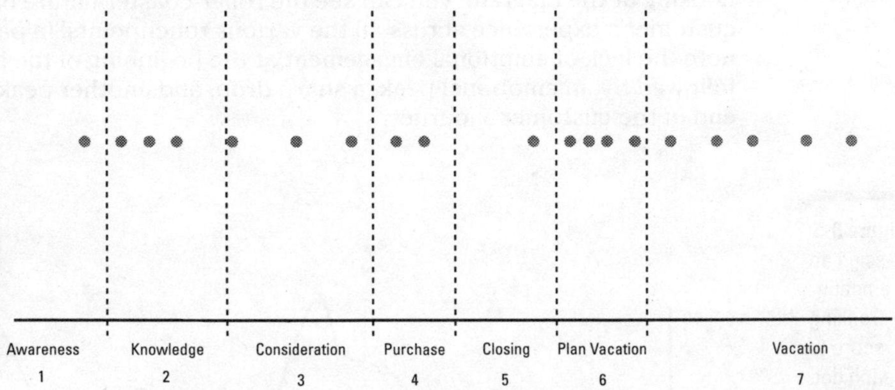

Figure 9-3: Add each of your customer touchpoints to the appropriate bucket.

Illustration courtesy of Roy Barnes.

TIP

If you have a lot of touchpoints, focus on mapping the major ones first. Shoot for 15 or 20 touchpoints for now. You can add more later.

3. **Place a *Y* axis on the left and add two labels: "High Emotion" and "Low Emotion" (see Figure 9-4).**

   Note that this scale doesn't indicate whether the emotion experienced by the customer is positive or negative. Rather, it tracks a *range* of emotion.

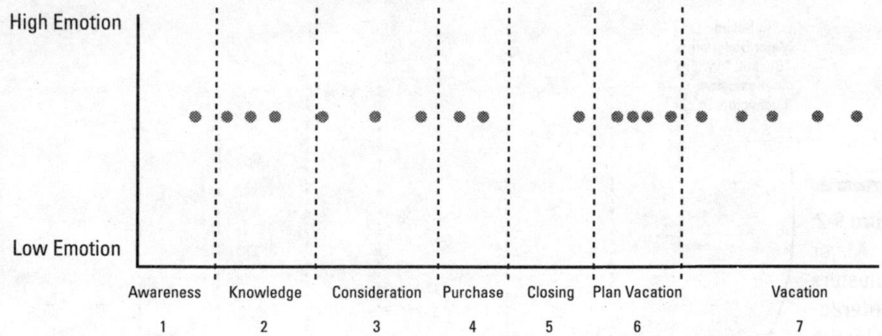

Illustration courtesy of Roy Barnes.

Figure 9-4: Add a *Y* axis and two labels to the diagram.

4. **Assign an emotion score to each dot (or touchpoint) on the diagram (refer to Figure 9-5).**

   You don't need to be terribly precise; you're just looking for a high-level picture of the customer's emotional experience at each individual touchpoint.

5. **Draw a line from one touchpoint to the next (see Figure 9-5).**

   Looking at the diagram, you can see the roller-coaster nature of the customer's experience across all the various touchpoints! In particular, note the lack of emotional engagement at the beginning of the journey, followed by an emotional peak, a sharp drop, and another peak near the end of the customer's journey.

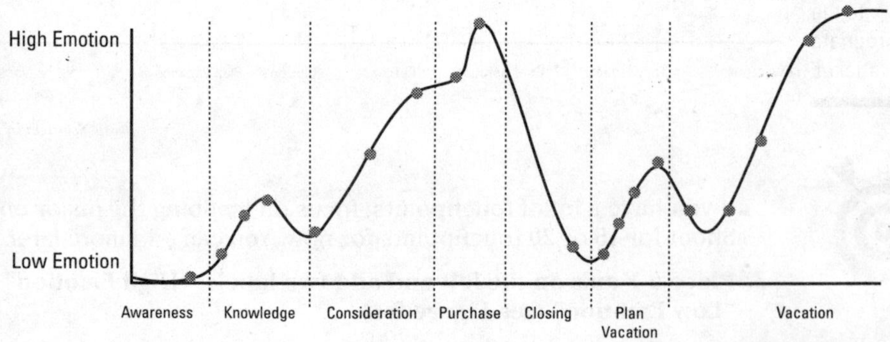

Illustration courtesy of Roy Barnes.

Figure 9-5: Assign an emotion-ranking score to each dot. Then draw a line from one dot to the next to grasp the roller-coaster nature of the customer's experience.

Using the emotion map to design your customer experience

So what can you glean from this emotion map? A few things of note. First, notice Touchpoint A in Figure 9-6. As you can see, at this touchpoint, emotions are quite high. But if you look at the next touchpoint, Touchpoint B, you see quite a precipitous drop in the level of engagement. That's because Touchpoint A represents the end of the purchase process, during which the customer has — through a fairly intensive sales process — been sold a week or two of time share. Touchpoint B, in contrast, represents the point at which the customer receives the invoice for the sale. Naturally, that's a bit of a low. But it's made even worse by the fact that there is a *six-week* gap between the two touchpoints. It's a little like going out on a date with a guy at the end of February, only to have him blow you off until Easter!

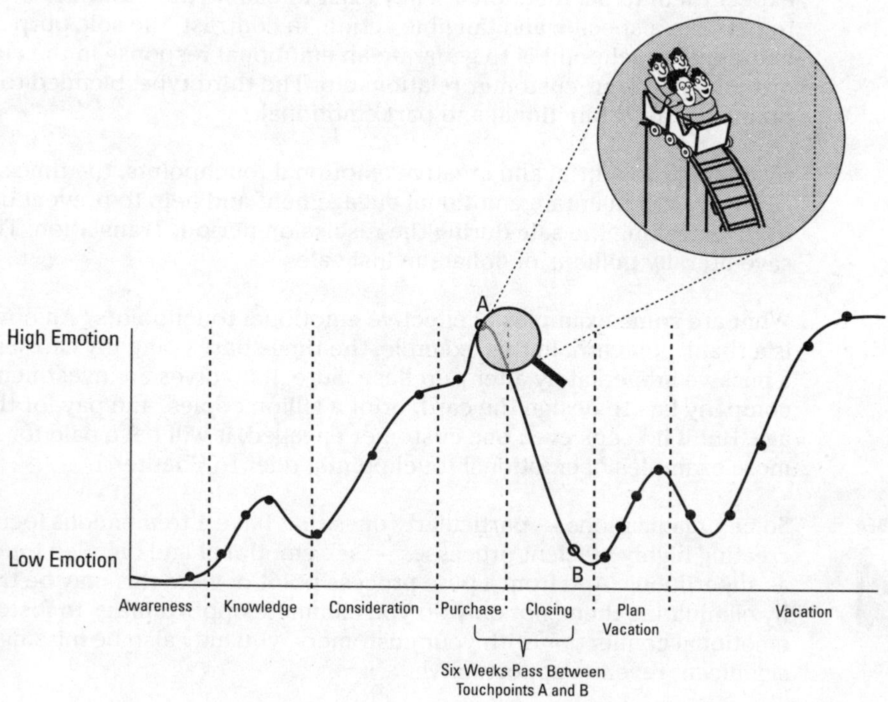

Figure 9-6: Notice the precipitous drop between Touchpoint A and Touchpoint B.

Illustration courtesy of Roy Barnes.

In some industries, going six weeks between touchpoints may not be such a big deal. But at this stage of a real-estate transaction like this one, it's a huge problem. Why? Because often, depending on your state and country of residence, real-estate transactions are subject to a *rescission period* — that is, a cooling-off period during which the buyer can cancel the sale without penalty. If you fail to emotionally engage your customer during this period, there's a very real chance he'll experience buyer's remorse and pull the plug on the whole deal.

You'll notice yet another dip in engagement occurs during the vacation period. It — along with the first dip in engagement we just discussed — forms what the company calls its "swimming pool." Although the stakes aren't quite as high for this second dip — that is, the rescission period has passed — it still indicates a gap in the customer's emotional experience that needs filling.

So what might this company do? And what can *your* company do, if faced with a similar problem? Simple: Create more touchpoints. In this case, the touchpoints should be *emotional touchpoints,* placed at Points 1, 2, and 3. As discussed in Chapter 7, there are three different kinds of touchpoints: functional, emotional, and blended. Functional touchpoints are just what you'd expect them to be: functional. They exist to enable the customer or company to perform a specific and tangible action. In contrast, the sole purpose of an emotional touchpoint is to generate an emotional response in the customer or to deepen your customer relationship. The third type, blended touchpoints, are part functional and part emotional.

By adding thoughtful and creative emotional touchpoints, the time-share company can maintain emotional engagement and help to prevent customers from cancelling the sale during the rescission period. Translation: They can save literally millions of dollars in lost sales.

What are some examples of effective emotional touchpoints? An obvious one is a thank-you card. In this example, the time-share company can send such a missive immediately after purchase. Sure, it involves an investment. The company has to design the card, print a zillion copies, and pay for the postage. But if it keeps even one customer engaged, it will have paid for itself. For more examples of emotional touchpoints, refer to Chapter 7.

REMEMBER

Some organizations — particularly ones that have a tremendous focus on creating highly efficient processes — see emotional and blended touchpoints as superfluous. And from a pure process point of view, this may be true. But by eliminating them, not only do you eliminate opportunities to foster an emotional connection with your customers, you may also be missing out on a significant revenue opportunity!

Part III
Essential Enabling Elements

web extras

Read about a great example of outstanding customer experience in a free article at `www.dummies.com/extras/customerexperience`.

In this part...

- Discover ways to manage customer feedback and foster dialogue.
- Find out how to build customer experience knowledge in your broader workforce.
- Discover the keys to assembling the right customer experience team.
- Find out how to embed customer experience into your organization's larger culture.

Chapter 10

Plan Up: Redesigning Your Touchpoint Program in Four Weeks

In This Chapter

- Understanding the key ingredients of a customer touchpoint redesign program
- Looking at an overview of the touchpoint redesign process
- Understanding the PADBES design methodology
- Showing your appreciation of the touchpoint redesign team
- Going bigger with larger-scale, cross-touchpoint redesign efforts

Touchpoint management is a major component of improving customer engagement. A *touchpoint* is, in a nutshell, any human interaction your customers have during the entire duration of their interaction with your business. Designing a plan for managing these touchpoints well is crucial.

It's a fact: We humans have grand visions and even grander appetites. We want to do big things, *fast*. All too often, however, our tendency is to take on too much, bite off more than we can chew, burn the candle at both ends, spread ourselves too thin, and other idioms that mean we try to do too much without taking the time to plan. Which is why all too often, attempts to tackle big projects, like redesigning your customer experience, go awry.

In our experience, no matter what type of project we're embarking on, the effectiveness of execution is directly proportional to two key factors:

- **How well defined the project is:** Our prescription for redesigning a customer touchpoint to foster an improved customer experience is pretty specific. No vague directives here!

- **How limited the project's scope is:** The work of the redesign team must be precisely aligned to deliver the specific requirements of your customer experience intent statement — nothing more, nothing less. (For more on developing a customer experience intent statement, see Chapter 6.)

In this chapter, you look at a process for improving your customer touchpoints, keeping these two factors in mind. Even better, you find out how to improve each touchpoint in just four short weeks using a proven, rapid-implementation methodology.

(Note that much of the rest of this book goes into a lot more detail on some of the topics covered here, but this chapter gives you a quick overview of how the whole process works. Also, for best results, consider reading Chapter 6 and Chapter 7 before you start this one.)

Six Appeal: Six Key Ingredients of a Touchpoint Redesign Program

Maida Heatter, a world-class chocolate dessert chef, once observed, "I am always amazed when someone tells me about a recipe that didn't turn out right, and then they casually add, 'but that might be because I used fewer eggs and baked it in a larger pan at a lower temperature and I used salad oil instead of butter.'" Similarly, as you're "baking" your redesigned customer touchpoint, you'll want to follow this recipe exactly to yield the desired results.

We've identified six critical ingredients for any touchpoint redesign. These are as follows:

- A firm 20-day time limit
- The right program manager
- A solid redesign team
- A strong stakeholder group
- A definitive customer experience intent statement
- A limited project scope

The following sections give you the lowdown on each of these ingredients so your customer touchpoint redesign program turns out just right.

Setting a firm 20-day time limit

Your redesign efforts should occur within a four-week — or 20 workday — span. During that period, members of the redesign team should be completely removed from their normal work responsibilities. (In reality, you'll find that the last week of the four weeks is more flexible, enabling team members to give their normal work responsibilities at least some minimal attention. But during the first three weeks, the team's redesign efforts will require their full concentration.)

Whoa!" you're probably thinking. "Execution in 20 days? That's a whole lot faster than we're used to working!" No kidding. But remember: The way you've been working is what got you reading this book in the first place. It's time to pick up the pace and change the cadence of execution.

Thanks for asking: 20-day rule FAQ

In case you feel you're a unique exception, here are our responses to a few frequently asked questions about the 20-day rule:

Q: Twenty days requires a pretty big investment in human resources. I mean, 20 multiplied by our average daily pay for five people comes out to more than $20,000. Is this the most appropriate use of our human assets?

A: Great question! What do the problems at the target touchpoint cost you in real dollars? Brand reputation? Goodwill? Repeat business? Employee frustration? Do the math, and then decide whether you think it's worth the investment.

Q: The scope of our redesign is bigger. Should we go 25 days (or longer)?

A: No. Limit your scope. Scope creep is death to touchpoint redesign work.

Q: I don't think we can free up people from their jobs to dedicate 20 days to the touchpoint redesign. Can we do it in 15 (or 10, or 5) days?

A: Not really. Yes, it's appealing to go shorter. But remember: These touchpoints are *broken.* If all you want is ideas on what to fix at a particular touchpoint, then sure, take five days and stop. But if you want to execute a change (and you do, right?), then the redesign team will need the full 20 days. Do it properly the first time and you will get your reward in the form of a well-implemented new process afterwards.

Q: We have already reengineered some of our customer processes. Can we shorten the 20-day process to take that into account?

A: If the reengineering efforts include a detailed mapping of the current path or journey that customers take when they interact with each specific touchpoint, then, yes, you can probably safely do the work in 19 days rather than 20. But if all you've done is map internal processes, plan on using all 20 days.

The 20-day time limit is at the very heart of a successful customer touchpoint experience redesign. Here's why:

- Having just 20 days of work time naturally limits the scope of work.
- Implementable ideas will quickly take precedence over wish lists.
- A short work schedule enables team members to temporarily leave their regular, day-to-day roles.
- Teams will be working *really* hard during this temporary assignment, at a pace they can't typically maintain for much longer than 20 days.
- Limiting the duration to only 20 days helps to remind team members that it's a sprint, not a marathon. Immediate speed is required.
- Attention deficit disorder (ADD) is rampant among senior leaders. Having teams begin and end their work in a short time frame enables leaders to maintain focus on the team.

Many people resist the 20-day time limit. It always seems too long or too short, never "just right." But having participated in several hundred touchpoint redesign efforts, we know from experience that 20 days works best.

Choosing the right program manager

We strongly recommend assigning one person the job of running your organization's ongoing touchpoint redesign process. This person will manage resources and logistics, and will also shepherd the redesign team and stakeholder group (discussed in the next two sections) through the touchpoint redesign.

The ideal candidate for this position has most of the following personal and professional characteristics:

- She is likeable and self-directed.
- She is fast on her feet, with a sense of urgency; flexible; and fearless in the face of power and politics.
- She isn't afraid to stick her nose anywhere and everywhere necessary to smooth the way for the touchpoint redesign team and its time-sensitive requests and inquiries.
- She is relatively well known and has some history with the organization.
- She is well organized and has a good project-management mindset.
- She has some process-reengineering skills and experience.
- She has good relationships across a broad cross section of the organization.

Think of a human synthesis of MacGyver, Radar O'Reilly from *M*A*S*H*, and Scotty from *Star Trek*. That's your person! (If you don't know who we're talking about, activate your Netflix account and spend the next few days figuring it out. Consider this part of your cultural awareness education.)

After a year or so of on-the-job experience, the customer touchpoint program manager will likely have one of the broadest and deepest understandings of how your organization actually operates. This role is a fantastic development opportunity for an up-and-coming, high-potential employee.

Assembling a solid redesign team

The touchpoint redesign team is a cross-functional group, ideally composed of five to seven individuals who have broad expertise in each of their individual parts of the organization and are able to understand and advocate for the customer experience within the touchpoint to be redesigned.

To be more specific, the redesign team should include the following:

- Subject matter experts (SMEs) from the targeted touchpoint (that is, the touchpoint being redesigned)
- SMEs from the touchpoints immediately upstream and downstream of the targeted touchpoint
- A balance of corporate or headquarters staff and field (directly customer-facing representation)
- A touchpoint outsider — someone not familiar with the particular workings of the targeted touchpoint

This last role — the touchpoint outsider — is particularly important. This person can help give those people who are too operationally close to the touchpoint an outsider's perspective and valuable input.

Here are a few more points to keep in mind:

- **Pass on passive types:** Members of your customer touchpoint redesign team should be doers. They can't just produce a plan or a set of ideas; it's their job to execute the changes they propose.
- **Be wary of senior managers:** Be cautious about enlisting managers or directors of the targeted touchpoint as members of the redesign team. These people may be too close to the inner workings of the touchpoint to be effective. Besides, a senior person from the touchpoint in question will likely be part of the stakeholder group anyway.

- **Pick your best and brightest:** Yes, we know what you're thinking: "I can't afford to pull my 'best and brightest' away from their daily responsibilities for 20 days! My business will fall apart!" But trust us: These are exactly the people you want redesigning your customer touchpoints. And remember, participation on one of these teams is a great developmental opportunity for high-potential employees who need "stretch and growth" challenges.

Ideally, you want to look for people with these qualities. (Note that this is also a pretty good list for customer-facing employees.)

- **Empathy:** The most essential quality for a touchpoint designer is empathy — specifically, empathy for the customer. Touchpoint designers must have an understanding of customers' goals and motivations; the context in which they live, work, or play; and how they think about the world. This insight ensures that the experience design actually meets customers' needs.
- **Insatiable curiosity:** When designing a customer touchpoint, you need employees who want to continually explore and understand problems and solutions. More often than not, this characteristic is the key differentiator between those employees who can imagine and create lasting experience engagements and those who can't.
- **Imagination:** As Albert Einstein said, "I believe that imagination is stronger than knowledge. I believe that dreams are more powerful than facts. Knowledge is limited. Imagination encircles." Imagination enables customer experience designers to upend traditional thinking and paradigms and to hit on new ideas that are not initially obvious.
- **Objectivity and self awareness:** Not every idea is a great one. In fact, very few are. The challenge, of course, is to have sufficient objectivity (and a manageable ego) to emotionally distance oneself from the situation to accurately assess options, thoughts, work, and self.
- **Networking abilities:** To be successful as a touchpoint designer, it is extremely helpful to be well connected in the organization. As in all organizational structures, there is the formal way of getting things done . . . and then there's the *real* way: through informal networks and connections. The more "wired" your candidates are, the speedier their execution, and the higher the likelihood of the project's success.
- **The ability to communicate clearly:** It's the rare person indeed who can write and speak well! The ability to effectively communicate across departmental or functional disciplines is critical to customer experience designers. Successful touchpoint redesigners must compose clear emails, hold face-to-face and virtual conversations (potentially crossing

numerous time zones and departmental and functional cultures), and perform countless other communication tasks. Great communication is an art. Look for communication artists.

- **The ability to shift context easily:** When redesigning touchpoints, employees are typically way out of their natural comfort zone. Design is not their "day job," and there's no manual to tell them exactly what to do. They will need to draw on their past experiences to help them solve the customer experience challenge in front of them. What you want in a touchpoint redesigner is someone who has the ability to readily transfer her experiences from one context to an entirely new one. This ability is rare!
- **A systems orientation:** Look for employees who naturally want to understand how the whole system behaves, not just the component pieces. Seeing the forest for the trees — viewing problems as parts of an overall system rather than reacting to specific parts, outcomes, or events — is the mark of a systems-oriented thinker.
- **Impeccable execution:** By "impeccable execution," we mean "the unparalleled ability to get things done." A touchpoint redesigner must work with a small, cross-functional team to map, create, and execute new processes and customer designs. Touchpoint redesigners must also be detailed-oriented enough to grasp and use basic project-management tools. It's difficult, deliberate, step-by-step work.
- **Business smarts and awareness:** It may sound ridiculous, but all too many employees fail to understand how their companies operate, even on a basic level. But touchpoint redesigners must understand how their business works. They must present a business case for each change, including a return on investment from any dollars they plan to invest. They must also be broad enough in their thinking to understand how changes in their industry, market, and environment may affect their business and customers.
- **Natural leadership:** Natural leadership is one of the most important qualities for touchpoint redesigners. But don't be fooled. "Leadership" doesn't refer to one's title or position in the company. Leadership is about one's ability to influence others. Taking on a new project or responsibility means managing the extent of your authority and, more importantly, exercising your influencing skills. Look for flexibility. A person who can roll with it when things go awry, yet be firm when the team needs a stronger hand at the wheel, is ideal.
- **Raw talent:** Having a real talent for customer experience design is a rare thing indeed. Those few employees who can take something half-baked, not well thought out, and incomplete and turn it into something amazingly engaging are to be treasured. When we find raw talent in a

prospective touchpoint redesigner, we are willing to overlook a whole host of other deficiencies. If they're talented and have a willingness to learn, they can be critical players on your redesign team.

REMEMBER

Remember, it's a customer-experience redesign *team*. Although it would be truly amazing to find someone with all these attributes, that's not likely to happen. We've run across only half a dozen or so of these "renaissance people" in our entire careers. In the end, you're putting together a team of people who together will create engaging customer experiences. As long as each team member possesses some of the qualities listed here, you'll be in good shape!

During the formation of the customer touchpoint redesign team, you must also designate a team lead. Although accountability for the team's output will lie with the program manager and stakeholder group (discussed next), the team lead will need to make day-to-day team decisions without their input. Because the team lead will likely be leading a group of his peers, he won't have authority over them in the traditional sense. That means he'll need to use a collaborative coaching style to engage his fellow team members, helping rather than directing. The ideal candidate is someone who can lead strong personalities without getting his own ego involved.

The importance of "influencers"

You may want to salt your redesign team with "influencers" — people who are influential within their peer group across the organization — to help build enthusiasm and support. Malcolm Gladwell wrote about these types of people in his book *The Tipping Point*, dividing them into three key categories:

- **Connectors:** These people are highly social in nature and likely have a long list of friends and acquaintances throughout every level of your organization. Connectors are experts at networking. They know what's going on at work and they tell their friends.
- **Mavens:** Mavens are considered to be experts in their field. As such, their peers look to them for their approval of a proposed change or course of action. Mavens are typically the builders, the engineers, or the process and system experts in your organization. They have a significant impact on the discussions and direction of the large social networks of which they are a part.
- **Salespeople:** Thanks to their persuasive abilities, salespeople are the ones who spur change. They are able to make new (and potentially threatening) concepts seem more understandable. As a result, they persuade people to buy in to your ideas, plans, products, or proposed changes.

It's extraordinarily helpful to have one or two of these influencers — be they connectors, mavens, or salespeople — on your touchpoint redesign team. Their enthusiasm and engagement can be catalysts to the creation of a more customer-centric culture in your organization.

Identifying a strong stakeholder group

Let us be clear: Anytime you redesign a touchpoint, you are seriously messing with the very fabric of the organization (well, at least a swatch or two). The redesign team is very likely to recommend changes to existing processes and procedures that somebody — who is in fact probably still working in the organization — thought were brilliant when they were designed. To that somebody, the redesign process feels a little like being told her child is ugly and is in need of major surgery.

So what to do? For each customer touchpoint redesign assignment, you must establish a separate and distinct stakeholder group. This group should be a formal entity. Its role is to help review the team's redesign strategy and to approve (or not) plans put forth by the redesign team.

The stakeholder group should be composed of two sets of senior leaders:

- Those responsible for managing the touchpoint being redesigned — also known as the touchpoint owner(s)
- Peers of the touchpoint owner(s) — that is, leaders on the same organizational level

The idea is that the peers can help to prevent the primary touchpoint owner(s) from resisting changes that are intended to improve the customer experience. (Often, a touchpoint owner is content with the touchpoint's status quo, even if that touchpoint is clearly broken. For whatever reason, some people just don't like change. Go figure.)

Planning a meeting with your stakeholder group

As you are pulling the stakeholder group together, the program manager should plan on having a quick meeting to go over the stakeholders' role, your expectations of them, and the rules of engagement. This meeting should cover the following regarding what's expected of them:

- Stakeholders have a big responsibility in the redesign process, but that doesn't mean they're members of the redesign team. Members of the stakeholder group should be coaches, not players.

- The redesign team may have a tendency to want to go beyond the original scope of the project. At times, stakeholders may need to rein them in.
- Stakeholders must walk a fine line between allowing creative thinking about how to deliver great customer experience and keeping solutions grounded in the reality of an operating business. If the redesign team proposes something crazy, stakeholders should look for the positive possibilities in the suggestion and redirect the team as appropriate.

  TIP

  Don't deflate the team. These are teachable moments! Too heavy a hand discourages teams, causing them to take only small, incremental steps that don't make a significant difference to the customer. On the flip side, not exercising enough control may result in the redesign team taking on too much in terms of scope or complexity.
- Stakeholders should help members of the touchpoint redesign team think through the financial implications of their proposed actions and solutions.
- When the redesign team needs a decision, stakeholders must give it to them as quickly as possible. If stakeholders don't have the authority to make a decision, they should obtain the decision from someone who *does* have the authority, preferably that same day. No lollygagging!
- Stakeholders must quickly arrive at a unified point of view when asked for a decision. Also, it's no good to appear compliant during the decision-making process, only to be defiant later on. Once the decision is made, all members of the stakeholder team must support it.
- Stakeholders should engage with the redesign team, but should not micromanage. Let the team work independently. You want fresh, new ideas that are a quantum shift from what's happening at the touchpoint today. You're not looking for small, incremental change. Push!
- How to say this nicely? Stakeholders must show up for scheduled meetings with the redesign team. Too many senior executives treat these meetings as optional. Unfortunately, this really messes up all the people who are counting on their presence, opinions, direction, and approval. Worse, the tight time frame means there's no time to reschedule these meetings. When forming the stakeholder team, it's crucial to get its members to commit to attending scheduled meetings. If someone can't attend a meeting, she should send a proxy — someone she trusts to speak and vote on her behalf. Failure to do so means surrendering the right to veto the team's subsequent suggestions and direction.

Working from a definitive customer experience intent statement

Chapter 6 discusses the critical work of creating a definitive customer experience intent statement. If you haven't already, you may want to head over and read that chapter, because now it's time to use this statement. Think of the customer experience intent statement as a set of architectural blueprints or engineering drawings. It clearly articulates the desired end.

Often, as the touchpoint redesign team settles down and gets to work, its efforts quickly morph from redesigning touchpoints to improving internal efficiency and/or reducing process costs. Although there's nothing wrong with either of these — indeed, improving efficiency and saving money are certainly both laudable goals and may well be an effect of the redesign team's efforts — they should *not* be the team's principal focus. Rather, the principal focus should be the experiential objectives outlined in the customer experience intent statement.

The program manager must keep an eye on the team to make sure it's always working from the customer experience intent statement. To help keep things on track, consider hanging large posters of the intent statement in the team's work area, installing screensavers with the intent statement on work computers, or doing anything else you can think of that keeps the "end" — the intended customer experience — in the team members' minds. If all else fails, a quick team field trip to your local tattoo parlor should do the trick! (Just kidding.)

Limiting the scope of your touchpoint redesign

In addition to the customer experience intent statement, you need to keep one other key document at hand: a well-written scope statement. This document helps you avoid scope creep, which is death to any touchpoint redesign. Taking an extra hour or two to develop a scope statement will save the redesign team many more hours later on.

The scope statement, developed by the program manager and stakeholder group, must be developed prior to the formation of the redesign team. The scope must be in place before any work begins during the 20-day work period. It should include the following:

- The name of the targeted customer touchpoint (that is, the touchpoint you are redesigning).
- The names of the other affected touchpoints both upstream and downstream of the targeted touchpoint. (Use a touchpoint map, or journey map, to identify these. For more on journey maps, see Chapter 7.)
- The scope of the project. This should define the problem to be solved, the deliverables, and the expected benefits.
- The exclusions, or what is outside the scope of the redesign effort.
- Any known issues, risks, or technology dependencies.
- Performance measures that may be affected by the redesign effort. These measures should be a mix of leading and lagging performance measures and can be both qualitative and quantitative in nature.
- The touchpoint owner and the stakeholder team.

Think of the scope statement as a contract of sorts, binding the redesign team to the task. That way, the statement is more likely to be written with the specificity needed. Vagueness is your nemesis here. The more information provided to the touchpoint redesign team, the better. Figure 10-1 shows a template for a scope statement. Feel free to use it to develop your own scope statement.

Avoiding the technology trap

The redesign team likely won't have time to address issues with major IT systems within your organization. Tinkering with almost any IT system is often very complicated and time-consuming. Plus, there's likely already a prioritized wish list of enhancements lined up in the IT developers' queue. Throwing a touchpoint redesign team's work in the midst of pre-existing priorities just doesn't work. Avoid this by limiting the scope of your redesign efforts to stay away from significant changes to IT systems.

By the way, great customer experience is hardly dependent upon systems. They help, of course, but many of your customer touchpoints can be redesigned to substantially improve the customer experience without factoring in the use of systems or technology. That doesn't mean there isn't work to be done in making the systems that customers *do* interface with more user and experientially friendly. We talk about what to do with larger-scope issues at the end of this chapter.

Customer Experience Touchpoint Team Scope Template

Touchpoint Name/Project Name: ______________________

One Paragraph Problem Statement/Rationale for Change:

____

____

Touchpoint Owner: ______________________

Impacted Touchpoints (Upstream and Downstream)

____

____

What is In-Scope?:

____

____

What is Out-of-Scope? (include technology limits if appropriate):

____

____

Existing Performance Metrics for Touchpoint:

____

____

Enabling Technologies of the Touchpoint:

____

____

Touchpoint Team Members and Home Department or Function:

____

____

____

____

Additional Anticipated Support Required:

____

____

Figure 10-1: A scope statement template.

Illustration courtesy of Roy Barnes.

Getting a Brief Overview of the Touchpoint Redesign Process

The first step of the touchpoint redesign process is to gather a redesign team. As mentioned earlier in this chapter, this team will be active for four weeks (or 20 workdays), assembling, working, and then disbanding. Broadly speaking, during that four-week period, the team will be responsible for the following:

- Assessing the current state of the customer touchpoint
- Brainstorming desired changes to enhance the customer experience
- Designing new touchpoint processes
- Executing the change

That last bullet — executing the change — is *very important.* This isn't just an "imagineering" exercise. This is hard work, with the absolute expectation of change at the end of the four-week period. No extensions, no excuses, no kidding.

After you have a few touchpoint redesigns under your belt, you may opt to run two or more redesign teams simultaneously. Often, when organizations get in the habit of continuously redesigning touchpoints, they find that they can complete up to 20 touchpoint redesigns over the course of a year. That's a lot of positive change!

Using the PADBES Design Method

You've selected a program manager, assembled your redesign team, and gathered a group of stakeholders to keep them in check. You've set a 20-day time limit, distributed your customer experience intent statement, and developed a scope statement. Now what?

PADBES, that's what. PADBES describes the process of touchpoint redesign. It's very similar to the software design cycle used by thousands of companies all over the world. It stands for the following:

- **Plan:** Describe what will be accomplished.
- **Analyze:** Analyze the current state.

- **Design:** Use the customer experience intent statement and scope document to design touchpoint changes.
- **Build:** Build the new touchpoint process.
- **Execute:** Deploy and implement the new approach.
- **Sustain:** Sustain, measure, and continuously improve the touchpoint.

Figure 10-2 shows the PADBES workflow from pre-work planning through ongoing sustainment.

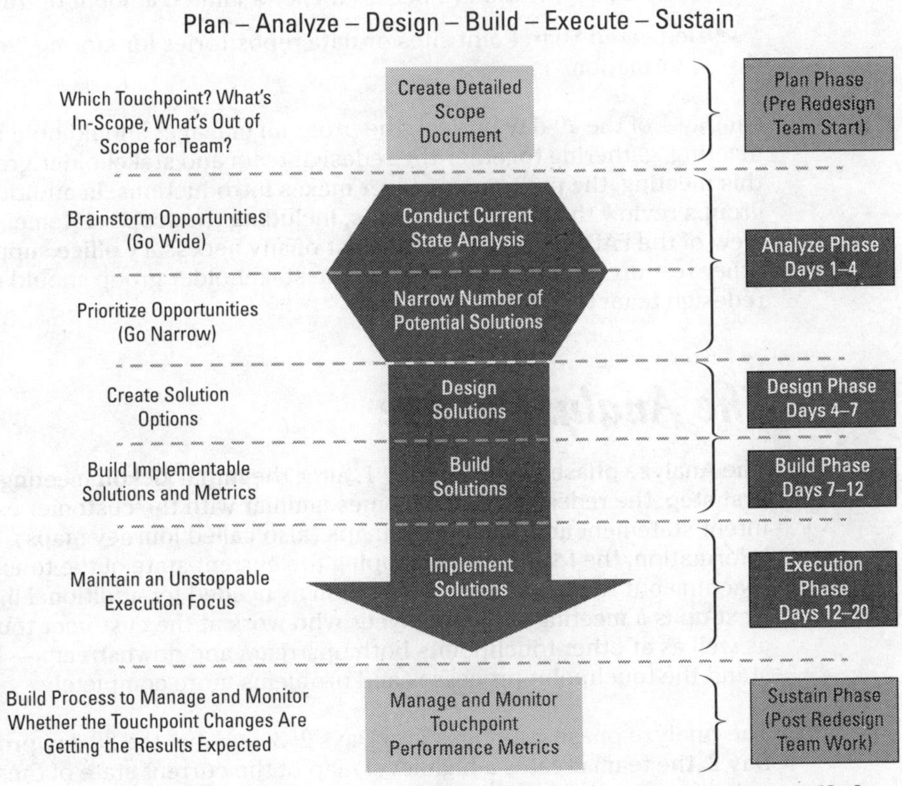

Figure 10-2: The PADBES workflow.

Illustration courtesy of Roy Barnes.

The major challenge for the touchpoint redesign team is the speed at which the PADBES process occurs. Given the 20-day work window, things need to move pretty rapidly. Next we look at which stages happen when.

The Plan phase

The Plan phase starts before the 20-day work window. During this phase, the program manager needs to assemble the redesign team and stakeholder group. She also needs to ensure the redesign team has access to the following:

- A dedicated team workspace
- Computers, printers, and basic office supplies and materials
- Local transportation (if necessary) or a limited amount of travel dollars
- Dedicated SharePoint sites or data repositories for storing files and information

On Day 1 of the 20-day project, the program manager should hold a kickoff meeting, gathering together the redesign team and stakeholder group. During this meeting, the program manager makes introductions. In addition, both groups review the initial documents, including the scope statement, an overview of the PADBES process, and a list of any necessary office supplies or other resources. After this meeting, the stakeholder group should leave the redesign team to begin work.

The Analyze phase

The Analyze phase begins on Day 1, after the initial kickoff meeting. As a first step, the redesign team becomes familiar with the customer experience intent statement and touchpoint maps (also called journey maps). Using this information, the team begins mapping the current state of the touchpoint, reaching out to the greater organization as needed for additional information. Next up is a meeting with employees who work at the customer touchpoint — as well as at other touchpoints both upstream and downstream — to understand the touchpoint processes and problems more completely.

The Analyze phase continues into Days 2, 3, and 4 of the 20-day project. On Day 2, the team creates a high-level map of the current state of the touchpoint (see Figure 10-3). The idea is to get a quick, clear visual representation of what's happening from both an internal (company) view and an external (customer) perspective. (We recommend using large sticky notes to build the map. This gives you a bit of extra flexibility as you work.) If a relatively bright sixth-grader could follow the map the team lays out, they've probably hit it just right. In addition, the redesign team should capture obvious process and customer blocks and hurdles, and identify dependencies and their impact on other touchpoints. Day 3 sees further analysis of the current state of the touchpoint, with the result being more-detailed workflow/process diagrams to further identify constraints and generate alternatives.

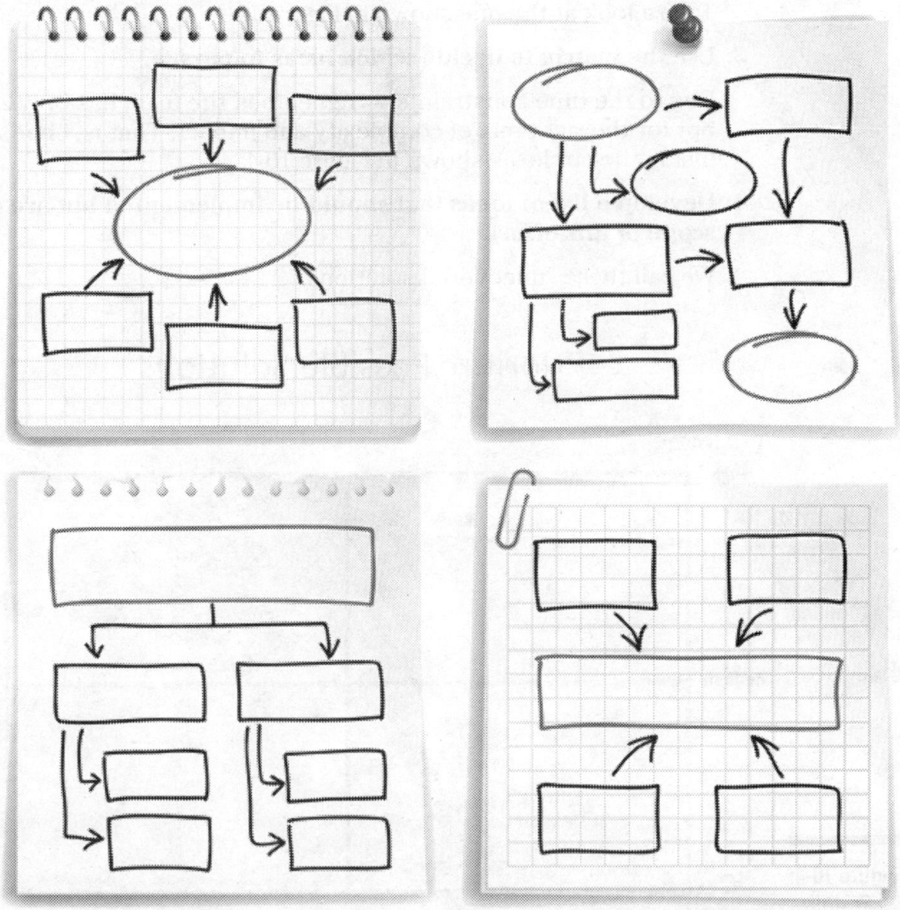

Figure 10-3: Map the process flow within the touchpoint.

Illustration courtesy of Roy Barnes.

With that complete, it's time for the redesign team members to begin brainstorming for solutions to problems and ways to enhance the customer experience, using the customer experience intent statement as their guide. The objective is to develop a list of feasible ideas that are within the scope of the redesign. To determine feasibility, the team should do the following:

1. **Rate each idea on the list in terms of complexity (how hard it will be to execute the idea) and impact (how much of a difference the idea will make to the customer's experience).**

If necessary, the team can use different metrics, such as cost, impact on other touchpoints, ease of maintenance — whatever makes sense for the situation.

2. **Position each idea in a simple, four-box matrix.**

   Take a look at the one shown in Figure 10-4.

3. **Use the matrix to decide which ideas to pursue.**

   Due to the time constraints — remember, the team has only 20 days — opt for the right mix of complexity and impact. That is, choose the ideas inside the circle, as shown in Figure 10-4.

4. **Develop a list of ideas that should be implemented but are outside the scope of this effort.**

   We call these "uncovered solutions."

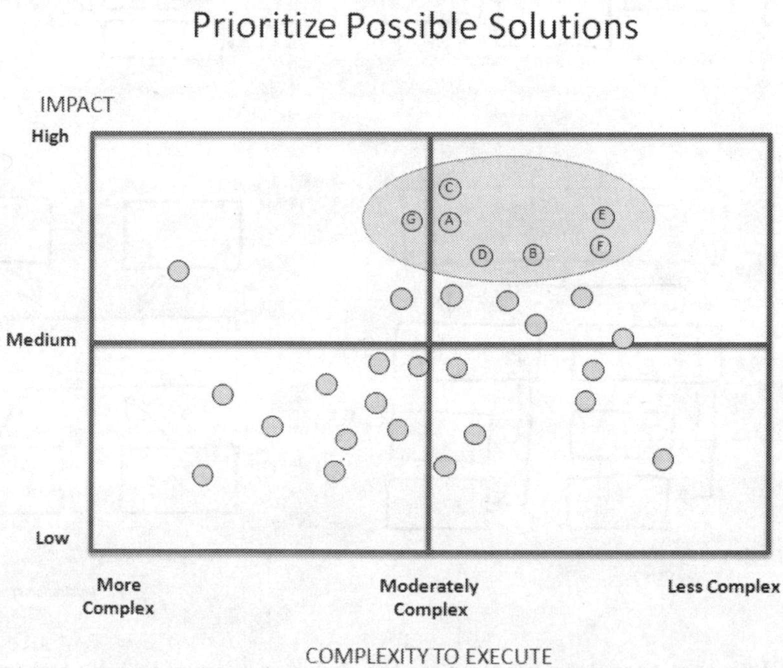

Illustration courtesy of Roy Barnes.

Figure 10-4: Prioritize possible solutions.

Tracking uncovered work and dealing with other hidden horrors

If you've ever been part of remodeling a house, building an addition, moving a wall, or even adding a new light switch, you've probably had the dubious reward of discovering some unforeseen problem and realizing that the job suddenly got bigger. Whether it's bad wiring, mold, asbestos, or a colony of creepy crawlies slithering behind your drywall, these hidden horrors quickly turn what should have been a simple task into a frustratingly pricey pit of problems.

Similarly, during the 20-day project period, the touchpoint redesign team will uncover all sorts of problems. Solving these problems may be either outside the scope of the redesign effort or too complex to complete within the allotted time. Nonetheless, it's critical that the redesign team members catalog all the additional work that needs to be done, even if they aren't the ones to do it. Often, this "uncovered work" will reveal some of the biggest problems in your organization in terms of the customer experience. Once this work is uncovered, it's imperative that the program manager and the organization's senior leadership follow up on it. If they don't, rest assured that these issues will remain. Solving problems is hard work. Solving deeply entrenched, creepy-crawly problems is even harder.

At the conclusion of the Analyze phase, usually on Day 4, the redesign team should meet with the stakeholder group for an hour or two to reveal findings, observations, and initial solutions, and to ask for any needed input. This is not a time to wing it. The redesign team should carefully prepare for this meeting, ensuring that its ideas are presented in a logical way. Failure to prepare may lead stakeholders to believe the team hasn't examined the situation carefully enough to suggest good ideas!

No matter how well the redesign team prepares, odds are the stakeholder group will *not* like everything the redesign team suggests! This is normal. It's critical that the program manager coach the redesign team members through the lows that may follow this meeting, helping them to pick themselves up and dust themselves off.

Using the stakeholder group's feedback, the redesign team should then narrow its scope and rethink its proposed solutions. At that point, the team can pinpoint which solutions to choose. The team should also begin identifying expenses associated with implementing the proposed solutions and maintaining them after they're live.

Riding the roller coaster

Redesigning a customer touchpoint is a little like riding an emotional roller coaster (see the following figure). When the project starts (Point A), the team will likely experience a mixture of excitement, trepidation, and uncertainty. At Point B, they may feel disillusioned by the amount of work to be done in a very limited amount of time. After brainstorming some new ideas, the team, full of enthusiasm, may experience a high point (Point C), only to plunge back down after those ideas are pooh-poohed by the stakeholder group (Point D). This goes on in an up-and-down fashion for the duration of the project. The program manager must be attentive to the team members' emotional state and coach them through both the highs and the lows. These ups and downs are a natural part of any rapid redesign project. It doesn't hurt to warn the team of this beforehand, so the roller coaster doesn't take them by surprise!

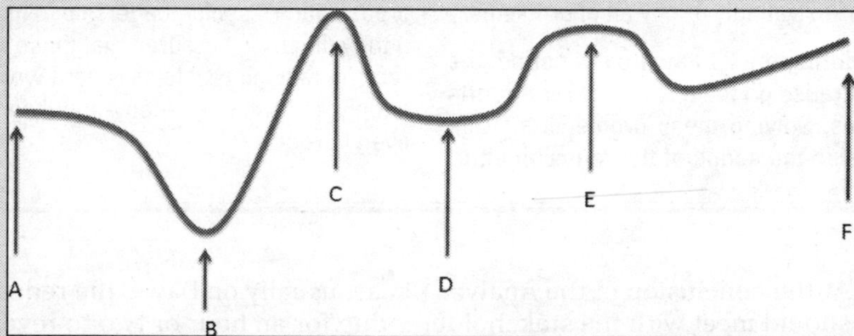

Illustration courtesy of Roy Barnes.

The Design phase

The Design phase kicks off on Day 5 and continues into the second week of the project. During this phase, the redesign team should do the following:

- Run proposed changes by the touchpoint operators.
- Meet with the stakeholder group to propose changes and seek approval.

You find out more about the Design phase in Chapter 8.

The Build phase

Starting in Week 2 and continuing until the beginning of Week 3, you're in the Build phase. During this phase, the redesign team "builds" the new experiential processes, collateral, and other solutions for the new touchpoint design. For example, the redesign team might build a new billing statement or inquiry-handling process. The Build phase is about creating something new that actually works to deliver a better customer experience. The Build phase begins the process of moving ideas into concrete reality. Frequent meetings with the stakeholder group during this phase help to keep the redesign team on track.

Often, changes made during this phase require new customer-facing collateral — brochures, marketing materials, and/or other communication pieces (or at the very least, modifications to existing materials). In this case, the touchpoint redesign team must coordinate with the organization's marketing/brand team to ensure these materials meet branding requirements. Touchpoint teams should not be in the business of revamping their organization's branding strategy!

The Execute phase

It's not enough to come up with ideas for change; the key is to implement, or execute, those ideas. This implementation happens in the Execute phase, which spans from the end of Week 3 through the final week of the 20-day period.

As they say in the military, "Every plan is good until the first shot is fired." This philosophy is true for touchpoint redesign work as well. And it's why we make such a fuss about ensuring that the redesign team focuses on executing the changes it proposes within the 20-day period.

In the Execute phase, your touchpoint redesign meets up with the reality of your organization's operating environment — the day-to-day chaos. The purpose of this phase is to get the proposed changes up and operating. It's almost impossible to predict what the reaction will be — from people and from existing processes — when you introduce your change into the mix, but we guarantee that you'll get some unexpected responses.

Knowing that something is going to go sideways should be a comfort to you. Things won't go as planned. So it's crucial that the redesign team leaves enough time to execute and then adjust its recommendations in real-life, real-time circumstances.

The Sustain phase

Just as human bodies sometimes reject transplanted organs or tissue, organizations have a tendency to reject anything new. In medicine, doctors combat this by administering immunosuppressive drugs to transplant patients. These drugs allow the new organ or tissue to gain a foothold of acceptance in the patient's body. Although it may be tempting to drug your entire organization into accepting change, most human resources offices frown on that.

The final presentation

After implementing the proposed changes, the redesign team will disband. First, however, its members must present their findings to the stakeholder group. This final presentation should (at a minimum) contain the following components:

- The customer experience intent statement
- The scope statement
- The names of the members of the touchpoint redesign team.
- What the team found that needed to be changed. (This should include what measures were in place to measure and monitor the touchpoint's performance, such as customer surveys, process performance management metrics, and so on.)
- The team's discoveries — issues working together, working inside the process, and so forth. This information is to help subsequent teams and the program manager pinpoint potential roadblocks and hurdles in subsequent redesigns.
- A description of the pre-redesign state of the touchpoint. (This presentation is best done in a process-map format.)
- A description of the current, post-redesign state of the touchpoint. (This step should include any redesigned customer-facing collateral or materials that were developed and are now in use.)
- The implementation steps that have been taken and what (if any) implementation work remains to be done.
- A description of all (existing, changed, and new) performance metrics that were put in place to monitor the future performance of the customer touchpoint.
- A costs and savings review. (This review should include what costs and/or savings the touchpoint team incurred during the redesign.)
- Issues uncovered that were outside the scope of this redesign project that should be addressed by another touchpoint redesign effort.
- Questions/discussion topics.

This presentation should be made using Microsoft PowerPoint, Apple Keynote, or similar software. Subsequent touchpoint redesign teams will likely reference the team's findings and observations, so it's best to have the final presentation in a format that is easy to distribute and access. The customer touchpoint program manager should maintain an online library of all presentations as well as all reference materials produced by the touchpoint redesign team.

In the place of drug therapy, the customer experience touchpoint program manager must carefully monitor the acceptance, adoption, and further implementation needs of each redesign. This is the Sustain phase, and it continues far beyond the 20-day window. Without constant and visible monitoring of touchpoint changes, most organizations will gradually drift back toward their original state, as if no change occurred.

The importance of communication

A critical aspect of the Sustain phase is communication, which helps to combat the "marathon effect." Imagine you're standing with 38,000 other runners in the start corral for the London Marathon. Bang! The starting gun fires and . . . nothing happens. Why? Because unless you're Kenyan, you're probably too far back to hear it. Even if you *do* hear it, you have to wait for the masses of people in front of you to get moving before you can cross the start line and begin your race. And by that time, the elite runners are already far down the road!

The same thing applies with a touchpoint redesign. Remember that the touchpoint redesign team has been off and running for 20 days. While the stakeholder group and employees at the redesigned touchpoint may be close on their heels, the rest of the organization hasn't even crossed the start line yet.

To avoid the marathon effect, an aggressive communications strategy is needed. Everyone in the organization must be made aware of what the touchpoint redesign team is doing and how its work will affect the rest of the organization. To achieve this, you must do whatever you can to publicize the touchpoint redesign team's work. Mention it in meetings. Provide updates in newsletters. Spread the word on your intranet site. If there's a quarterly staff celebration, make sure the touchpoint work is highlighted. The idea is to show the rest of the organization that the senior leadership views the touchpoint work as critically important.

REMEMBER: People notice what is talked about and what isn't. If what was a major initiative several months ago no longer commands attention, employees will quickly shift their attention to the next new flavor of the day.

Measuring performance

A fall-off in execution over time is natural. The only remedy is to constantly monitor and report on the ongoing execution effort. So during the Sustain phase, you want to keep track of which parts of your organization have implemented the touchpoint change and which parts have continued to use the change over time, and report on your findings.

A simple tracking tool, like the one shown in Figure 10-5, can help you keep track of which of the redesign team's recommendations have been implemented, and which are still in use 6 and 12 months after the team completes its work. The program manager must then publish a list of which areas of the company are doing well in this regard, as well as which areas aren't. Otherwise, odds are the customer experience won't be up to par.

TIP: Here's a best-practice tip: Use the performance metrics that each of the teams presents and make sure those metrics are highly visible on the organization's balanced scorecard or on its list of regularly published KPIs (Key Performance Indicators).

Region	% of Recommended Touchpoint Changes Implemented	% of Touchpoint Changes Still Being Executed (6 months)	% of Touchpoint Changes Still Being Executed (12 months)
Northern	100%	95%	95%
Southern	88%	50%	55%
Eastern	90%	80%	80%
Western	100%	98%	95%

Figure 10-5: Tracking implementation is key.

Illustration courtesy of Roy Barnes.

We talk more about this in Chapter 15, but be warned that significant momentum is often lost when the performance of the customer experience changes implemented isn't consistently monitored. Remember that past redesign teams will be substantially disheartened if their hard work and implemented changes slowly fade back to the original state.

Recognizing and Rewarding Team Members

If you want to inspire innovation in your organization, it's imperative that you recognize and reward those employees who display it. That goes double for your touchpoint redesign team. Recognition and rewards could range from a gift card for a dinner out for each team member at the conclusion of the project to a shout-out at the next company meeting. However you do it, you must ensure that members of the touchpoint redesign team are publicly and privately celebrated for their work.

One client, the CEO of a large gas and electric utility company, made it a practice to drop in on touchpoint redesign team members, chat for a few minutes, and thank them for their effort. Not only was this obvious senior-level acknowledgment appreciated by team members, but their peers — who saw the CEO come in, sit down, and shoot the breeze — were impressed, too.

TIP

Look at what behaviors are formally recognized and rewarded in your organization. Are employees recognized for meeting safety requirements? Are they rewarded for meeting sales goals or for reducing costs? Members of touchpoint redesign teams need to be celebrated in the same way. In order to become "real," touchpoint redesign work must be endowed with the same visibility as other efforts.

Chapter 11

Can We Talk? Managing Customer Feedback and Fostering Dialogue

In This Chapter

- Looking at three rules for handling customer feedback
- Understanding the difference between CRM systems and EFM programs
- Seeing what an EFM program can do for you
- Getting your EFM program up and running
- Keeping in mind special considerations with social media

Suppose you've been single for a while. The dating scene is pretty wretched. Then one day, you encounter a fabulous person. Destiny! Fireworks! This person appears to meet every single one of the requirements on your unreasonably detailed list.

So what do you do? You watch every little action, observe every little gesture, and look for any clues of your beloved's interests. You listen and capture every like and dislike. You soak up every conversation, hanging on each word.

What you're *really* looking for is some actionable data out of all the unstructured feedback that you're receiving. You want to extract key phrases and sentiments to gain previously unknown insight — information that you can use to deliver a better romantic experience.

Sound unromantic? Maybe, but with the information you glean, you put forth new offers and opportunities in the hope that your love interest will bite. All the while, you maintain steady (but not smothering) contact, helping your mate-to-be understand the depth of your attentiveness. Look how selfless you are!

The truth is, you should give your customers this same level of attention, listening to their feedback and establishing and maintaining an ongoing dialogue. Indeed, this is the very basis of a profitable relationship. Meaningful conversation, curiosity, shared insights, and your clear intention to immediately respond to any concern signal your willingness to partner with your customer for your mutual success. The bottom line? When you listen to and act on feedback and maintain a dialogue with your customers, you make them happy. And happy customers buy more, refer more, and maintain their loyalty to you over time.

This chapter covers the rules of engagement when it comes to dealing with customer feedback, the systems you can use to manage this feedback, and special considerations for social media.

3-2-1 Go! Three Hard-and-Fast Rules for Dealing with Customer Feedback

When it comes to dealing with customer feedback — be it good, bad, or indifferent — there are three hard-and-fast rules:

- **Take action.** This is the step that people skip most often. But there's no point in surveying customers or soliciting other kinds of feedback if you have no intention of acting on it. If you go that route, you're just creating one more bad customer experience. When you have data, take action.

  REMEMBER: Collecting feedback is of no value unless an action or change occurs.

- **Communicate your action.** When you take action after receiving feedback, spread the word! Showing people that you listen to their feedback helps to ensure that they'll continue to offer feedback in the future. And if you decide *not* to take action, it's worthwhile to explain why. Bad news is better than no news! You may also decide to communicate other actions you've taken instead, but whatever you do, don't just say nothing. In your silence, people will come to their own conclusions about your actions (or lack thereof), and those conclusions will almost always be negative.
- **Ensure satisfaction.** It's important to make sure that customers who provide feedback are satisfied with the outcome of their communication with you. That means following up with every single person who provides feedback. First, thank everyone who gives you feedback for communicating with you, even if that communication was a complaint. Next, if the feedback is indeed a complaint, attempt to resolve the customer's problem. Finally, ask the customer whether he's satisfied with how you handled his feedback. If not, ask what resolution he'd like to see. If you haven't met the customer's expectations, do what you can to resolve the issue.

Alphabet Soup: CRM versus EFM

Over the last 10 to 15 years, companies all over the world have collectively poured millions of dollars into buying and using customer relationship management (CRM) software. This software is designed to manage a company's interactions with current and future customers — in other words, to track, manage, and enable the dialogue. In essence, CRM software organizes, automates, and synchronizes activities in sales, marketing, customer service, and technical support.

What has been the return on this investment? Generally, pretty disappointing. By themselves, most CRM systems just aren't up to the task of helping organizations deliver an exceptional customer experience. Yes, robust CRM platforms can remember a customer's birthday. And yes, they can slice and dice customer segment preferences as effectively as a Ginsu knife. But these systems aren't particularly good at the softer side of interactions, like knowing when and how best to respond to a particular customer's failed service experience.

CRM systems document and analyze things like buying behaviors, likes and dislikes, contact details, demographic information, and so forth. In other words, they know everything about your customers — except how they felt about their actual experience.

Enter enterprise feedback management (EFM) programs. The term *enterprise feedback management* describes the process of systematically collecting, analyzing, consolidating, and then using all sources of feedback to improve your customer experience, business results, and overall profitability. Where CRM systems tell you the who, what, where, and when of a customer's experience, the EFM program tells you the how and why.

REMEMBER

EFM programs provide information, direct from the customer, about feelings and perceptions of actual product and service experiences. EFM programs don't just aggregate feedback from multiple sources across multiple channels; they also disseminate real-time, actionable information across the company, and the best ones enforce accountability for follow-up and service lapse recovery. An EFM program isn't just a piece of software — it's a way of doing business.

TIP

In more advanced organizational implementations, data gathered from a robust EFM program can provide valuable input into a company's CRM system, merging information about attitudes with information about behaviors and transactions and helping to pinpoint synergies between the two. New services, products, niches, and markets will naturally evolve from the resulting insights — meaning more money for your organization!

Getting with the Program: Making the Case for an EFM Program

Consider all the different ways money can flow into and out of your organization. Money can flow in the form of cash, credit cards, debit cards, and bank checks. Sometimes, money flows in at cash registers or point-of-sale kiosks. Other times, it flows in as a direct transfer from someone's bank account. On occasion, someone may even stop by your place of business to pay a bill in person! Some money trades hands at your most basic customer touchpoints. Other cash movements occur at the corporate level. Accounts payable and payroll transactions bring yet another layer of complexity to the movement of money.

No matter where they come from, in most organizations, all these streams of money are consolidated into one central accounting system, ensuring completeness, accuracy, and usability from a reporting perspective. Can you imagine what would happen if this weren't the case — if these financial transactions *didn't* flow through a single accounting system, were not followed up on, and were never reconciled? Chaos would reign!

Now try replacing the phrase "financial transactions" with the words "customer feedback." This gives you a pretty good picture of how most companies in the world should operate but don't. Customer, vendor, employee, and even performance feedback is collected, but it's not consolidated into a central processing system. As a result, the data is often stuck in different "silos" within the company, its value unrealized.

For example, many organizations collect customer feedback using point-of-sale surveys or comment cards. These same organizations may also perform internal quality checks or use third-party mystery shoppers to measure performance. And yet, these different types of feedback are never consolidated into one centralized database, nor are they shared with customer touchpoint managers for follow-up and customer recovery.

But these examples are only the tip of the iceberg. Think of the many additional ways in which customers can provide feedback. For example, customers may

- Google your website and fill out a feedback form you've supplied there
- Send you an email to share their feedback
- Call your toll-free number

- Write you a letter
- Complain about you on the Internet on social media, their blog, and so forth

Then ask yourself these questions:

- Can your organization currently integrate feedback collected from any of these methods?
- Are you set up to capture feedback in ways that are most convenient for your customers rather than most convenient for you?
- Is feedback immediately delivered to the right manager or employee in a simple, consolidated fashion? Or does it trickle in sporadically, through multiple channels, over a number of weeks or, worse, months? (This scenario is compounded even further when multiple types of feedback are involved, such as that from employees, vendors, and partners.)
- Does your company have an easy way to ensure that someone is following up on each piece of feedback, regardless of how the customer, vendor, or employee chose to share it with you?
- Is someone being held accountable to fix any problems that are uncovered? Are tools being used to ensure that follow-up action is occurring? Is positive feedback channeled back to the front lines or to training programs for reward and replication?
- Do you know how these various types of feedback influence each other? For example, how might declining employee satisfaction affect customer experience? And how will declining customer experience affect customer loyalty and, eventually, your revenues?

TIP

If you answer "No" to any of these questions, you need an EFM program.

In an EFM program, feedback is collected, consolidated, analyzed, and immediately made available to front-line supervisors and managers to improve operations and customer experience. The information is widely accessible up and down the organization, with different reports, roles, and permission levels available for different types of users.

An EFM program integrates and analyzes all the disparate sources of customer feedback, including surveys, recorded call center interactions, web forms, social media/online content, and others. The idea is to turn all this raw input into meaningful and actionable insight.

EFM versus traditional customer research

In case you're wondering, operating an EFM program is not the same as managing traditional customer research. Traditional customer research typically involves a deep dive on a set of issues and may involve quantitative analysis, lengthy consumer/customer interviews, surveys, focus groups, and so forth. It often takes many months to complete and even longer for findings to be revealed. Most organizations conduct traditional customer research to answer a specific question, like what product or service demands innovation or how customers feel about a particular new feature.

In contrast, the idea behind EFM is to unearth and resolve customer experience problems in real time. EFM is all about how well the organization performs during a particular interaction or transaction. When you capture feedback on as many interactions as possible, EFM offers a real-time view, enabling you to capture information about every customer rather than just a sample of a few.

Although traditional customer research and EFM are two different things, in an ideal scenario, they are highly integrated, with one informing the other (and vice versa).

Looking at the benefits of an EFM program

A well-designed, properly executed EFM program offers numerous benefits. It is especially useful in helping you understand your relationships with customers, employees, partners, suppliers, and others. Some specific examples of the benefits of EFM programs include the following:

- Consolidated survey management
- Support for real-time, customer-driven response
- Consolidated customer insight analysis
- A holistic journey/touchpoint map–wide view of the customer experience
- Speech and text analytics as well as data-mining capabilities to leverage open-ended comments and input
- Data to conduct statistical correlation and regression analysis to understand the key drivers of a thriving customer experience
- The ability to pinpoint specific team/employee training needs
- The ability to ensure prompt service-lapse recovery — in other words, fixing problems quickly so they don't recur
- The ability to "save" customers (and their lifetime value) before they permanently leave you
- The ability to compensate employees based on quantitative customer measurements
- Integrated reporting of all feedback, from all your touchpoints

- The creation of quantitative linkages between specific customer experience performance and financial results, allowing the creation of return on customer experience (ROCE) metrics
- The ability to drive customer experience consistency across the organization by sharing results widely
- The ability to deliver better internal service by tying into help-desk processes and other HR and IT systems
- Support for many HR responsibilities, including compensation and performance reviews, input into a balanced scorecard, customer service training needs, competency evaluations, and hiring evaluations for recruitment purposes

Real-time feedback, consolidated from all sources, enables managers to make an immediate impact. When customers and employees see or hear that their input is actually being put to use, they become increasingly engaged in your business overall.

For "before" and "after" assessments of the implementation of an EFM program, see Figures 11-1 and 11-2. Figure 11-1 illustrates the *silo mentality* of many businesses. Feedback data is collected in various locations by different means. Input received from customers sits and gets stale. Often, specific customer requests or complaints are left unattended. Nothing is available to consolidate feedback and enable action. Time-starved operating managers are forced to sift through multiple reports, surveys, and sources to try to make sense of disjointed information. No accountability is possible.

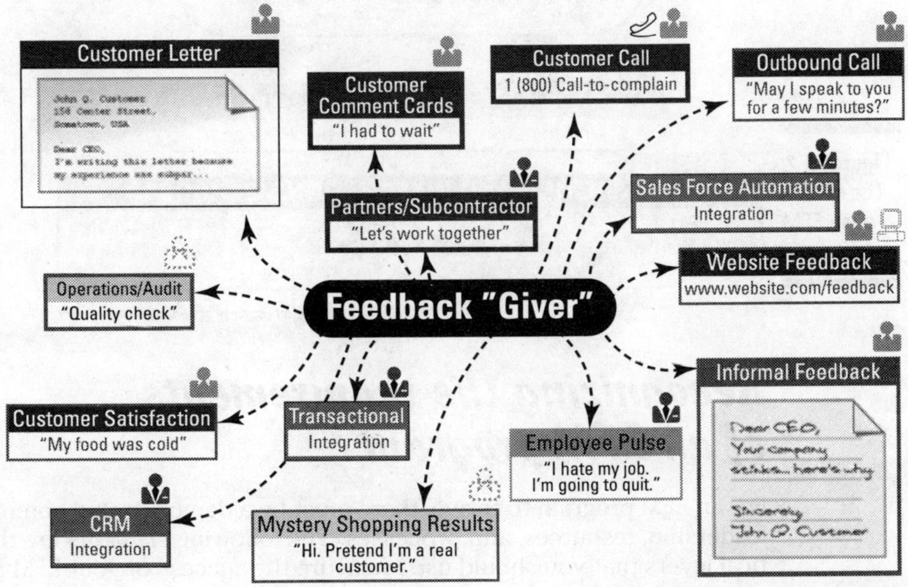

Figure 11-1: The silo mentality of many businesses. Chaos reigns!

Illustration courtesy of Mindshare/InMoment.

Figure 11-2 illustrates the possible flow of information after the implementation of an EFM program. Data is transformed into actionable information. It is consolidated, summarized, analyzed, and delivered to the appropriate manager, in a usable format, and in real time, when it is still fresh and actionable. People are held accountable for following up on the feedback.

Figure 11-2: The results of an EFM program.

Illustration courtesy of Mindshare/InMoment.

Recognizing the requirements of an EFM program

For an EFM program to thrive, there must be a demonstrated commitment of leadership, resources, and processes. The following elements are the main tactical levers that you should use to ensure the success of your EFM program:

- Senior management's commitment and involvement. Implementing an EFM requires leadership to do something with the information that is gathered. Employees will only be committed if their bosses are.
- Compensation and reward structures that use real, not just hearsay, quantitative data for measuring customer experience improvement are putting your money where your mouth is. What gets compensated gets attention.
- Make sure that all employee nonfinancial recognition and appreciation programs are using EFM customer feedback as the basis of recognition. A robust EFM can provide great customer stories that can be used to drive the customer-centric culture you want.
- Employee engagement with customer experience rises when real-time feedback from customers is provided to the front-line workforce. An effective EFM can provide near instantaneous feedback from which employees can measure their success in delivering the experience intent you desire.

REMEMBER

EFM goes hand in hand with building a customer-centric culture. Chapter 14 discusses customer-centric culture in more detail. For now, just be aware that many of the foundational elements that need to be present for a customer-centric culture to flourish also need to be present for EFM systems and processes to work well.

Making It So: Implementing Your EFM Program

So how do you get an EFM program up and running? After you obtain the backing of key executives, we recommend a phased approach, starting small and ultimately building toward a fully functional EFM program. In general terms, the phases are as follows:

1. Inventory all existing customer feedback sources.
2. Consolidate the questions that customers are being asked.
3. Fill in the missing gaps in your touchpoint feedback collection.
4. Identify linkages between employee experience and customer experience.
5. Develop a more advanced EFM program.

The following sections address each of these phases in more detail.

Phase 1: Inventory all existing customer feedback sources

Like the British Empire of old, you may be part of a far-flung organization with a lot of dots on the map, all representing different sources of feedback. Job #1 is to centralize and automate the gathering and management of this feedback. This process enables a more systematic approach to assessing customer experience across channels of interaction.

Start with this activity. For each customer touchpoint on your map, ask yourself the following questions:

- Is this a touchpoint we should be listening to?
- Are we listening there today?
- What means/methods/vendors are we using to capture feedback today?
- How frequently do we receive and gather feedback?
- Is the feedback gathered at this touchpoint stored? For how long?
- Is the feedback gathered at this touchpoint centrally accessible?
- Is the feedback gathered at this touchpoint passed on or consolidated elsewhere? Or is it sitting in isolation?
- Who is responsible for administering the feedback-gathering process at this touchpoint?
- Who is responsible for ensuring an appropriate (timely, helpful, and so forth) response to feedback at this touchpoint?
- Do we have the ability to provide real-time or near-real-time dialogue at this touchpoint?

You need to focus on more than just touchpoints, however. Odds are, dozens of different departments in your organization have conducted their own surveys and feedback programs, all independent of the others, without sharing the resulting information. Indeed, it's entirely possible that every single department that interacts with customers has its own survey or feedback-collection program! And you, Sherlock, are going to have to find them all.

To do so, you'll likely have to interview a number of different people from each department or functional area. Here's what you'll want to ask:

- Has your department ever conducted a survey or used some other type of tool to get feedback from your department's or the organization's customers?
- What tool did you use to conduct the survey or obtain the feedback?

- How well did it work for you?
- How often do you do it?
- Do you regularly ask for feedback in any other ways?
- How long have you been collecting information?
- Where do you keep this information?
- Who has access to your customer feedback/survey results?
- How do you respond to concerns or issues that customers raise?
- Is there other information about or feedback from your customers that you'd like to have but aren't currently getting?

The answers to these questions, and to the ones earlier in this section, will give you a strong sense of your organization's feedback sources.

No matter how tempting it may be, do not use old information for your new feedback collection program! Start with a clean slate of up-to-date feedback.

Phase 2: Consolidate the questions that customers are being asked

Chances are, many of the surveys conducted by the various parts of your organization ask the same or similar questions. In this phase, you want to identify between two and five questions that seem to be asked everywhere. This process enables you to perform regression analysis to determine which touchpoints are your key business drivers (among other things). For example, if you ask customers to rate their overall satisfaction and experience at each individual touchpoint, you can then determine which touchpoints have the strongest impact on overall scores.

Here are a few examples of questions you probably already ask at every touchpoint:

- What's your overall level of satisfaction with our company?
- What was your level of satisfaction with your company service/sales person?
- Based on this interaction, what's the likelihood you would recommend this company to a friend or colleague?
- Do you have any comments or concerns you'd like to share?
- Would you like a response from one of our customer-service representatives to tell you what we've done to respond to your comments or concerns?

Then pinpoint between two and five additional questions that you may want to ask at each individual touchpoint (as opposed to all of them). Every touchpoint is different, so you'll probably want to know different things about each one. Take your time here. Talk with the touchpoint owner and operators and ask them what really drives experience at that particular touchpoint.

Phase 3: Fill in the missing gaps in your feedback collection

After you've completed Phases 1 and 2, step back and ask yourself the following question:

> Where are we not creating the opportunity for dialogue today that we know we want to get better at creating for customer conversations tomorrow?

When you have the answer to that question, it's time to set some priorities. For which touchpoints should you activate new listening and dialogue capabilities first? Factors that may influence how you set your priorities include the following:

- Historically speaking, where do customers feel most frustrated?
- Where is the organization (internally) having the most problems?
- Where are the biggest opportunities for improvement in customer experience?
- Where are potential revenue and/or cost-savings opportunities?
- Are there special considerations with respect to systems/IT limitations or opportunities?
- Are there touchpoints that may be eliminated or that may soon undergo significant change, in which case it may not be worth collecting feedback?

With your priorities in hand, meet with your organization's market/customer research team (if you have one) or a group of representative leaders from across the business to discuss how best to align all these different surveys, centrally administer them, and have the data deposited for all parts of the organization to use.

Setting a feedback response standard

As you begin aligning your feedback efforts, you must set, communicate, and enforce a feedback response standard. Determine how much time is allowed to pass from when a customer provides feedback until

- The feedback is acknowledged
- The feedback is address and responded to
- The customer acknowledges resolution

Simply establishing this standard creates a vast improvement in how your organization handles customer feedback. Imagine if you said, "Every piece of customer feedback must receive a response within four hours." While it's true that merely *discussing* such a standard — let alone implementing it — will likely cause some members of your organization to keel over, it's also true that doing so will improve your business. Our advice? Set a standard. Then make it your new mantra. *Ommmmmmmm.*

Phase 4: Identify linkages between employee experience and customer experience

The Gallup Organization, the Employee Engagement Group, and others have done phenomenal research on the direct correlation between varying levels of employee engagement and the impact on the customer experience by those employees. Simply put, the more engaged your employees are, the happier and better the customer experience will be. (Chapter 13 covers this in a lot more detail.)

So it makes sense that the next logical step in implementing your EFM program is to make sure that employee feedback is solicited routinely. By the way, "routinely" doesn't mean every two years. We know of more than a few organizations that solicit formal employee feedback only once every two or three years. What a waste of time and money! The workforce, their assignments, and their attitudes change much more frequently than that. Conducting a survey every two years lets some senior leader somewhere say, "We did it!" But it doesn't sincerely and meaningfully study the cause and effect between employee attitudes and their impact on customers.

Ideally, you should solicit employee feedback more than once a year. Indeed, many companies take quarterly employee pulse surveys, with a full-blown survey on an annual basis. Employee feedback should then be integrated with customer feedback to provide a more holistic view of causal relationships and the organization's performance.

With this kind of information, you can investigate whether the engagement and attitudes of a particular individual or group are resulting in greater customer experience, customer satisfaction, or customer dissatisfaction.

Phase 5: Develop a more advanced EFM program

When your organization reaches this phase, you're ready for additional data inputs. For example, you can integrate transactional and financial data, other kinds of feedback, more robust diagnostics (such as predictive analytics), and accountability and follow-up tools. For this phase, you may want to engage an external, dedicated EFM company — one that does this kind of work for a living.

Getting Social: Some Social Media "Need to Knows"

Recent years have seen the development of a new channel for customer feedback: social media. Today, sites like Facebook, Twitter, and others give millions of people the chance to "hold the megaphone," potentially broadcasting their opinion of your business to hundreds or even thousands of their friends and followers. This phenomenon can be great, as when someone shares a story that puts you in a flattering light and it goes viral. Or it can be terrible, as when a million people get wind of a screw-up on your part.

So how do you respond to this flood of feedback? First, you have to find it. Fortunately, lots of tools are available to help you find postings that mention your specific organization live, as it happens. These include the following:

- Google Alerts (`www.google.com/alerts`)
- IceRocket (`www.icerocket.com`)
- Twitter Search (`twitter.com/search-home`)
- TweetGrid (`tweetgrid.com/search`)

Social media: Definitely not optional!

Although many believe that social media is used primarily by teenagers and college kids, that's simply not the case. Facebook has reported that its fastest-growing demographic is age 35 and up! Moreover, a recent Cone Business study in social media revealed that of the 60 percent of Americans using social media, 93 percent think that a company should have a social media presence, and 85 percent believe companies should use social media to interact with consumers. Translation: If you're not on social media, you're missing out!

As Richard Hanks, founder of Mindshare, says: "Using these tools is a little like stretching a net across a river in an attempt to snare fish. Sure, you might catch the occasional carp, but you'll also wind up with a lot of old boots, plastic bottles, hubcaps, and tires." In other words, these tools may reveal social buzz about your organization, but that info may not reveal much in the way of actionable data that you can actually use to improve customer experience.

REMEMBER

In general, ideas and opinions shared on social media are much less structured than those shared by customers taking a phone or web survey, where feedback can be quantified and tied to a specific store, employee, or incident. This characteristic makes feedback shared via social media much more difficult to report and act on.

For example, suppose someone complains about your company on Twitter. Using one of the aforementioned tools, you unearth her tweet. From her feedback, you know she's unhappy. But you probably *don't* know which touchpoint was involved, which employee upset her, when the incident occurred, or which product or service she was attempting to use. (She can only convey so much in 140 characters, after all!) In other words, you can't immediately act on this feedback.

To use this feedback effectively, your organization must have its finger on the pulse of social media at all times. There must be someone monitoring key social media sites for posts and comments that mention your company, products, services, or employees. This person should also respond to feedback and manage your organization's social media presence.

Responding to feedback

As you've probably guessed, it's not enough to collect feedback via social media. Your organization must also respond to it — quickly, and with a message from an actual human being rather than an automated response.

Sometimes, the feedback you receive via social media will be positive. "I love my new XQJ-11 widget!" or "Got awesome service at my neighborhood McWendee's!" In that case, great! A simple "thank you" will suffice (although you're free to probe for more details so you can reward the appropriate employees for a job well done).

More often, however, the feedback will be negative. "My latte was cold. StarPeets #FAIL." Despair not! A free-floating complaint represents a brilliant opportunity, enabling you to demonstrate your organization's dedication to customer experience as well as your desire to listen and respond to customers' concerns. Even better, if the complaint draws comments from other customers with the same concern, you have the chance to reach out to an entire group.

Often, you'll find that when you respond promptly to customer concerns and complaints, the once-disgruntled customer will subsequently post positive comments about how quickly you replied and how well you resolved his problem. The end result? Improved customer experience and long-term loyalty.

WARNING!

Of course, you can't please everyone — particularly the gripers and whiners who sometimes use social media as a bully pulpit for bitching and moaning. When you come across these people, the best tactic is to apologize for not meeting their expectations and encourage them to provide more specific feedback. Looking like you sincerely care is what matters most. If you sincerely follow up, other readers will appreciate it — even if the original whiner keeps complaining. No one loves a troll for long! Be pleasant, sincere, and open . . . *twice*. If the person continues to complain, let it go.

To help streamline the feedback you receive via social media, consider giving customers an easy way to provide additional, more helpful, more structured information. How? Include a link in your response that directs the customer to a brief survey. (Tip: Don't call it a "survey." Instead, say "Would you please provide some additional information so we can better meet your needs?") You can use this survey — it should take one to two minutes, tops — to collect more structured information about the customer's problem, such as where the problem occurred, when the problem occurred, who was involved, and so on.

REMEMBER

Be sure the information provided by the customer can be ported to your organization's EFM program so it can be shared company-wide, managed, and responded to appropriately.

Mini Case Study: Social Media Fail at the Florida DMV

Recently, I (coauthor Roy) celebrated my birthday. That meant that, in addition to being a year older, I was due at the Florida DMV to renew my driver's license. I knew I would have a long wait — but I had no idea how long it would turn out to be.

After I'd been there for two hours, the electronic board that indicated who was next in line stopped working, remaining frozen on the same set of numbers for some time. No staff person from the DMV made an announcement of any kind. Naturally, I grew increasingly frustrated. So I did what any self-respecting modern person would do: I turned to Twitter. I posted a tweet in which I observed that the DMV's system was down and asked if anyone at the DMV knew when it might come back up. Their response? An automated tweet noting that Mondays and Fridays were their busiest days. This was interesting, but not useful, as it was a Tuesday.

I tweeted that I appreciated the irrelevant information, but could someone please inform the 100 or so people waiting at the DMV whether we should stay, go home, or just give up driving? In response, I received — you guessed it — an automated tweet noting that Mondays and Fridays were the DMV's busiest days.

Finally, two hours after the system went down, it came back to life. An hour and a half later, I emerged from the DMV, brand new license in hand. Thirty minutes after that — some six hours after I had entered their offices — I got another tweet from the DMV, this one from a living person: "Are you still at the DMV office?" *Argh.* Too late!

Maintaining your social media presence

Of course, social media enables you to do more than collect feedback. It also allows you to broadcast your own messages — to hold up your end of the dialogue with your customers, so to speak.

At the very least, your company should maintain its own Facebook fan page (`www.facebook.com`) and Twitter account (`www.twitter.com`). You can also establish a presence on sites like digg (`www.digg.com`), LinkedIn (`www.linkedin.com`), YouTube (`www.youtube.com`), Google+ (`plus.google.com`), and others. Investing in a formal social media presence demonstrates your organization's desire to communicate with your customers as well as to solicit both positive and negative feedback from them.

So what to share on said social media platforms? Although you may be tempted to promote your products, services, and all-around awesomeness, don't! No one on social media wants to follow a company whose contributions to the conversation are limited to canned marketing pitches. Instead, participate by sharing information that others will find helpful, valuable, or interesting.

The benefit of this approach is that your brand will become a trusted resource in the social media community, and your customers will be more likely to come to your social media pages to leave feedback. Remember: Social media is all about relationships and relevance.

All that being said, don't dip your toe into the social media pond unless you're serious. In other words, unless you're ready to dedicate the resources needed to properly maintain your social media presence, it's best to just stay away. There's nothing worse than a company who has a Facebook page but never updates it, holds a Twitter account but never tweets, and so on. It just looks bad.

Along the same lines, don't limit your social media interactions to automated responses. An automated response to a real human problem never works. If you aren't committed to providing timely responses to feedback from an actual, breathing human, don't play the social media game. You'll just end up making people upset!

Chapter 12

Building Customer Experience Knowledge in the Broader Workforce

In This Chapter

- Sizing up your team
- Taking care of your customers' basic needs
- Helping employees understand their individual roles
- Insuring employees get the same customer experience as customers
- Showing employees what's in it for them

Coauthor Roy relates the following story: One summer, I found myself prepping for a training session for 30 employees of a gas and electric company. It was a good-sized company — it boasted a market capitalization of around $8 billion and catered to roughly 1.5 million customers, spread over a couple states.

These weren't just any employees. They were linemen. It's no stretch to say that linemen are the unsung heroes of our digital lives. These are the people who, during and after every storm, make sure the electricity stays on — and work tirelessly to restore it when it doesn't.

Where I live, in Florida, we have a special spot in our hearts for linemen. In 2006, Florida was battered by three hurricanes within six weeks. Linemen from ten surrounding states converged on our communities to put the "grid" back together. We love those guys!

Nevertheless, linemen are a tough crowd. For the most part, they're introverts who would much rather be working outside, 30 feet up in the air, than sequestered indoors at a corporate training facility. That much was evident to me, as I organized my session notes, by their body language. They slouched in their seats, arms crossed, with the requisite battered baseball cap pulled down tight over their eyes.

Finally, it was time to begin. A company representative kicked things off by asking the audience one simple question: "How many of you, during the course of your career, have had any training on customer service?" The answer? No one. Not one hand raised, and no one spoke. You could practically hear the sound of crickets in the room.

These guys were not rookies. Many of them had been hard at work for 20, 25, 30, or more years! Among them, they had just under 500 combined years of work experience. And yet, not one of them had received customer service training. Nothing on how to present a professional image. Nothing on how to manage angry customers. Nothing on how to de-escalate an interpersonal conflict. Nothing on reading body language. Nothing on listening without interrupting. *Nothing.* And yet, each one of them — and the other 400 of their peers I trained that fall — have dozens of interactions with customers each week! That's close to half a million customer interactions per year.

I was — and remain — astonished by companies who throw their employees into customer interactions with absolutely no training, no counseling, and no practice!

No doubt, this same company provided hundreds of hours of customer experience training for its call-center employees. But as you've just seen, those employees aren't the only ones who interact with customers. *Everyone* who interacts with customers — be they external or internal — should receive some training on basic customer interaction skills. In this chapter, you find out how to put customer experience front and center for your broader workforce.

Judgment Day: Assessing Your Team

If you want to get better at anything, whether it's running a marathon or improving customer experience, you have to be honest with yourself (and with others) about where you're starting from.

Of course, one way to assess this is through customer feedback, surveys, and dialogue. All three can provide a tremendous amount of information about customer experience. But you can also do a little self-assessment to gauge your performance in delivering a great customer experience. To do so, we recommend that you and five to ten other people whose opinions you value complete the following questionnaire:

1. **Rate the quality of your team's physical performance (on-time, on-scope, on-budget) with your customers.**

   1 = Poor; 5 = Good; 10 = Consistently excellent

2. **Rate the degree to which you understand your customer's expectations.**

   1 = Not sure; 5 = I think we get it; 10 = 100 percent clear

3. **Rate how frequently you meet the customer's expectations.**

   1 = Rarely; 5 = Most of the time; 10 = Always

4. **Rate the frequency with which employees in your organization consistently deliver on the customer experience intent.**

   1 = Rarely; 5 = Most of the time; 10 = Always

5. **What three words would your customers use to describe their interactions with your team?**

6. **What emotions do your processes and behaviors create in your customers?**

The point of this exercise is not to achieve the highest possible score (although that would be nice). Rather, the idea is to begin a dialogue on how effectively you and your team are delivering the experience you envision. After you answer the questions, get together for a bit of a discussion. We promise you, it will be long and fruitful! Find out which points the group agrees on and where their opinions differ (and why). Your goal is to come to a consensus on where you need to begin.

REMEMBER

When you know where you are right now, you can work to improve.

Addressing Six Basic Customer Needs

As a first step, it helps to remind employees of the six basic needs of all customers. If you can build the following basics into your workforce as a preliminary step, you'll be well on your way to improving customer experience!

Friendliness

Friendliness is the most basic of customer needs. All people make snap judgments about each other. When you first meet someone, it takes that person only about three seconds to develop a first impression of you. To ensure that first impression is positive, be friendly. Every good interaction starts with a warm, sincere, and authentic greeting.

REMEMBER

Friendly never fails, and you never get a second chance to make a first impression.

Competence

Have you ever been served by a very nice and friendly but utterly clueless employee? (Don't answer that. We know you have.) Unfortunately, friendliness really isn't enough. Every customer-facing employee must be able to respond competently to at least 80 percent of the customer inquiries and questions that she's likely to receive. Putting clueless employees in front of your customers just isn't fair! If you're in the habit of turning inexperienced employees loose on unsuspecting customers, stop it. (Hint: If you overhear one of your employees saying to a customer, "I'm sorry; it's my first day," that's your clue that you are short-changing your employees on both their developmental and tactical training.)

Understanding and empathy

Honest care is what customers really want. Unfortunately, developing it in your workforce is no small feat. Why? Because fostering genuine empathy is hard. We've talked with therapists who, even after a couple decades of professional practice, still don't consider themselves experts at it!

REMEMBER

Note that sympathy is not empathy. Sympathy is what one person feels for another when he is going through a difficult experience. For example, if Person A is having a terribly stressful day, Person B may feel sad for him. That's sympathy. Empathy takes those feelings to much greater depths. People who are empathetic not only feel bad for the other person, but they also have some understanding of what he's going through.

The key word here is *understanding.* For an employee to truly understand what a customer is feeling, she must listen and show patience. That takes practice, however. With training, your employees can learn to view each customer's unique circumstances and feelings without criticism or judgment.

Fairness

We all need fairness. It's no surprise that customers become annoyed and defensive when they feel they're being subject to unfairness! If your organization engages in practices that are unfair to certain customers — for example, end of month sales discounts that make customers who bought earlier in the month feel like stooges — stop. Customers are like elephants: They never forget. If you engage in unfair practices, your customers will remember.

Control

Remember the game Chutes and Ladders? Whether you won or lost depended solely on which square you landed on. It was random. Players had no real control over the outcome. Needless to say, unless you were under the age of five, it was a frustrating game! Customers are likewise frustrated when they feel they have no control over the outcome of their situation. Simply put, customers must feel that they have an impact on the way things turn out. Don't herd your customers or send them all down a single path. If you give customers even just a little bit of control over their situation, they will feel less constrained.

Options and alternatives

Lastly, customers should be helped to understand that there aren't other, more effective ways of solving their immediate problem — or if there are, that those solutions will be pursued. Don't leave them wondering whether there was a better way to get their mission accomplished.

Aligning Employee Performance with the Customer Experience Intent Statement

Often, employees have no idea what is expected of them. That's because business leaders, managers, and supervisors fail to communicate this critical information with employees.

REMEMBER

As a business leader, manager, or supervisor, it's your job to clearly articulate to all employees your expectations with regard to customer experience (and every other aspect of their jobs).

So what *are* your expectations with regard to customer experience? To identify them, look to your customer experience intent statement. (For information about developing your customer experience intent statement, see

Chapter 6.) For example, suppose your customer experience intent statement reads something like this:

> At every point of interaction with us, we want consumers to feel that we are easy to do business with, that choosing and using our products and services is understandable and straightforward. We build a sense of confidence. Our consumers should have a sense of trust and assurance that we are always looking out for their best interests and security. Our consumers should be freed from any worry concerning their purchase. They should feel a pride of ownership knowing that our product matters and that they have made the right and best choice by choosing us.

If you deconstruct the customer experience intent statement into its component pieces, you can use those pieces to foster powerful dialogue about how each individual, in his or her role, can help deliver each specific intent.

For example, with a customer service agent, you could foster discussion by asking the following:

> How can you help customers view us as a company that is easy to do business with? Do you see things in your job that may prevent a customer from feeling that way?

With a technical support representative, you might pose the following question:

> You interact with customers who are struggling to use different products and services of ours. What can we do to help you make those products more understandable and straightforward?

With an accounts receivable clerk, you might ask:

> What specific actions do you take in your payment-solicitation calls to help provide the customer a sense of confidence in our company?

With a web designer, you might pose this question:

> How can our self-service web portal be redesigned to instill a sense of trust and assurance in customers?

REMEMBER

Customer experience is created across all interactions and at every single one of your touchpoints. That means each and every employee who interacts with customers needs to collaboratively define exactly how he is going to meet your company's customer experience expectations. Each employee must deconstruct the customer experience intent statement for his specific job.

Some employees will find they can deliver on every element of your intent statement, while others may be able to address only one or two elements. That's okay! The important thing is to have the discussion. Once you do, it's more than fair for you to hold employees accountable for results. In other words, define what success looks like and get out of the way!

One thing you'll hear during these discussions is what we call "castle talk." We call it that because of the siloed nature of most organizations. In too many organizations, each department is in its own realm, responsible for its own task. These departments don't take the holistic customer view because all too often, it's just easier to blame the other guy. Here are some examples:

- We can't deliver the experience because of limits in legacy systems.
- We can't deliver the experience because the salespeople don't tell the truth about what the product will do.
- We can't satisfy the customer because dispatch gives them unrealistic times for delivery.
- We can't finish the proposals on time because we can't get the pricing quotes from Finance.

Yes, these types of "blame some other part of the organization" statements may be accurate. And yes, the technological infrastructure and business systems and processes can diminish from a customer's experience. But the fact remains that the most important variable in the mix is the employees themselves.

You will always face these types of problems. In the meantime, however, it's important to stress that customer experience typically starts — and stops — with a human interaction between customer and employee.

Extending the Experience Intent to Internal Customers

Usually, when you talk about the "customer," you're referring to external customers — the people who buy your products and services. But there's another kind of customer: the internal customer. That is, employees and other stakeholders.

Obviously, you understand the importance of taking care of your external customers. (At least, we hope you do!) But the truth is, successful organizations also take care of their *internal* clientele.

Why bother worrying about internal customers?

Why bother worrying about internal customers? Well, for one thing, it's the right thing to do. But apart from that, catering to your internal customers can have an effect on the experience of your external ones.

Here's an example: Suppose someone on your design team is having trouble with her laptop. The folks at IT should make as much of an effort to resolve the problem as a customer service representative would to help out an external customer who calls for assistance. Why? Because if they don't, it could hinder that design team member's ability to complete her work. And that could result in a delay in the launch of a key product. And *that* could cause all your customers who are waiting for the launch of said product to be terribly disappointed. See the connection?

The fact is that there's a direct link between your internal customers and your external ones. Whether a receptionist, a store manager, or a call-center representative, every person in your organization — that is, every internal customer — is critical to the delivery of a great product or service. It's imperative that you do everything possible to enable every employee to complete her work in a timely manner.

On a related note, taking excellent care of your internal customers has a direct impact on your organization's culture and work environment. When you take care of your internal customers, they feel valued. They feel *appreciated.* This positive feeling is sure to seep into your employees' interactions with external customers, thereby improving *their* experience, too.

Improving the internal customer experience

So how can you improve experience for internal customers? Simple. You apply your customer experience intent statement to your internal customers as well as your external ones. (Again, you can find information about developing your customer experience intent statement in Chapter 6.) After all, you took the time to identify what you want your external customer to experience when interacting with your organization; is there some good reason why your employees shouldn't expect this same level of service?

Here are a few other tips to keep in mind:

- **Beware a "castle" or siloed organizational structure.** This type of structure often leads to bad behavior because employees in one functional area don't know, don't like, or don't trust employees in other areas. Obviously, this can have a pernicious effect on the experience of your internal customers.
- **Create internal service standards.** Define clear standards for response times for email messages, phone calls, and internal requests. Holding employees accountable for responding to coworkers' communications within a predetermined period of time can help tear down the castle walls between different internal groups.
- **Establish a performance review process.** This step enables different functional areas to talk openly and honestly about how well they are meeting each other's needs.
- **Conduct surveys.** If you're *really* serious about improving your internal customer experience, your internal customer engagement survey methods and practices should be as robust and holistic as your external "voice-of-the-customer" protocols. A twice-yearly internal customer satisfaction survey can go a long way toward fostering progress in internal customer satisfaction levels!
- **Swap jobs.** You've heard of house-swapping. You may even have watched *Wife Swap* on TV. But have you ever tried job swapping? With job swapping, employees from dependent departments swap jobs for a week or two to experience the day-to-day realities of their fellow workers. Most employees find it pretty easy to kvetch about employees in other departments, but their tune typically changes after they've walked a few miles in their colleagues' shoes.
- **Do ride-alongs.** If you don't have the resources (or the stomach) to support job swapping, consider implementing ride-alongs. In a *ride-along,* a person from one department shadows an employee from another. In this way, employees discover the ways in which what they do affects others.
- **Be social.** Make the effort, by whatever means necessary, to introduce work teams from different functional areas and enable them to socialize as regularly as you can.

Answering "What Does This Mean for Me?" and "How Will This Help Me?"

Obviously, improving customer experience — external and internal — involves making some changes. And as you probably know, most people don't love change.

Almost without fail, when an organization introduces change, employees have two questions: "What does this mean for me?" and "How does this help me?" Regardless of whether they ask these questions out loud (and most won't), trust us: That's what they're thinking. So you need to be ready to answer them, even if they don't ask.

We recommend that you hit your employees with a one-two punch. For your first punch, explain to your staff what the changes are, why they are needed, what impact they will have on customer experience, and — most importantly — what impact they will have on the employees' jobs.

The second punch is more tactical, and as such, requires a bit more thought on your part. First, you must get to the real root of the question. You could argue that the question "How does this help me?" *really* means "How will this help me in my job?"

But you have to dig even deeper than that. Because for most people, their job is a key aspect of their identity. This is true to such an extent that in many countries, including the United States, people frequently ask "What do you do?" when meeting someone new. For many people, we are what we do.

It follows, then, that for many of us, "what we do" has great purpose. Tapping into this purpose is an excellent starting point if you're tasked with building a case for change. So in our view, when someone asks (either silently or aloud) "How does this help me?" they're actually asking "How will this bring more meaning to my life, improve my self-esteem, and/or boost my self-worth?" It's this question that Punch #2 must address. And it's a toughie.

To do this, you must construct better stories with more meaning, stronger logic, and an emotional connection to what you're trying to achieve. Julie Dirksen, who maintains an excellent blog called *Usable Learning* (`usablelearning.com/blog/`), uses the example of course catalog listings for two photo-editing classes to illustrate the difference between simply conveying information and forging that emotional connection.

Here's the description for the first class:

> **Class A: Photo-Editing for Beginners**
>
> Lesson 1: Working with Layers
>
> Lesson 2: Photo-Editing Tools
>
> Lesson 3: Working with Special Effects and Filters
>
> Lesson 4: Using the Pen Tool

And here's the description for the second class:

> **Class B: Photo-Editing for Beginners**
>
> Lesson 1: How to Merge Two (or More) of Your Favorite Photos into One Glorious Work of Art
>
> Lesson 2: How to Rescue Your Almost Perfect Photo from the Trash Bin
>
> Lesson 3: How to Make Grandma Look 20 Years Old Again
>
> Lesson 4: How to Remove Acne, Warts, and "Photo-Bombers" with One Quick Stroke of Your Pen

Which class would *you* rather take?

As you develop your story in your effort to get employees on board, consider the following questions and imagine how your different types of employees — hourly, supervisory, managerial, field staff, and so on — might answer them:

- What's in it for me?
- What can I do with it?
- What can it do for me?
- How will it enhance my skills?
- Will this change how I do my job?
- Will this help my career in the short term or long term?
- How will this be accepted by my work group?
- Who is on the losing end of this change?
- Is this really possible or appropriate to do?
- What will I have to abandon that I'm doing now?
- What is the real value of this to me?

Are you unable to answer each of these questions for all of your target audiences? If so, then pump the brakes. Going full speed ahead without these answers will spell your doom. Why? Because a) You don't know enough about the change you want to bring about; b) You don't know your audience very well; or c) All of the above. Take the time to understand the on-the-ground impact of what you're proposing. If you're not sure what the impact will be, then ask!

Chapter 13

Assembling and Managing Your Customer Experience Team

In This Chapter

- Linking customer experience with good hiring practices
- Identifying and improving key behaviors and traits
- Hiring the best people by using the BEST approach
- Making the most of the interviewing process
- Inspiring and rewarding employee commitment

A few months back, my wife and I (coauthor Bob) decided to eat out with some friends in a hip (and crowded) part of Boston. There was a wait at all the restaurants in the area, so we decided to put our name on the waiting list at a couple of different establishments.

At one restaurant (I'll call it Restaurant A), the hostess and waitstaff seemed rather, well, *surly* — not only to each other, but to the customers as well. "The bar area is too crowded," she informed us curtly when we asked to put our name on the list. She then demanded my cellphone number and suggested we wait outside. "But you had better be in the area when we call you or else we'll have to give your table to the next person in line," she said rudely.

Huh.

At another restaurant — I'll call it Restaurant B — it was a different story altogether. Although just as busy as Restaurant A, the hostess and waitstaff were a delight. "I'm so sorry we don't have a table available right now," the hostess said with a smile. "But I promise you, it will be worth the wait. The food's great!" She encouraged us to cozy up to the bar and promised to find us when our table was ready.

During our wait, we observed that the hostess did indeed personally scour the bar to find each party as its table became available. Moreover, we discovered that the bartenders, waitstaff, and busboys appeared to be having a blast while working! Their camaraderie was evident and even seeped into their interactions with us.

About 25 minutes into our wait at Restaurant B, we received a call from Restaurant A. "Your table is ready," snapped the hostess. "But we can only hold it for a couple of minutes." But by that point, we would not have left the comfortable surroundings of Restaurant B to battle the unpleasantness at Restaurant A even if we had been offered a free meal. Needless to say, we stayed put.

After a great meal, one of our friends remarked, "Is it me, or does everyone at this restaurant seem like they're having a great time?" He continued: "Heck, *I* wouldn't mind working here!"

It's simple: If your employees are fired up about working for your organization — if they're *engaged* — then your customers will benefit! An engaged workforce is critical to customer experience. That's why employee engagement has become one of the hottest topics around.

No matter what size your business, if you can't deliver a positive customer experience, you *will* lose business. And the way to deliver a positive customer experience is through engaged employees. So how do you ensure your team is engaged? More often than not, the key to an engaged workforce is hiring the right people. Beyond that, it's about managing them properly. For more on both, read on!

The Missing Link: Linking Good Hiring Practices and Customer Experience

Grab a pen and paper and write this down:

> The customer experience does not start with the customer.

Yes, the customer is a key part of a successful customer experience. But successful organizations understand that it is *employees* who are the principal drivers of customer experience.

Unfortunately, many organizations fail to see this link between customer experience and their employees. Nowhere is this failure more evident than in their hiring practices. These companies place a premium on finding candidates with the right skills and education, but fail to identify prospective employees who display the behaviors and traits that define success in their firm — the traits and behaviors that lead to outstanding customer experience. Worse, many of these organizations fail to identify what those behaviors and traits even *are!* (We do just that in the next section.)

Don't believe us? Consider the American department store Nordstrom. In the retail world, Nordstrom is *the* standard in terms of customer experience. Not surprisingly, this is no accident. Nordstrom understands that the employee is the captain of the customer experience team, and hires accordingly. In other words, it doesn't simply hire retail associates with the appropriate skills and education. Rather, it hires retail associates who have the prerequisite skills and education — *and* who have the behaviors and traits they've identified as key to the company's success. In other words, hire employees who can deliver your customer experience intent.

Here's the deal: Great customer experience is an outcome — more often than not, the result of an interaction between an engaged employee and an engaged customer. Covering the employee side of the equation by assembling an exceptional customer experience team is critical.

Recognizing the Importance of Behaviors and Traits

As we mention in the preceding section, hiring managers often place a great deal of emphasis on a candidate's education and skills. And rightly so! Education (that is, what people know, usually indicated by diplomas and certificates) and skills (in other words, what a person can do, such as technical writing, accurately interpreting lab results, or what have you) are important. Having the necessary education and skills is similar to having Jacks or better in poker — you need them just to stay in the game!

But often, it's a person's behaviors (that is, how he acts or reacts to specific circumstances) and traits (those things that define the candidate's personal nature, such as integrity, honesty, accountability, enthusiasm, and so on) that get him promoted in the workplace. In fact, if you were to ask a leadership team to define the common attributes of the top 10 percent of their workforce or to define their most engaged employees, they would most likely outline a common set of behaviors and traits — rather than education or skills — that all these individuals possess.

The fact is, the most engaged employees are engaged because of behaviors and traits they exhibit, not because of their skill set or the educational degrees they hold. Understanding the behaviors and traits that reflect your organizational values and will result in the delivery of your customer experience intent is an important first step in ensuring you're hiring the right people in the first place!

An example of a company that hires based on behaviors and traits is BMW. BMW typically hires people who are driving enthusiasts and therefore can identify with consumers interested in buying one of the company's "Ultimate Driving Machines." Apple is another example. When you walk into an Apple store, you're likely to enjoy an amazing customer experience. This isn't because Apple hires highly technical people to man its Genius Bars — it doesn't. Rather, Apple hires people with a high aptitude for customer service (a trait) and then trains those people on the technical nuances of its products (a skill).

Identifying key behaviors and traits

So how do you determine what behaviors and traits are most important for your organization? Your best bet is to gather a cross-sectional group of leaders and list the employees who consistently embody excellence at your company. (The actual number of names depends on your company's size; target the top 10 percent.) It doesn't matter how junior or senior the employees are or what area they work in. Then start listing the behaviors and traits that make these individuals shine. (Be sure to limit your list to personal qualities rather than achievements.)

For example, say one of the employees on your list, John, who is an architect, always lands the best projects. Why? Is it because he's a great architect, which you can attribute to education and skills? No. It's because he's tenacious, creative, and resourceful. These are traits. In addition, John surrounds himself with the best people, chases clients the company never would have pursued otherwise, modifies his business development plan to incorporate new findings based on proposal wins and losses and subsequent contact with clients, and is dogged in following up and following through. These are behaviors.

If the people on your list all possess the same 15 behaviors or traits, you can assume these are the distinguishing characteristics you should be looking for in new hires and candidates for promotion. Of course, education and skills are important. But a candidate needs those to merely get her foot in the door or to suggest adequate performance. You don't want adequate — you want *excellent*.

Here are several behaviors and traits commonly associated with high performance and high engagement (your requirements may differ):

- Enthusiastic
- Solution-oriented
- Team-oriented
- Selfless
- Optimistic
- Passionate about learning
- Asking "Why not?" rather than simply saying, "That won't work"
- Passing along credit and accepting blame
- Going above and beyond

Identifying negative behaviors and traits

Behaviors and traits also have an effect on the opposite end of the employment spectrum: causing some employees to get fired or laid off. Often, the first employees to be let go exhibit certain behaviors and traits — in this case, those that define low performance and low engagement. If you were to ask a group of human resource executives whether they fired more accountants because they couldn't add (or more designers because they couldn't design) or let go of more accountants or designers because of a certain behavior or trait, they would unanimously say that the majority of people they've let go in their careers were the result of disruptive behaviors and/or traits rather than skill-based characteristics.

Following are several behaviors and traits commonly associated with low performance and low engagement. Naturally, these are behaviors and traits you want to avoid:

- Negative
- Pessimistic
- History of absenteeism
- Showing a "me first" attitude
- Egocentric
- Accepting credit but passing along blame
- Focusing on monetary worth ("I'm not being paid to do that")

Based on my experience, people who model the aforementioned high-performing traits will accelerate their career, while those who model the low-performing behaviors and traits . . . well, they won't.

REMEMBER

Your employees are *you.* They are the face of your business. As such, they can help — or hurt — your brand. When your employees provide an excellent customer experience, it results in repeat business. When they don't — when they're disinterested (or worse, rude) — it can and will result in lost customers.

Improving behaviors and traits

The good news is that just as employees can add to their education and improve their skills, they can, with effort, modify their behaviors — when they know which behaviors your organization considers valuable. You can help them along by recognizing and rewarding the behaviors you want to promote (and punishing the ones you want to discourage).

Note, however, that traits are a little more difficult to improve. People's traits are generally just part of their DNA. For example, say you work in hospitality, and your organization values extroverted personality types. Odds are, any introverts in your midst will have a hard time becoming extroverts. In that case, the correct response may be to counsel introverted employees to shift their careers toward a less extroverted career path within the business — say, switching from the front desk to the finance department.

Using the BEST Approach for Hiring Your Team

We use the acronym BEST to describe the process that managers should use to weave behaviors, education, skills, and traits into their employee selection and hiring process. This acronym was coined by one of the authors of this book, Bob Kelleher. (He describes the BEST process in more detail in his own book, *Employee Engagement for Dummies,* also published by Wiley.)

The trick to hiring the person with the right combination of behaviors, education, skills, and traits is knowing what behaviors, education, skills, and traits will yield superior performance for the job you seek to fill and developing a job description that takes these into account. This determination involves some thinking on your part.

First, define six to eight performance objectives for the position, which should relate in some way to your customer experience intent. (These objectives will vary based on the position and your needs.) Then, with these performance objectives in hand, consider what behaviors, education, skills, and traits a candidate needs in order to meet them. For example, if you've established a performance objective of leading the social media advertising campaign for the company's six divisions within the desired budget and timeline, then the applicable behaviors, education, skills, and traits may include the following:

- **Behaviors:** Shows initiative, is a self-starter, collaborates, exhibits autonomy, exhibits self-discipline
- **Education:** Bachelor's degree in communication, master's degree in digital media preferred
- **Skills:** Outstanding written and oral communication skills, knowledge of current social media and search optimization trends, expertise in mobile technology applications
- **Traits:** Creative, tenacious, competitive, high achiever

This information serves as the foundation for the position's job description.

TIP

If you wind up with several behaviors, traits, educational credentials, and skills in your list, consider dividing them into two categories: absolute and desirable. Behaviors, traits, educational credentials, and skills in the "absolute" category *must* be present or the candidate is not eligible for the position. Desirable behaviors, traits, educational credentials, and skills are "nice to haves." In other words, they add value to a candidate.

TIP

Not sure what behaviors, education, skills, and traits best serve a given performance objective? Think about the employees you currently have who are excelling in a position like the one you seek to fill and pinpoint their BEST characteristics. For example, if you're looking to hire a sales/account executive, take an inventory of your current high-performing sales/account executives and determine what behaviors, education, skills, and traits they possess. This assessment gives you an idea of the BEST requirements for that position.

Figure 13-1 shows a worksheet we've designed to help you develop a job description that factors in the BEST model — what we call a "BEST Profile." Feel free to modify or copy it and use it in your own organization.

B.E.S.T. Profile

Requisition/Position Description

Req. #:

Date Posted:

Requisitioner **Date Requested** **Desired Start Date**

Complete the Appropriate Information about the Position

Replacement for:
New Position:
Budgeted (salary):

Full-Time *(36 – 40 hours)*
Part-Time *(number of hours)*
On-Call *(number of hours)*
Temporary *(length of service)*

Position Description

Title: **Grade:** **Reports To:**

Location of Position: **Service Line:** **Dept. #:** **Section #:**

Click arrow to open menu

Describe at least 6 performance objectives expected (long and short term):

1
2
3
4
5
6

Behaviors, Education, Skills, Traits (B.E.S.T.) Requirements

Competencies required for this position (see page 3 for examples):

Behaviors and Traits Required:

Degree or education level: **Focus of study or discipline:** **Professional Certifications or Registrations:**

Yrs. Experience in similar position: **Years Total Experience:**

Skills Needed *(including language skills)*

Prospects

Any internal candidates? Name(s): **External candidates? Name(s):**

Candidate Sourcing Options

For advertising purposes, describe what the employee will be doing in the position, primary responsibilities, selling points, etc.:

All positions will be posted on [list sites]. Please list other potential sourcing opportunities

Approvals

Requisitioner: HR Manager:

Supervisor: VP or CSCM:

Two additional pages of instructions and samples included with full versio

Illustration courtesy of Bob Kelleher.

Figure 13-1: Use this sheet to hire the BEST candidates.

Asking the Right Questions

A candidate's résumé says a lot about his education and skills — the E and S in the BEST profile. But a candidate's behaviors and traits — the B and T in the BEST profile — are often at least as important as his education and skills. Indeed, a candidate's behaviors and traits are likely the truest barometer of his performance level and his ability to fit in at your organization. Odds are, however, you won't find *that* information in a résumé.

So, how do you find out about a candidate's behaviors and traits? After you've identified the behaviors and traits you're looking for, you must map these into your interviewing process. Most likely, your existing interview process stresses past assignments and accomplishments too heavily. Although these factors are necessary in evaluating candidates' experience and qualifications for the job, they don't necessarily speak to the deeper issues of how those candidates will perform according to your company's priorities or how well they'll work within your corporate culture. It's up to the interview team to ask the right questions in order to capture this information.

Based on the theory that past behavior is the best indicator of future responses, the *behavioral interview* has become popular in recent years — and with good reason. Behavioral interview questions require the interviewee to provide concrete, narrative examples of past situations. Often, these responses reveal the degree to which the candidate possesses the behaviors and traits identified as essential to top performance within your organization. Such questions avoid the typical hypotheticals ("Where do you see yourself in five years?") and instead focus on how an individual has responded to specific situations in the past. Obviously, you'll need to tailor your questions to the position's responsibilities and context, but here are a few examples of typical interview questions and their behavioral interview counterparts:

Typical interview question: What was the biggest accomplishment in your last job?

Desired trait: Creativity

Behavioral interview question: Describe the most creative work-related project you've carried out, and describe why you succeeded with this project.

Typical interview question: Are you a team player?

Desired behavior: Collaboration

Behavioral interview question: Give an example of a time when you were able to successfully complete a project on a team where there were personality conflicts.

Typical interview question: What major challenges and problems did you face at your last job?

Desired trait: Resilience

Behavioral interview question: Describe a difficult and tense situation in which some people were losing hope and you were able to influence them in a positive direction.

Here are a few more questions you might ask that pertain specifically to customer experience:

- Describe a situation in which you went the extra mile to support a customer. What was the customer's reaction?
- Describe the best customer experience you've ever had. Why was it special?
- Describe the worst customer experience you've ever had. What would you have done differently, had you been on the other side of the exchange?
- Describe a time when you dealt with a frustrated customer who you felt was right, but you were unable to help due to company policy. What did you do? What do you now wish you had done?
- How would you respond if a customer were to make a request that violated your employer's policy?
- Talk about a problem you've solved in a unique or unusual way. What was the outcome? Were you satisfied with it?
- Describe a time when you performed above and beyond the call of duty to meet the needs of a customer or client.
- Give an example of a situation in which you had to adjust your approach to a prospect/customer based on the person's body language, socioeconomic status, education, or other background influencer.
- How fast are you on your feet in dealing with customer concerns? Do you like to improvise or do you prefer to work from a script?

REMEMBER

The idea is to craft questions that are targeted toward the *specific* behaviors and traits that are unique to your organization, your customer experience intent, and the position. Although traits like enthusiasm, patience, selflessness, and optimism may be desired in almost any company, there are differences in positions' requirements that require tailored inquiry. Examples may include a job that requires travel, involves client or customer interaction, includes management of other staff, or requires working remotely.

Review the BEST profile to develop your own set of questions to tease out each candidate's behaviors, education, skills, and traits. For best results (no pun intended), write down your questions in a customized candidate evaluation form. Figure 13-2 shows a blank version of this form, which you can copy or use as the basis for your own. (Note that this form includes fields for "Rating" and "Weight." We fill you in on these in a moment.)

Candidate Evaluation Form

Candidate: ____________ **Position:** ____________
Interviewed By: ____________ **Date Interviewed:** ____________

Summary Notes:

Rating Scale:
3 = Expert/excellent match
2 = High/good match
1 = Satisfactory/acceptable
0 = Unsatisfactory

Weighting Factors:
3 = Critical
2 = Important
1 = Helpful

Education/Skills	Rating		Weight		Score
1. Educational Background:		×		=	
2. Technical Skills:		×		=	
3. Related Experience:		×		=	

Behaviors/Traits	Rating		Weight		Score
4.		×		=	
5.		×		=	
6.		×		=	
7		×		=	
8.		×		=	
9.		×		=	
10		×		=	
11.		×		=	
12.		×		=	
13.		×		=	
14.		×		=	
15.		×		=	
16.		×		=	
17.		×		=	
OVERALL SCORE					

Closing Questions and Information

1. What aspects of the job sound particularly appealing? ____________
2. What aspects of the job are of concern to you? ____________
3. References requested? **Y N** References provided/date? ____________
4. Thank applicant for their time commitment.
5. Follow-up time-frame given ________ Follow-up action ____________

Illustration courtesy of Bob Kelleher.

Figure 13-2: A candidate evaluation form.

Assessing the Candidate's Answers

Of course, knowing what questions to ask is only half the battle. You must also assess the candidate's responses to these questions to determine whether she is the right fit for the job and for your organization as a whole. Fortunately, this section offers a few ideas to help you make the best choice!

Weighting questions

After your interview, think about which behaviors, education, skills, and traits are most important for the position in question, and then weight your questions accordingly. Here's how we do it:

- We assign questions designed to elicit *helpful* behaviors, education, skills, and traits a weight of 1.
- Questions meant to uncover *important* behaviors, education, skills, and traits receive a weight of 2.
- Questions designed to reveal *critical* behaviors, education, skills, and traits get a value of 3.

For example, suppose you're interviewing candidates for a position as a customer service representative. In that case, you may assign questions designed to illuminate the candidate's skills and education a weight of 1, but assign questions that pertain to revealing a candidate's personality a weight of 3. Or, if you're interviewing candidates for a position that involves working from home or a remote office, you may weight questions that pertain to independence more highly than those related to cultural fit.

Rating answers

In addition to weighting the questions, you want to rate the candidate's answers. We generally assign a rating of 3 to answers that indicate an excellent match, a rating of 2 to answers that are a good match, a rating of 1 to answers that are satisfactory or acceptable, and a rating of 0 to answers that are unsatisfactory.

Scoring candidates

So, how do you use this info? If you refer to Figure 13-2, you'll notice that the candidate evaluation form includes a "Rating" column, a "Weight" column, and a "Score" column for each question. To score the candidate's answer to a question, you simply multiply its rating by its weight. For example, if a question is weighted a 3, and the candidate's response is a 2, you enter 6 in the "Score" column. You can then add the scores for all the questions to determine an overall score for the candidate. This score can then be compared to the scores of other candidates to determine who is the best fit.

Engaging Employees to Improve Customer Experience

It's not enough to hire a crack team. You must work to *engage* your staff after you've hired them. Employee engagement is often described as "the capture of discretionary effort" — *discretionary effort* referring to employees going above and beyond. We agree, but we prefer this definition:

> Employee engagement is the mutual commitment between an organization and an employee, in which the organization helps the employee meet his or her potential and the employee helps the organization meet its goals.

It is this mutual commitment that truly defines employee engagement and results in discretionary effort. It's also what makes employee engagement a win-win for both the employer and the employee.

What kinds of traits and behaviors do engaged employees display? According to Gallup, engaged employees

- Show consistent levels of high performance
- Have a natural drive for innovation and efficiency
- Intentionally build supportive relationships
- Are clear about the desired outcomes of their roles
- Are emotionally committed to what they do
- Have high levels of energy and enthusiasm
- Are always busy improving things

- Create positive things on which to act
- Broaden what they do and build on it
- Are committed to their company, work group, and role

Although the benefits of employee engagement are evident, engagement is at an all-time low in the American workplace. Gallup's 2013 *State of The American Workplace Report — Employee Engagement Insights for US Business Leaders* concludes that only 30 percent of the workforce is engaged. Worse, 52 percent are disengaged, and 18 percent are *actively* disengaged. To put this in perspective, do what *Fast Company* contributing editor Mark Crowley did: Imagine you're part of a rowing team. You and two others are paddling your butts off, while five of your teammates are idly enjoying the scenery, and two more are attempting to sink the boat. Odds are, your crew will *not* win this regatta!

Now consider the impact of low engagement on your customer experience. Ask yourself: Is it even possible to offer a positive customer experience if 7 out of 10 of your employees are not engaged? (Answer: Probably not.)

So how can you boost engagement? Here are a few ideas:

- **Drive engagement with a sense of purpose:** Companies that know their own purpose, values, customer experience intent, and strategic plan, and that believe in corporate social responsibility, are better able to win over the hearts and minds of their employees. And not surprisingly, employees who are duly won over are significantly more likely to be engaged! In fact, according to research by Jim Collins, author of *Good to Great: Why Some Companies Make the Leap . . . And Others Don't* (published by HarperCollins), firms that focus on purpose outperform their peer groups by a factor of six.
- **Engage employees through leadership:** A *manager* manages processes, programs, and data. *Leaders,* on the other hand, guide people, build followers, and steer organizations to success. Leaders are the ones who define and uphold an organization's principles. And it's leaders who really drive engagement in an organization. In particular, you must train your first-line leaders to foster an engaged culture. Why? Because the #1 driver of employee engagement is an employee's relationship with his boss.
- **Drive engagement across generations:** People of different generations (Baby Boomers, Generation Xers, and Millennials) have different motivational drivers — which means they become engaged in different ways. Smart managers drive engagement by adjusting their communication, leadership, oversight, recognition, and patience levels when leading a department populated by people of different generations.

- **Drive engagement through team development:** Working with great coworkers, helping each other out, and having great camaraderie, trust, and love for one another is engaging. In other words, a great team environment can engage a person as much as a great job!
- **Drive engagement through branding:** Many firms focus all their branding efforts on their product brand — what they do. But they invest virtually no time communicating their employment brand — who they are. Ideally, what you do and who you are should be like two sides of the same coin. Engagement is about capturing your employees' heads and hearts. Firms that spend all their time branding what they do most likely are making an intellectual connection with their employees. But *true* engagement occurs when you make an emotional connection. This occurs only when you can define who you are and even why you exist. When that happens, engagement flourishes!
- **Engage employees through gamification:** For years, neuroscientists have known that people whose lives involve fun and enjoyment are healthier. The same is true of employees. One way to introduce fun as an engagement driver is to embrace the growing trend toward *gamification* (using game mechanics and rewards in a nongame setting to increase user engagement and drive desired user behaviors). Good gamification programs reward people for behaviors they're already inclined to perform or required to perform, increasing their engagement and enjoyment. In other words, gamification makes the things you have to do more fun. And injecting fun in the workplace goes a long way toward increasing employee engagement.

To drive engagement, you must also have a firm grasp on what motivates your people. Commit to a robust communication culture built on transparency, honesty, and consistency; and create a line of sight for employees that reveals where your company is going, how you're going to get there, and exactly what role your employees will play in the journey. Finally, recognition, discussed next, is an important ingredient in your engagement stew.

TIP

Shameless plug: For more information on employee engagement, read *Employee Engagement for Dummies* by Bob Kelleher, coauthor of this book.

The Rewards of Rewarding: Recognizing and Rewarding Performance

If you have a child — or, for that matter, a dog — you know that positive reinforcement is key. It's not enough to simply tell said child (or dog) how you want him to behave; you must also recognize his good behavior with a kind word and perhaps even reward him with, say, a treat. (Sausages, anyone?) The same is true in business. You must recognize and reward performance — including performance that pertains to customer experience.

Driving and rewarding high performance is imperative. "A" players want to work with "A" players. If said "A" players perceive that your organization rewards mediocrity in others, they will quickly disengage and disappear!

Rewards — think compensation, promotions, perks, and the like — must be tied to an individual's performance. Conversely, if an individual is not making the grade (for example, he performs in such a way that the result is poor or insufficient customer satisfaction), there must be a negative consequence. This may include the withholding of a bonus or raise, or slowed career advancement. Otherwise, that employee's behavior simply won't change.

REMEMBER

In and of themselves, rewards don't foster customer service. But they do reinforce achievement, which drives your customer experience.

Designing your total compensation strategy

When it comes to compensation, some managers use what we call the "peanut-butter approach" to paying their employees. That is, they simply use "number of employees" as the denominator in their salary or bonus pool and spread everything around evenly, like creamy peanut butter on a piece of bread.

No doubt this practice is born of good intentions: Managers don't want any particular employee to be disappointed or feel slighted. Managers may even think this approach will satisfy all their employees equally, or use the "We're a team!" excuse to justify their distribution strategy. But the sad fact is that this approach is about as effective as a paper parasol in a typhoon. It simply doesn't work. Why? Because employees are not created equal, nor do they achieve equal results. In other words, business is not kids' T-ball — not everyone deserves a trophy.

If your goal is employee engagement and, by extension, awesome customer experience — and it is — then rewards, including pay, must be tied to performance and achievement.

If you don't reward your high performers more than your average and below-average employees, you won't incentivize your high performers to continue with their high-performing ways, nor will you incentivize your average and below-average employees to improve. Over time, this will result in a culture of mediocrity. It can erode employee engagement, as high-performing employees perceive that their achievements aren't being recognized.

To reinforce the importance of high performance, successful firms pay their "stars" — those high-performing people who routinely achieve results, as well as embrace the firm's values — a disproportionately high amount. Indeed, we often tell clients that they should pay their top performers so much that the competition could never afford them. It's money well spent! As for everyone else, go with slightly above or slightly below the industry standard.

What about bonuses? Early in our careers, merit-increase pools were often in the double digits. (Yep, those were the good old days!) But these days, and for as long as most people can remember, merit rewards have been in the 3 percent to 4 percent neighborhood. This decrease has created a challenge for managers: How do you allot such a small pool to adequately reward your top performers and maximize engagement?

We'll tell you how *not* to allot it: by using the peanut-butter approach. Take great care in determining who gets what. For guidance, look to the compensation matrix in Figure 13-3. You can use this matrix to help you divide a merit pool or even a bonus pool. Although other factors — such as an employee's position in her salary grade, the employee's tenure in the position, market conditions, and so on — may be at play, this tool offers managers a great place to start. Make sure to keep it fair; leave personal favoritism aside.

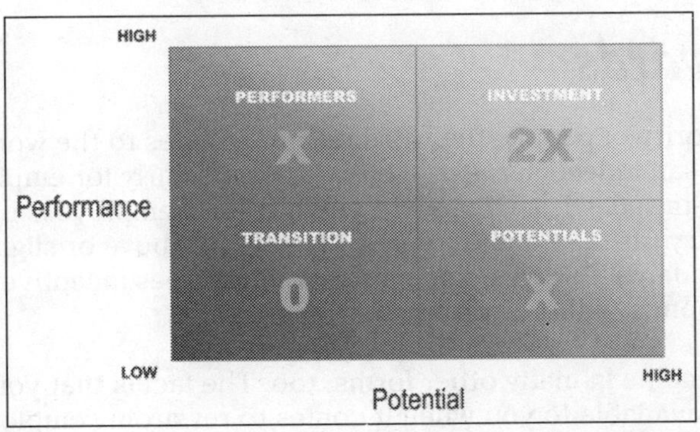

Figure 13-3: A compensation matrix.

Illustration courtesy of Bob Kelleher.

Looking at Figure 13-3, if X is the average reward, then

- *Transition employees* (the 10 to 20 percent of employees who aren't quite making the grade) should receive no merit increase. Not to be harsh, but they shouldn't be rewarded for failing to perform. If you're inclined to give them something, just remember: Your top performers will, in effect, subsidize it. As any elementary school kid can tell you, that's no fair!
- *Investment employees* (the 10 to 20 percent of employees who really matter — who function above and beyond the norm and define the standard for exceptional performance) should earn double the average merit increase or bonus. They should be rewarded extra for their excellence.
- *Performers* (the 30 to 35 percent of employees who are strong and steady workers but don't yet display their full potential) deserve your average bonus.
- *Potentials* (the 30 to 35 percent of your talent pool who haven't yet reached their potential because they haven't yet had time to develop) deserve your average bonus.

The fact is, *homo sapiens* have been programmed through thousands of years of evolution to look for causal relationships — how A connects to B, and so on. Once people see these connections, they change their behaviors to produce the desired results. In other words, the sooner your employees realize that recognition and rewards are linked to the execution of your organization's customer experience strategy, the sooner you'll start to see the results you want!

Other rewards

For the vast majority of people, the word *reward* equates to the word *money*. And yes, money can indeed serve as a reward, particularly for employees in, say, commission-based sales. Obviously, you'll reward employees by paying them a base salary (as mentioned, preferably slightly above or slightly below the industry standard). And yes, you can offer employees incentive compensation, such as bonuses and/or profit sharing.

But rewards can come in many other forms, too. The fact is that you have any number of tools available to you when it comes to rewarding employees, with money being just one of them. Here are a few more ideas:

- Promotions
- Training and development

- Task team or committee involvement
- Time off
- Flextime

Non-tolerance for non-conformance

One of the biggest challenges facing leaders in just about every firm, regardless of industry or nation, is dealing with someone who is a top producer but who rubs everyone the wrong way. On the one hand, leaders don't want to sacrifice the gains made by this employee. But on the other hand, this employee's bad behavior is causing other employees to disengage — which, as you've discovered, will likely lead to a lesser customer experience.

First, you must recognize that sometimes a firm's most talented and brilliant employees are also the most difficult to deal with. In many instances, they've earned the right to be treated a little bit differently. But there is a line. And when that line is crossed, leadership must take action. Otherwise, leaders risk losing credibility and eroding engagement. Leadership must pinpoint and communicate this line. If someone crosses it, even if that person is a top performer, it's up to leadership to show that person the door. (There was a reason Steve Jobs was fired from Apple his first time around. Even with his brilliance and talent — not to mention the fact that he founded the company — there came a point when Apple's board of directors simply got fed up with Jobs' arrogance and infamously difficult personality!)

Most of the time, these people can be reeled in with a simple talking-to. Firmly saying that their behavior will no longer be tolerated is the first step. Of course, leaders worry that such a discussion will prompt said person to quit. In fact, they may be so worried about this that they'll avoid having the conversation altogether. But the fact is, these people — we call them "organizational cancer" — rarely quit. And if they do, you'll usually recover from their lost production by way of a gain in coworkers' engagement levels. The bigger issue is what happens when the organizational cancer stays and grows. This is where leadership comes in. Effective leaders understand that the loss in production is a cost of doing business, but allowing said behaviors to go unchecked risks derailing a healthy culture and polluting the organizational waters.

Remember: Your employees are watching every move you make and the ones you don't. Although top performers may have earned the right to a bit of special treatment, having different rules for different people is a major disengagement driver! Perhaps the chief people officer at a *Fortune* "Best Place to Work" company put it best: When asked the secret behind his company's success in always making the top 100 list, he answered, "We simply don't let our rock stars trash the hotel room!"

Consequences for poor performance

There are any number of causes for poor performance, whether it pertains to customer experience or any other area of your business. Arguably, these causes can be grouped into two categories: aptitude-related causes and attitude-related causes.

Aptitude-based performance issues or disengagement: When an employee's skills are lacking

Generally speaking, if an employee is experiencing aptitude-based underperformance, it's because his job competencies don't meet the minimum requirements for the job. Usually, this occurs when an applicant overstates his qualifications and/or the hiring team doesn't effectively qualify a candidate. It can also occur when an employee is promoted sooner than his competencies allow — in other words, when people are promoted "above their pay grade."

Don't let this discourage you from hiring or promoting people into stretch assignments. More often than not, talented people grow into their jobs and should be stretched beyond their current capabilities. There are times, however, when people just don't have the competencies to succeed, regardless of their admirable behaviors and traits.

Symptoms of aptitude-based underperformance include the following:

- An increase in quality issues
- A shift in focus to reactive (rather than proactive) tasks and duties
- An increase in task delegation
- Delays in deliverables
- Reluctance to embrace new assignments

Attitude-based disengagement: When an employee's behavior is the issue

Although disengagement and performance problems can certainly stem from a lack of aptitude, the vast majority of performance issues that arise in the workplace have their roots in the employee's attitude, or in a behavior or trait that is not productive. (Refer to the discussion of B and T, or behaviors and traits, in the earlier section "Using the BEST Approach for Hiring Your Team.") This is especially true for performance as it relates to customer experience.

The warning signs for attitude-based disengagement include the following:

- Attendance issues
- Lack of energy or excitement about the job
- Loss of camaraderie
- Quality issues
- Customer-service issues
- Unwillingness to work additional hours when necessary or go above and beyond

Most performance issues that relate to customer experience stem from attitude rather than aptitude. For this reason, managers must always be on the lookout for changes in an employee's attitude, mood, and/or behavior.

Need help figuring out what to do with an underperforming employee? Use the culture matrix shown in Figure 13-4. As shown, employees who have both low aptitude and low attitude should be sent packing. Employees with low attitude but high aptitude should be counseled or sent to your competitor. Employees with high attitude but low aptitude should be trained and developed, and employees with high attitude and high aptitude should receive their own star on your company's walk of fame.

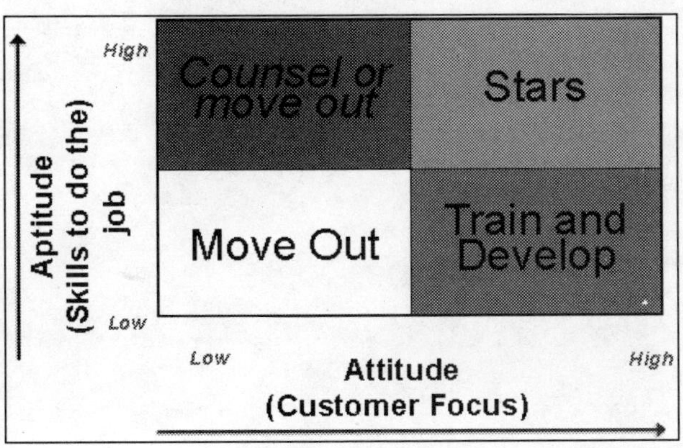

Figure 13-4: The attitude/aptitude matrix.

Illustration courtesy of Bob Kelleher.

Part IV

Making it Stick

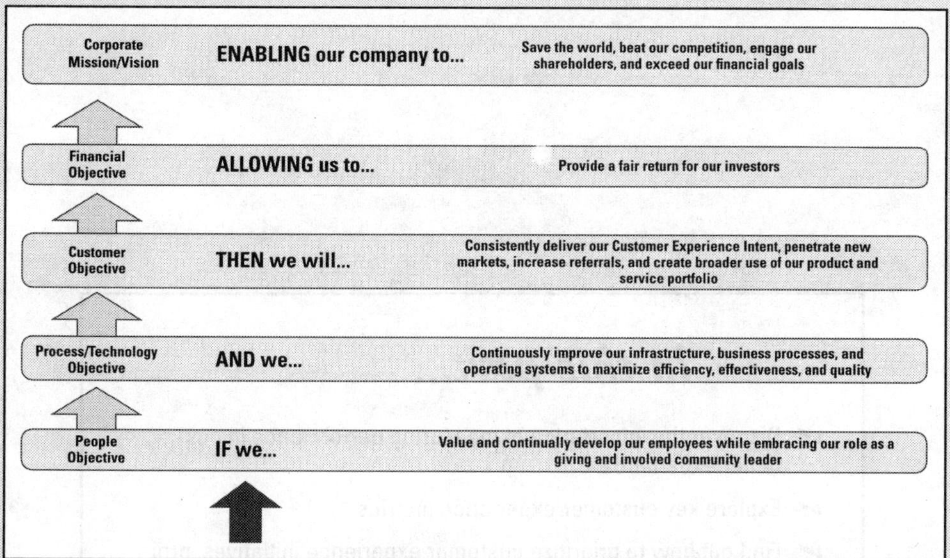

web extras

Find out how text analysis tools can help you to sort through customer comments in a free article at `www.dummies.com/extras/customerexperience`.

In this part...

- Discover the importance of measuring performance in customer experience.
- Explore key customer experience metrics.
- Find out how to prioritize customer experience initiatives, projects, and programs for best results.

Chapter 14

Creating Your Customer-Centric Culture

In This Chapter

- Setting SMART goals
- Seeing the value of an integrated internal customer communications campaign
- Getting leaders and employees to buy in

News flash: No matter what your business model, the very existence of your organization depends on your customers and clients. And yet, it seems that countless organizations — indeed, whole industries — fail to recognize this simple fact. Take the airline industry in the United States.

Every time we fly a U.S. carrier, we're reminded that many of these companies don't seem to consider the customer experience at all. If they did, they wouldn't nickel and dime passengers at every opportunity. It's so bad, we half expect them to put pay boxes in the lavatories! But if you try traveling on almost any international carrier — Thai Airways, Cebu Pacific Air, and Emirates Airlines (among others) come to mind — you'll quickly notice a difference. These airlines practice a customer-centric business approach. The customer is embedded in their culture . . . and it shows in the customer experience.

So what does it mean to have a "customer-centric culture"? To answer that, it helps to have some understanding of what we mean by "culture." One writer, Shawn Parr, whose piece "Culture Eats Strategy for Lunch" was featured in *Fast Company* in January of 2012, defines culture as follows:

> . . . a balanced blend of human psychology, attitudes, actions, and beliefs that combined create either pleasure or pain, serious momentum or miserable stagnation.

In other words, your company's culture can lead to engagement or disengagement, alignment or disjointedness, innovation or complacency. Companies with strong customer-centric cultures have processes in place that communicate and reinforce their customer-centric values, train their employees on these values, measure the results to ensure compliance and success, and hold people accountable. They also hire the right people and understand the unique behaviors and traits in employees that foster excellent customer experience.

So how can *your* organization become more customer-centric? We'll answer that question by asking another: Have you ever tried to lose 10 pounds but failed in your efforts? Most likely, this failure was because you went on a "diet" rather than changing your lifestyle to embrace healthy eating and exercise. The same thing often happens when organizations attempt to improve customer experience or spearhead other similar efforts. They "go on a diet," so to speak — launching new initiatives and campaigns — but they don't really change their lifestyle. To *really* see results, you must embed your efforts to improve customer experience into your company's culture.

What does that mean in practical terms? At a bare minimum, it means three things:

- **Identifying specific goals:** It's not enough to declare that you want to improve customer experience. You must outline how you plan to do so. Clearly articulating the "how" is the first step to shifting people's behavior in the right direction and realizing your customer experience intent.
- **Effectively communicating goals (and your progress on meeting them) to your staff:** By "communicating goals," we mean communicating not only goals that pertain to your customer experience, but *all* goals. Good communication fosters engagement — which, as we discuss in Chapter 13, drives the delivery of a positive customer experience.
- **Getting buy-in from leadership:** Any new initiative is doomed to failure without buy-in from leadership. To avoid torpedoing your customer experience efforts, take extra care to get everyone on board!

In this chapter, you find out about all three of these key steps.

Setting Specific Goals the SMART Way

Are goals important? In a word, yes. If you don't believe us, consider that a simple web search for the word *goals,* minus hits pertaining to soccer, yields nearly 700 *million* results. We agree, then, that it's essential to set goals. After all, if you aim at nothing, you'll hit every time!

It's not enough to just set goals, however. No matter what area of business you seek to improve — be it customer experience, productivity, or something else — you must set the *right* goals. That's where SMART goals come in. SMART goals are

- **Specific:** The more specific you make your goals, the better your results will be. Lack of specificity results in ambiguity — and ambiguity can't be measured. Goals should specify what you want to accomplish, why you want to accomplish it, when you will work toward the goal, and who will be involved.
- **Measurable:** You promote the behavior you measure. That means you must set measurable goals. As you establish your goals, ask yourself what your metrics are. Are they fair? If not, prepare for your employees to disengage and for customer experience to suffer.
- **Achievable:** Nothing is more demoralizing than pursuing a goal that you simply can't attain. Although you should always set stretch goals (those "hard but possible" targets) to drive employees to achieve, remember that there's a fine line between stretch goals and impossible ones.
- **Relevant:** Also known as "Realistic"; think in terms of whichever one makes the most sense for you and your organization. Individual goals should jibe with overall company goals. For instance, if improved customer experience is a key organizational goal, you also need to establish specific, measurable customer experience–related goals at the individual level.
- **Time-bound:** You must establish deliverable dates and deadlines. Goals that lack completion dates are not goals; they're suggestions.

So, how do you go about setting SMART goals?

Here's a step-by-step guide:

1. **Define your specific goal, focusing on the what and the why.**
2. **Outline the steps that must be taken for the goal to be met.**
3. **Define the time frame required to meet the goal.**
4. **Select a *goal manager* (someone to manage the process of meeting the goal).**
5. **Consider the expected outcomes.**

   Ask yourself:

   - What will be different?
   - How will the organization benefit?
   - What will we gain by achieving this goal?

6. **Consider the tradeoffs and obstacles.**

   Ask yourself:

   • What will we have to give up to achieve this goal?

   • What obstacles or difficulties exist or potentially exist? How will we manage them?

When you set SMART goals for your employees, you must give them the equipment, resources, and support they need to attain them. Failing to do so will lead employees to conclude that either you're being unrealistic, you're out-of touch with their day-to-day realities, or their work isn't that important — a definite disengagement driver.

To reach a goal, you must have disciplined focus. A goal without focus is merely an idea. Nowhere is this truer than in business. Perhaps entrepreneur and author Jim Rohn said it best: "Discipline is the bridge between goals and accomplishments." Often, however, people allow themselves to be distracted (A.D.D. anyone?) and lack the discipline to complete what they start out to do. Other times, they jump into something in a reactionary way, without evaluating its impact on their overall goal.

There's no doubt about it: Change is hard. In a recent study, leaders of some 300 major change transformations were asked what, if anything, they could have done to make their change effort go more smoothly. Far and away, the #1 answer was that they wished they had spent more time on the people side of the change. In our experience, implementing new technologies and new process protocols is infinitely easier than fundamentally changing employee behavior. Changing people's behavior is tough!

Look, improving your overall customer experience is going to take some time. If you follow our redesign recommendations, rapid change will occur at the customer touchpoint level. But changing your organization's culture takes substantially longer. Don't expect it to happen all at once. Other activities will no doubt be competing for your audience's attention. Getting and keeping employees engaged with your customer experience efforts requires you to do an extraordinary job of publicizing your efforts. When you consider how many initiatives, programs, and job duties are fighting for your employees' attention, you come to see that maintaining "mindshare" is no small feat! That means you need to treat your effort to embed customer experience into your culture as a campaign. Think Eisenhower and D-Day, or landing a man on the moon, or, better yet, a presidential campaign! Your job is to get a new "way of doing business" elected.

Developing an Integrated Internal Communications Plan

A key part of any campaign is an integrated communications plan. As you begin your campaign to embed customer experience into your organization's cultural fabric, you have to employ all the tools that a modern-day political campaign may use, including those nasty robo-calls and social media blitzes. And although yard signs might be one toke over the line, cubicle posters might be a nice touch!

If you find the political campaign metaphor distasteful, try thinking in terms of how major movie studios market a new movie. Not too long ago, a sequel to the famous Will Ferrell movie, *Anchorman: The Legend of Ron Burgundy,* came out in theaters in the United States. The sequel wasn't great, but the depth and reach of the pre-release marketing was staggering. Every possible media channel was flooded with promotional teasers for the movie, and the lead actor, Will Ferrell, appeared on dozens of different news and entertainment shows in character. It's not hard to imagine that people in the target market were hit with at least 100 different messages about the movie! Along a similar vein, movies like those in the *Shrek* franchise and, more recently, Disney's popular movie *Frozen,* are known for using co-marketing campaigns with fast-food companies and other major retailers as a way of widely promoting their movies. The idea, of course, is to cut through the day-to-day media noise to capture the consumer's awareness and interest. Needless to say, this approach takes thought, creativity, planning, money, and a *lot* of effort!

You need to think of your efforts to embed customer communications planning along these lines. The purpose of your integrated communication plan is to create awareness, understanding, and buy-in to your organization's deep commitment to the customer. The challenge for you as a customer change leader is getting your employees to pay attention to your customer experience messaging in the busy, noisy, chaotic, everyday life of your organization!

The components of your internal communications campaign

You and your team need to answer four critical questions as you develop your internal communications campaign:

- Who are all the different audiences within your organization that you must reach?
- What channels in your organization can you use to send messages about the need to focus on customer experience?

- What message do you want to put through each channel?
- When do you want to communicate your message?

Possible audiences

Here are some categories to consider when attempting to determine the different audiences within your organization that you need to reach:

- Temporary/seasonal staff
- Union/non-union staff
- Contract workers/representatives
- Regular employees (hourly wage)
- Supervisors
- Specific departments
- Managers
- Directors
- Vice presidents
- Executive team/company officers
- Board of directors
- Headquarters staff
- Field staff
- Regional staff

Possible channels

Here are some possible channels for communicating your message:

- Internal text messaging
- SMS messaging
- Voicemail blast messaging
- Internal emails
- Internal white papers
- Video messages lasting two or three minutes each
- Your company's intranet site
- A dedicated intranet web page
- Internal-facing blogs

- Personal face-to-face meetings
- Pre-shift meetings
- Departmental meetings
- Quarterly meetings and business reviews
- Annual departmental meetings
- Annual enterprise-wide meetings
- Brown-bag lunches
- Special internal events
- Paycheck stuffers
- Posters, displays, and other advertising media
- Personal, handwritten notes of support and/or recognition from senior executives to staff
- Swag (coffee mugs, hats, notebooks, water bottles, and so forth)

For best results, you want to target certain types of employees with messages via specific channels. Figure 14-1 provides a visual example of which employees might receive messages through which channels. (This is for illustrative purposes only; think carefully about which channels will be most effective for different employees in your own organization.)

Possible messages

There are various messages that you may want to push through your various channels. They include the following:

- The overall vision for customer experience in your organization
- Competitive and market threats to your business
- Why you must improve customer experience
- Your customer experience intent
- Your customer touchpoints
- How you're going to redesign your customer experience
- What employees need to do differently, and why
- The timeline for rolling out new customer-focused initiatives
- Success stories
- Customer letters (positive or negative)
- The financial impact of what you're doing

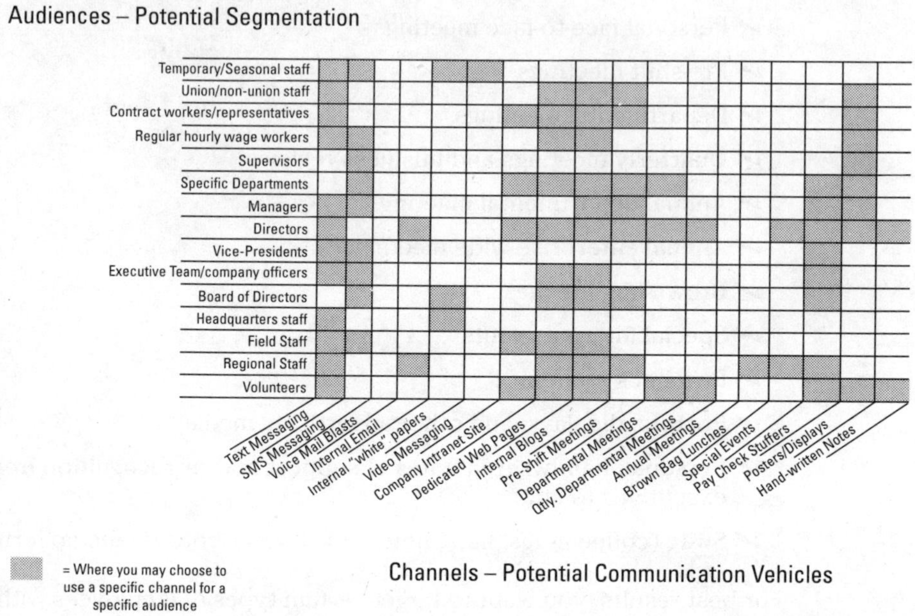

Figure 14-1: Using different channels to reach different audiences (for illustrative purposes only).

Illustration courtesy of Roy Barnes.

Delivering the right messages to the appropriate employees is critical. For guidance, see Figure 14-2. It illustrates which employees might receive which message in the context of a pre-shift meeting. As with determining which channels are best for which employees, you need to think carefully about which messages are appropriate for which staff members. You also want to consider when those messages should be sent.

TIP

It's a good idea to build a matrix like the one shown in Figure 14-2 for each communication channel in your organization. Doing so enables you to quickly see which audiences, channels, or messages are being missed.

Communicating your vision

Communicating your customer experience intent and the specific goals to achieve that intention is critical. You must also convey to your employees that what you're undertaking is a marathon, not a sprint. You and they are going to be in this for the long haul.

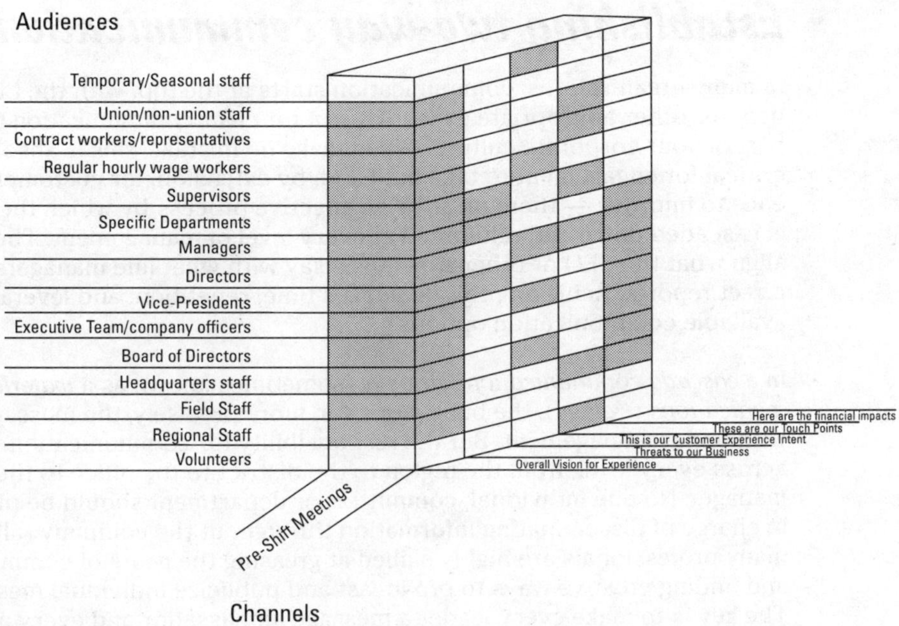

Figure 14-2: Which message should go to which staff member (for illustrative purposes only).

Illustration courtesy of Roy Barnes.

Unfortunately, the long-term nature of embedding customer-centricity in your culture can result in a lack of alignment over time. After all, if a company neglects to articulate a clear vision or to stick with a solid communication plan over time — whether about customer experience or any other area of business — it can hardly expect its employees to invest more than the bare minimum on realizing it. Everyone has some form of attention deficit disorder; other initiatives, programs, and tasks inevitably rise up and shift people's focus away from this priority. In one oft-quoted study, conducted by Robert S. Kaplan and David P. Norton in 2001, a mere 7 percent of employees reported that they fully understood their company's business strategies and what was expected of them in order to help achieve the company's goals. Yikes! Talk about a lack of focus and alignment.

REMEMBER

Successful companies don't allow miscommunication to happen. Employers or leaders who articulate a clear vision and strategy find that employees help them reach their goals quickly and more efficiently. Indeed, according to recent research by Dale Carnegie Training, employees indicated that working in a company that encourages open communication with senior leadership has a significant impact on their level of engagement, which in turn can help drive improved customer experience. To cultivate an engaged culture, open and consistent communication -- about your customer experience efforts and everything else — must become part of the air your employees breathe.

Establishing two-way communication

In many organizations, communication starts at the top, with the CEO, president, or other appropriate executive. But for clear communication to become part of your corporate culture — and make no mistake, this is absolutely critical for engagement to take hold and, by extension, for customer experience to improve — there must be an effective process by which the message is cascaded down and reinforced at every level of management. The goal is to align what the CEO or other executives say with what line managers tell their direct reports. Achieving this goal takes time, repetition, and leveraging of available communication options.

In a *cascade communications strategy* (sometimes known as a *waterfall communications strategy*), the buck stops (or, more precisely, the message starts) with upper management. But the responsibility for communication is shared across every level, from the region to the district to the office to the line manager. No one individual, committee, or department should be placed in charge of disseminating information throughout the company (although many professionals are highly skilled at greasing the gears of communication and finding creative ways to broadcast and publicize individual messages). The key is to make every leader a message ambassador and every management level responsible and accountable for informing the next.

In addition to communication waterfalls, for top-down communication, you also need *communication fountains* — that is, vehicles to propel communication from the bottom up. For engagement to truly take hold, employees must feel comfortable communicating questions, concerns, and observations upward.

Generally, this type of communication comes in one of two forms:

- **Questions:** Managers at all levels must answer questions in such a way that the overarching message is reinforced. If the answer is beyond a manager's knowledge, he must push the question to the next level while assuring the questioner that an answer is forthcoming. (Of course, it's important to deliver on this promise. The responsibility lies with the manager who has posed the question to his superiors.)
- **Feedback:** Whether it's positive or negative, managers must be provided a means by which to funnel employee input to the people responsible for processing and, if warranted, incorporating it. Employee engagement surveys — conducted a couple times a year, with interim pulse surveys as needed — are one mechanism to ensure that this happens. Communicating those results back is the way to complete the loop. Companies that establish a continuous and frequent feedback loop between managers and employees virtually guarantee alignment.

From cascades to fountains . . .

Until the late 1990s, the predominant business model was a "command and control" governance structure, which focused on cascade communications. In this model, the all-knowing, all-seeing boss would typically declare the direction and path along which the organization would proceed, while the rest of the organization was expected to say "Yes sir!" and get busy implementing the game plan. More recently, organizational leadership has taken a much more fluid approach to setting and communicating the direction and path, featuring more communication fountains. This approach has had some tremendous advantages over the old command and control model. For one, it makes organizations more innovative. They are faster to market and can more rapidly respond to quickly changing market conditions. The not-so-great news is that an awful lot of balls (communication priorities) tend to be up in the air, and sometimes it's difficult to determine which are the most critical to ensuring the success of the organization's current and future health.

Realizing the importance of a communication protocol

We've never met a manager who says managers shouldn't communicate openly and frequently with their employees — but often they don't. See, for many managers, communication falls in the category of "should do" rather than "must do." And when you're busy, "must do" trumps "should do" every time.

That's where a communication protocol comes in. A *communication protocol* is a formal process that outlines the types of information to be communicated to an organization, as well as identifying the person(s) responsible for communicating particular topics. The protocol also outlines the audience, frequency, and suggested communication vehicles.

REMEMBER

A communication protocol, which should be displayed in all common areas such as lobbies and conference rooms and distributed to all new hires, ensures that communications align with the company's key strategic priorities, whether they're specifically related to customer experience or some other initiative.

Just as important, the protocol represents a set of company commitments to employees. These might include the following:

- Leaders will be held accountable for fulfilling their communication responsibilities and will be assessed on the effectiveness and timeliness of their communication.

- Employees will receive regular updates about the progress, initiatives, and changes that affect them directly and indirectly.
- Each communication milestone will provide opportunities for employees to ask questions, contribute ideas, and give or receive feedback.

In turn, the expectations for employees must also be clear. All employees are responsible for sharing information and giving feedback to help the company reach its goals, thereby reinforcing the desire for employees to communicate "up" and bolstering the mutual commitment shared by employer and employee.

Implementing a communication protocol has several benefits. A communication protocol does all the following:

- It defines communication expectations for both employees and leaders.
- It builds consistency in communicating the firm's mission, vision, values, and strategy.
- It helps create alignment with employees at all levels.
- It builds in circular communication. This includes communication between those in a traditional hierarchy, such as the boss and subordinate, as well as communication between business units and departments and communication that leverages task teams and focus groups.
- It helps ensure shared accountability, from the top to the bottom.
- It assists in the communication of messages 13 times, which is the number of times some experts believe an employee needs to hear something to absorb it. (That's true of most other adults and kids, too, by the way.)
- It means leveraging all the available communication venues and tools — for example, town hall meetings, brown-bag lunches, personal notes, company-wide emails, vlogs (video blogs), department meetings, and so on.

Building a communication protocol

To build a communication protocol, you need a cross-sectional team of executives (preferably including the "top dog") along with a cross-sectional group of key influencers, or connectors. The first thing this team should do is assemble a draft of the communication protocol. (This will take the group anywhere from two to eight hours.) Figure 14-3 shows a template for teams in this phase to help guide them in their efforts.

Message	Communicator	Audience	Frequency

Figure 14-3: A communication protocol template.

Illustration courtesy of Bob Kelleher.

When drafting the protocol, the team should consider the following:

- How can we build in the communication of metrics that are key to our strategic plan (for example, growth, profit, employee engagement, customer service, quality, and so on)?
- How can we ensure that staff members are given an opportunity to communicate up?
- How can we build in redundancy in messaging between levels?

When the draft is complete, it should be sent to those who report up through the CEO (and perhaps their direct reports as well) to obtain additional input. This key step will also help you get buy-in. Once the input has been received and appropriated, the protocol can be finalized (see Figure 14-4).

With a finalized protocol in hand, the team's next move is to build a plan to roll out the protocol. But be careful to get solid commitment before you sound the trumpets. You'd hate to create false expectations.

REMEMBER

The launch of a communication protocol is great news and will be embraced by employees as, to quote Martha Stewart, "a good thing." That being said, you'll likely meet resistance from middle management, who will likely view the protocol as "one more thing to do that takes time." To overcome this roadblock, educate them on the protocol's benefits as well as on how to be an engaged participant in the protocol. Over time, they'll see that the administrative effort involved in maintaining a robust communication protocol will be offset by the gain in their employees' alignment and engagement and, by extension, improved customer experience.

Messenger	Topic (Examples)	Venue	Audience	Frequency
CEO	Customer/client success stories Recognition of key contributors Customer satisfaction metrics updated company-wide Recent wins Net revenue growth to plan Gross revenue growth % repeat business % new business Shrinkage and returns	Company email	All employees	Monthly or quarterly
Division Manager	Same as above, but metrics and success stories will be for the division level	Conference call or video conference	Divisional employees	Monthly following CEO communication
Business Unit	Same as above, but the metrics and success stories will be for the business unit level	Town-hall or all-hands meeting	Business unit employees	Bi-weekly or monthly
Department	Same as above, but the metrics and success stories are at the department level	In-person department meeting	Department employees	Weekly or bi-weekly

Figure 14-4: Sample communication protocol.

Illustration courtesy of Bob Kelleher.

Getting Leadership Buy-In

Leadership buy-in is a key driver of improved customer experience. Before we say more on this topic, however, we want to clarify the difference between the terms *leader* and *manager*. A manager manages processes, programs, and data. Leaders, on the other hand, guide people, build fellowship, and steer organizations to success (read: make money and grow). Leaders set the direction; managers follow the plan to get there. Yes, managers are indispensible when it comes to creating and monitoring policy. But it's leaders who define and uphold an organization's principles. And leaders are the ones who really drive engagement (and, by extension, improved customer experience) in an organization.

The things that define customer experience — service, attention to detail, cohesion, collaboration, openness, empowerment, and inspiration, to name a few — are largely the province of an organization's visionaries, role models, innovators, and counselors. These leaders may not hold the loftiest titles or pull down the biggest salaries. Nonetheless, they make their mark on the company culture, inviting multiple perspectives and team decisions while retaining — and communicating — a strong sense of personal accountability.

When it comes to improving customer experience, it is incumbent for your leaders — your rank-and-file visionaries *and* your senior leadership — to walk the talk. That means routinely speaking with customers or visiting clients, having their own incentives tied to improved customer engagement, and highlighting success stories at every possible chance. Demonstrating their visible support is key for a customer-centric culture to gain and sustain traction. *All* senior leaders need to speak the language of customer engagement and behave in demonstrably committed ways.

Frustrated by the lack of a client-focused culture at his organization, one CEO we know stamped this message on everyone's paycheck envelope: "This check comes to you courtesy of our clients." Although there are more graceful ways to make this point, employees within the organization got the message!

So how do you get your leaders to buy in? We'll be honest: It's not always easy. Often, leaders — including many *many* CEOs and CFOs — are highly analytical. As such, they are more comfortable with hard data. Unless you do the work outlined in Chapter 2, customer experience is likely to be seen as, well, a bit "soft."

If you're lucky — or unlucky, as the case may be — there may also be an outside market driver that you can use to make your case. This might be losing a key account, experiencing a noticeable drop in sales, your CEO receiving a scathing letter from an irate customer, and so on. This type of "burning platform" is often the impetus for change.

In addition to believing in and being able to articulate your customer experience intent, top leaders must also be held accountable for customer results. Elsewhere in this book, we discuss the importance of measuring your progress in your efforts to improve customer service. The same applies here. Unless a CEO and her leadership team are measured on customer experience, the CEO is unlikely to be pushed to lead differently. Only when senior managers are measured and judged on customer experience criteria will they be motivated to measure up.

WARNING!

Because most senior leaders are more comfortable working their left brain (analytical, sequential, objective) than their right brain (random, creative, subjective), they may be prone to relegate the primary responsibility for customer engagement to, say, the head of sales rather than championing the cause themselves. Don't let that happen. If your customer experience efforts are largely driven by your sales organization, employees may perceive them as just another flavor-of-the-month program to drive revenue. Senior leaders *must* support efforts in the customer experience arena to minimize the risk of it being viewed as a touchy-feely, lip-service-only, customer-satisfaction initiative. If the CEO lacks the time or talent to champion customer experience, then someone else at the senior level must be identified — someone senior enough to give customer experience credibility and, preferably, someone who's perceived as having the ear and support of the leader.

Harnessing Innovators and Early Adopters to Speed Buy-In Among Employees

Sorry, we have a bit of bad news for you. It's not enough to just get buy-in among your leaders. You must also take steps to ensure your rank-and-file embrace your efforts to embed customer experience in your company's culture. But just as a politician need not win 100 percent of the vote to be elected to office, you and your communications effort don't have to persuade everyone to jump on board either. Rather, you just need to win over the "right" people.

So who are the right people? To answer that, we turn to Malcolm Gladwell, author of *The Tipping Point* (published by Back Bay Books). According to Gladwell, any group of 50 or more people will include the following types of individuals:

- **Innovators:** Innovators, which comprise roughly 2.5 percent of the population, are the creators. They're the people who bring new thoughts, practices, and processes into an organization. If you're reading this book, you may be one of these brilliant, fantastic, and — dare we say — good-looking people!
- **Early adopters:** Early adopters make up about 13.5 percent of the population. Early adopters love the new stuff that innovators dream up. They're the beta-testers. It's in their nature to poke, prod, test, and often

buy anything new. They can't help themselves! If you're someone who buys the latest technological gadgets on the day they're released, you may recognize yourself in this description.

- **Early majority:** This describes 34 percent of the population. The early majority observes the shenanigans of the innovators and the response of the early adopters. Typically, they have reservations about new ideas or practices, but if the early adopters get on board, then the early majority is usually soon to follow.

In other words, if you want a large group to accept a new idea or innovation, you really need just 16 percent of its members — the innovators and the early adopters — to buy in! But without buy-in from those two key populations, your initiative is going nowhere because the early majority will never tip over in support of the new initiative. Why? Because the following types of individuals make up the rest of your organization:

- **Late majority:** This group, which, like the early majority, is made up of 34 percent of the population, will go along with the new idea, but only after the innovators, early adopters, and early majority buy in. If you fail to achieve buy-in from those three key groups, you'll fail to achieve buy-in from this group, as well.
- **Laggards:** This group, comprising 13.5 percent of the population, is all about passive-aggressive behavior. These people will say things like, "Yes, what a great idea!" but will do absolutely nothing to advance the idea further. Why? Because the laggards are quite happy with the status quo. Unless they're shoved into doing something new and different, they simply won't change. Ever. Instead, they'll do whatever it takes to divert your attention and energy from the change you want to bring about. Don't bother trying to convert these legions of laggards. It's a waste of your energy.
- **Losers:** Ah . . . the last, soul-sucking 2.5 percent. This group consists of the "death eaters" of your organization. They're even less likely to convert than your laggards. Our advice? Get rid of these people. They do far more damage than good.

REMEMBER

These categories — innovators, early adopters, early majority, late majority, laggards, and losers — have nothing at all to do with organizational hierarchy. There are likely to be as many losers and laggards in senior leadership roles as there are in deeper levels of the organization.

REMEMBER

For best results, focus your energy where it will do the most good — on the innovators and early adopters. If you can sell them on your customer-centric vision, the rest of the organization will soon tip in your favor. (See Figure 14-5.)

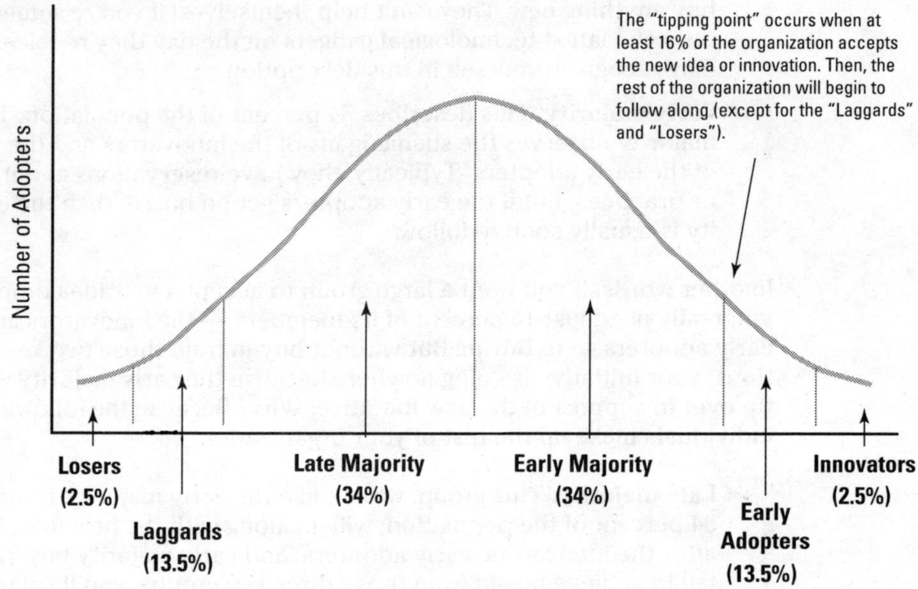

Figure 14-5: Adoption of innovation over time.

Illustration courtesy of Roy Barnes.

Chapter 15

Measure Up: Measuring Performance

In This Chapter

- Identifying key objectives and strategizing to achieve them
- Developing the right metrics to determine how well you're achieving your objectives
- Evaluating and acting on your customer data
- Building and reviewing a customer performance dashboard
- Sharing your customer performance metrics with the organization at large

Unless you can provide hard quantitative data, measurements, and facts about your customer experience, the leaders (and others) in your organization just won't take your work seriously. That's why you need to make sure that not only are you measuring the results of your customer service efforts, but that those measures are as noticeable as Donald Trump's combover.

In this chapter, we look at how to identify the metrics you need to focus on to meet your objectives. You also find out how to create a customer performance dashboard — that is, a means for keeping track of all those key metrics.

Using the Balanced Scorecard Approach to Identify Key Objective Areas

There's not a successful business in the world that doesn't pay very close attention to its key measures of success. In some organizations, these key measures may be strictly financial. In more enlightened companies, however, there's a balanced mixture of metrics.

The question is, what's in the mixture? For the answer, look to Bob Kaplan and Dave Norton, both of whom are distinguished professors at Harvard. They invented what's called the "Balanced Scorecard" approach to implementing strategy.

According to Kaplan and Norton, the mixture of metrics pertains to four key objective areas:

- **Financial:** For example, "To provide a fair return to our investors."
- **Customer:** For example, "To consistently deliver our customer experience intent, penetrate new markets, increase referrals, and foster broader use of our product and service portfolio." Just to be clear: We're not talking about what your *customer's* objectives are. We're talking about what *your* objectives are with respect to your customers — that is, what your organization wants to deliver.
- **Process/technology:** For example, "To continuously improve our infrastructure, business processes, and operating systems to maximize efficiency, effectiveness, and quality."
- **People (employees):** For example, "To value and continually develop our employees while embracing our role as a giving and involved community member."

Simply identifying these objectives isn't enough, however. Kaplan and Norton say there must be balance and synergy among them. That is, in order for an organization to achieve its mission and vision, its employees must be well-trained and engaged.

Additionally, its business processes must operate efficiently and effectively, with appropriate technology working in support of those business processes. If these two elements are in place, then it's more likely that customers will receive the value they pay for and the experience they want. And if customers are happy and buy more products and services, then the organization can achieve its financial objectives.

Finally, if these financial objectives are met, then the organization is in a position to achieve its overall mission and vision. (See Figure 15-1.)

This model works brilliantly, but it demands a broader perspective than many business leaders traditionally exhibit. It's incredible how many CEOs and CFOs fail to recognize the cause-and-effect relationship of sustained strategic performance! As a result, many organizations never fully execute major aspects of their overall strategy. But think about it:

- If your business processes were efficient and effective but your employees hated their jobs, would you have a successful organization in the long term?
- If your employees were happy but the key business processes or the enabling technology and infrastructure were lacking, would you have a successful organization in the long term?
- If your employees were happy and your processes and technology were brilliant, but your customers hated your product or service offerings, would you have a successful organization in the long term?

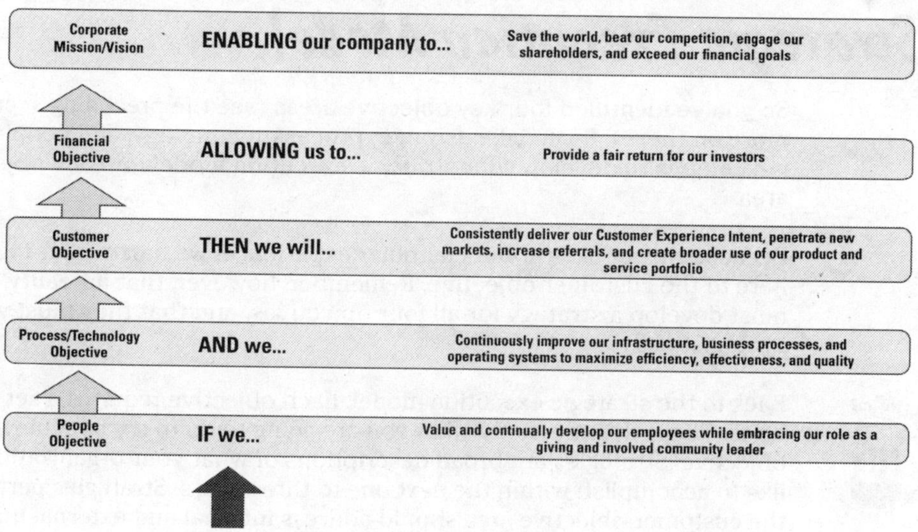

Figure 15-1: The cause-and-effect relationship between objectives. (Read from the bottom up.)

Illustration courtesy of Roy Barnes.

No, no, and no.

Look, we get it. Sometimes, given unique market or economic circumstances, you may have to shift priorities or change focus among each of the four major objective areas. Like recently. During the recession, companies placed a tremendous emphasis on efficiency. Thousands of organizations got lean by whittling down their workflows and cutting heads. That's all fine and good — even necessary at times. But to sustain a business for the long term, each of the four objective areas must be simultaneously managed.

A good customer experience is an outcome. It's the result of complex processes, behaviors, and attitudes. To use a cooking analogy, you can't bake a magnificent chocolate cake if you don't use primo ingredients, proper baking techniques, and a working oven! Everything must be finely tuned to produce the desired result. Likewise, you can't meet your customer objectives if you don't deliver on the financial, process/technology, and people fronts. Caring about the customer experience also means caring about everything else that goes into it!

"This is all fascinating," you're thinking. "But what does it have to do with metrics?" Good question. But we're not ready to answer it yet. Keep reading . . . we promise it will all make sense!

Top Model: Developing Your Strategic Execution Model

So you've identified four key objective areas (see the preceding section for more on these): financial, customer, process/technology, and people. Your next step is to develop your strategic execution model for each objective area.

Because this book is about customer experience, we narrow our focus here to the customer objective. Remember, however, that in reality, you must develop a strategy for all four objectives, and that they must work synergistically.

REMEMBER

Back to the strategic execution model. Each objective requires a set of strategies. These define exactly what you are going to do to try to achieve that objective. Strategies are broad descriptions of what your organization would like to accomplish within the next one to three years. Strategies pertaining to the customer objective area should address internal and external market challenges, essential program components, desired customer behaviors, specific aspects of customer experience, and the performance of customer processes.

To illustrate, we use the customer objective from the previous section: "To consistently deliver our customer experience intent, penetrate new markets, increase referrals, and foster broader use of our product and service portfolio." What strategies might you employ to achieve this? Here are a few ideas:

- Increase your overall customer engagement score.
- Embed your customer experience intent into the workforce.
- Build your presence in the Malaysian and Indonesian markets.
- Increase referrals from third-year clients.
- Double the number of products and services utilized within your portfolio by existing clients.

"Still fascinating," you're thinking. "But again, what does this have to do with metrics?" We're glad you asked . . . and we're ready to answer. As you implement your strategies, you need some way of determining how effective they are. And that, friends, is where metrics come in.

The Meter's Running: Identifying Key Metrics

Coming up with literally dozens of customer metrics is surprisingly easy. Spend ten minutes searching for "customer service metrics" online, and you'll see what we mean. But when it comes to metrics, it's quality, not quantity, that counts. Sure, you could measure what percentage of your customers own chocolate labs or wear their hair in a Jimmy Neutron pompadour. But unless you're a veterinarian or you run a hair salon (and maybe even then), that information would be useless.

When developing metrics, coauthor Roy often thinks of Mrs. Baker, his high-school chemistry teacher. She was very safety conscious — understandable, given that she was supervising a room full of teenagers with access to explosive chemicals. Perhaps more relevant, Mrs. Baker instilled in her students the importance of developing a hypothesis before conducting an experiment. It was good advice then, and it's good advice now. After all, isn't implementing a strategy the same as conducting an experiment? You think the strategy will help you attain your goal, so you put it in place to find out. So as you're identifying key metrics, think of it as developing your hypothesis. Ask yourself, "What do you want to measure? Why? What results are you expecting?"

While you're at it, keep these points in mind:

- It's possible to have too much of a good thing. As mentioned earlier, metrics are about quality, not quantity. Having too many customer measures blurs focus and prevents alignment.
- Don't use overcomplicated measures. A relatively intelligent person should be able to grasp your key measures without too much explanation.
- Precision often masquerades as a poor substitute for substance. You want precise measures where you need them, and broader measures where you don't.
- Just because it's possible to measure something doesn't mean it's useful. Stick with the measures that matter.

- Be clear and specific. Don't just have an "overall revenue" measure unless it really includes everything — international operations, one-time exceptions, the whole shebang.
- Most measures are lagging indicators — that is, they're after-the-fact outcomes. (We discuss these in more detail in the upcoming section "Lagging measures versus leading measures.")

REMEMBER

The idea is to pinpoint which critical few customer metrics are most important to you, your customer strategy, and your organization's overall objectives.

Good measures monitor and communicate progress on strategies. Selecting just a few critical metrics is difficult, but extremely important.

In our experience, the measures that provide the most value are those that answer these basic questions:

- Are you improving or declining?
- In which areas are you falling short over time?
- Are you appropriately responding to and following up on all service lapses?
- Which operational areas of the organization are improving key drivers?
- How is Unit *X* performing relative to the target set for it?

Also, when evaluating a metric, ask yourself, "Does this measure help me understand whether we are achieving our strategic customer objective?" If the answer is no, get rid of it (or at least reduce its visibility).

Sample customer metrics

Need some help coming up with customer metrics? The following list contains several sample metrics to help jump-start your brain.

- Abandonment rate/customers lost
- Annual sales per customer
- Average customer size
- Average duration of customer relationship
- Awareness percent
- Brand development index
- Brand penetration
- Brand recognition
- Category development index
- Complaints
- Complaints resolved on first contact

- Customer acquisition rate
- Customer lifetime value
- Customer loyalty
- Customer profitability
- Customer satisfaction
- Customer service expense per customer
- Customer visits to the company
- Customers per employee
- Direct price
- Frequency (number of sales transactions)
- Hours spent with customers
- Market share
- Marketing cost as a percentage of sales
- Number of ads placed
- Number of customers
- Number of proposals made
- Number of trade shows attended
- Penetration share
- Percent of revenue from new customers
- Price relative to competition
- Relative market share
- Repeat volume
- Response rate
- Response time per customer request
- Retention rate/loyalty
- Return rates
- Sales per channel
- Sales volume
- Share of requirements
- Share of target customer spending
- Total cost to customer
- Unit market share
- Wallet share
- Win rate (sales closed/sales contacts)

Lagging measures versus leading measures

Earlier, we mentioned lagging and leading measures. What, pray tell, are these?

REMEMBER

A *lagging measure* is one that follows an event. It tells you what happened. In contrast, a *leading measure* signals a future event. It tells you what's coming. You can think of a lagging measure as something you see in the rear-view mirror of your car. In contrast, a leading measure is something you see through your windshield.

Lagging measures are output oriented. They are typically easier to measure but harder to improve or influence. Leading measures are input oriented. They're often harder to measure but easier to improve or influence.

Obviously, unless you're TV psychic Miss Cleo, it's much easier to see the past than it is to see the future. But being able to see the past just isn't as helpful. After all, which information would you rather have — news about an accident that has already occurred or a warning about one that's about to happen?

Yes, it's fine — and appropriate — to use lagging customer measures. You do need to be apprised on historical performance and trends. But leading, predictive measures can help you prepare for what's coming.

Here's a simple example. Suppose you want to lose weight. Your current weight is a lagging measure, and it's easy to gauge. You step on the scale, you make a sad face, and you have your answer. But how do you actually reach your weight-loss goal? By tracking two leading measures: calories consumed and calories burned. These two indicators are easy to influence — you just eat less and exercise more. But until recently, these have been very hard to measure. (Nowadays, of course, you can use an app on your phone to calculate how many calories you've consumed and how many calories you've burned. But that wasn't always the case. You added all your snacks today, right?)

"Gaming" metrics

When choosing measures, sometimes people attempt to manipulate the process to suit their own needs, consciously or not. This is called "gaming" the measurements — and it's a not-so-subtle way to avoid responsibility and accountability for performance. Here are just a few of the ways that people try to game the system:

- **Constantly redefining and rewriting the metric:** Often, people find that if they keep tweaking the measurement, they won't have to report on their actual results.
- **Making one of your measure's targeted performances too easy to achieve:** If people constantly make their target, they won't ever really have to discuss their *actual* performance.
- **Setting the target performance range too wide:** If you have too wide a range, then relatively poor results may go unnoticed.
- **Infrequent reporting:** Some people may try to set the reporting frequency to annually, semi-annually, or quarterly, when in fact it should be monthly. This is just a delaying tactic.

- **Creating all new metrics:** Another delaying tactic. By creating all new metrics, the measure owner can reasonably argue that more time is needed to assess the results. (You find out more about measure owners later in this chapter.)
- **Creating an incredibly complex measure:** In this common tactic, the measure owner creates a metric that only a rocket scientist could understand. The result? Confusion through obfuscation.
- **Going deep on other people's measures:** If someone seems overly interested in the performance of other measure owners' measures, he may be attempting to divert attention from his own. We're just sayin'.
- **Creating measures for which data can't be gathered:** Perhaps the most brilliant "avoidance of accountability" tactic. If the data for the measure can't be gathered, then the measure owner can't reasonably be expected to report on performance!
- **Arguing for a change in measure ownership:** It's not uncommon for the ownership of a measure to change over time, especially as it becomes clearer who *should* own the measure. But some measure owners attempt to "pass the trash" to some unsuspecting rube.
- **Claiming a lack of relevancy:** As a last resort, some measure owners may claim that their measure isn't the most appropriate method to ensure the achievement of the overall strategic objective. Beware.

So how do you combat this? Simple. Acknowledge these bad behaviors upfront. The earlier you talk about them, the better. We recommend doing so as you begin identifying your customer objectives and strategies. Nothing is quite as effective as showing people all the tricks and behaviors they may be inclined to use *before* they consider using them! And if, despite your best efforts, these behaviors start to surface, flag them right away.

Blind Data: Analyzing Customer Data

The subject of analyzing customer data could fill a book. In fact, it has: We highly recommend *Delivering and Measuring Customer Service* by Richard D. Hanks (published by Duff Road Endeavors). This section hits just the highlights to give you some clue as to how to evaluate results, uncover the implications, and determine how best to act.

Data types

First, take a look at a few basic types of data that you'll be using to evaluate your customer's experiences (see Table 15-1). You'll use this data to track your key measures.

Table 15-1 Data Types

Type of Data	*Examples*
Absolute metric	82% of customers were greeted immediately.
Relative metric (versus peers)	We are four points below the competitor in our market.
Relative metric (versus goals)	We are under budget by 5%.
Relative metric (versus benchmark)	We are 3% above the region average.
Relative metric (versus competitors)	We have improved our market share by 6%.
Relative metric, over time	Complaints have declined by 4% since last month.
Causal and noncausal relationships	Customers greeted immediately are 80% more likely to return (probably causal). The increase in calls to the service center is driven by our increased advertising (probably not causal)

Kinds of analysis

Now we review a few of the kinds of analysis you can use to understand this customer data and suss out potential action steps.

Level 1: Straightforward analysis

The simplest forms of analysis are as follows:

- **Raw scores, rankings, and lists:** With this type of analysis, you can break down your data in terms of units and employees, geographies, pieces and parts, and so on. Results are presented in simple form, typically showing your highest and lowest performers (versus peers and/or goals). Results may also compare performers across attributes.

- **Trending over time:** This type of analysis shows directional patterns over time. It may also show a comparison of trends versus goals and/or trends versus benchmarks.
- **Distributions and histograms:** These analyses outline the distribution of answer responses, comparing parts of a whole.
- **Matrices:** A matrix compares two or more variables — for example, importance versus performance — for easy, quadrant-based classification.
- **Unit-oriented analysis:** This type of analysis is created specifically for the use of location or team managers.

Level 2: More complex kinds of analysis

More complex forms of analysis include the following:

- **Basic regression and correlations:** You use these analyses to determine the strength of direction or relationship between two or more variables, or to determine cause-and-effect relationships between inputs and desired outcomes.
- **Key driver analysis and measures:** This type of analysis can help you discover and measure the primary drivers of the customer's overall experience, identify what drives their willingness to return and to recommend, and measure performance against key drivers (for the entire company and/or for individual business units).

Benchmarking

Finally, there's benchmarking. With benchmarking, you compare results either internally across functional areas or externally against competitors.

Building a Customer Performance Dashboard

To help you keep track of your metrics and data, you'll want to place them on a dashboard of sorts. As shown in Figure 15-2, the ideal customer performance dashboard has nine columns:

- **Customer Strategies:** This column contains a list of your customer strategies.
- **Customer Measures:** These are the measures you use to determine your performance.

Customer Strategies	Customer Measures	Measure Definition	Owner	Frequency	Target	Current Actual	Results	Last Actual

Figure 15-2: A customer performance dashboard. Feel free to use this template for your own purposes!

Illustration courtesy of Roy Barnes.

- **Measure Definition:** This column features a common definition of the corresponding measure.
- **Owner:** This column indicates who "owns" the measure.
- **Frequency:** This column indicates how frequently results on the corresponding measure should be reported.
- **Target:** This column outlines the target — that is, the performance goal.
- **Current Actual:** This column contains the most current results.
- **Results:** This column indicates the results according to a range of acceptable performance.
- **Last Actual:** This column shows the last reported results. So, for example, the last actual column may contain data that is a month old, from a quarter ago, or even a longer period of time.

For more on each of these columns, read on!

The "Customer Strategies" column

Earlier, in the section "Top Model: Developing Your Strategic Execution Model," we talk about developing your customer strategies. You want to write those down in the "Customer Strategies" column in statement form. Here are some examples of strategy statements:

- C1: Deliver our customer experience intent.
- C2: Improve price, value, and delivery proposition.
- C3: Deliver innovation and industry best practice solutions.
- C4: Provide strategic expertise to our clients.

TIP

When writing down your strategy statements, it helps to number them as we've done here: C1, C2, and so on. That way, you have an easy way to reference them.

The "Customer Measures" column

The metrics for each strategy (refer to the section "The Meter's Running: Identifying Key Metrics") go in the "Customer Measures" column. As mentioned, these metrics are what you use to determine whether a strategy is working. Some sample measures for the example C1 strategy from the preceding section, "Deliver our customer experience intent," are as follows. (Note that each metric has a unique identifier, derived from the strategy number and an accompanying letter.)

- C1a: Percent overall customer satisfaction
- C1b: Percent onboarding satisfaction
- C1c: Percent of escalated complaints (compared to same month last year)
- C1d: Percent of customers exhibiting preferred behaviors

The "Measure Definition" column

You'd be surprised how often people in a group think they're on the same page when it comes to the definition of a measure, only to find out they're not. To avoid this hiccup, make it a point to clearly define each measure. Rewrite the measure in simple terms — something a sixth-grader could understand. The measure definition should spell out exactly what's being measured.

As an example, try defining measure C1b: Percent onboarding satisfaction. It seems clear enough, but there are two potential areas of confusion:

- What kinds of customers are you talking about? New customers? Residential clients?
- What operating division is being measured?

To help clarify, you might write the measure definition as follows:

> Percent onboarding satisfaction of new residential customers in the southeastern division

The "Owner" column

If you want to create a substantially better customer experience, you must establish a *measure owner.* In other words, you must assign responsibility for tracking and improving each measure to a specific individual. (Note we said *individual.* Don't assign ownership to a committee or team. You can, however, assign a separate *data reporter* to gather information about the measure and enter it into the dashboard.)

Establishing who owns a measure can be tricky. In many cases, customers touch so many different parts of the organization it's hard to pin down who exactly should be responsible for what. But do this you must.

The measure owner is responsible for the following:

- Ensuring that the measure is clearly written and is understood by all involved.
- The timeliness and accuracy of the measure result.
- Reporting on progress toward achieving the strategic goals tied to the measure. (Be aware, however, that the measure owner may or may not have complete reporting structure authority for measure achievement. For example, it may be that not all the staff responsible for moving a measure's results report to the measure owner — say, the chief customer officer. Even so, the measure owner is responsible for reporting on progress with the measure.)
- Explaining past performance and outlining any planned corrective measures.

The "Frequency" column

The "Frequency" column is where you indicate how frequently the metric should be measured and reported.

So, how often should you measure something? It depends on what you're measuring. Generally speaking, however, the more frequently you measure, the quicker you can build a data history, spot performance trends, and determine whether the actions you're taking to improve customer experience are actually working.

REMEMBER

Just for the record, measuring annually is in no way helpful from an action/response perspective. Semi-annual measures aren't much better. Sure, these measures are interesting from a tracking perspective, but they don't give you much time to correct your course. That's why we're strong advocates for measuring on a quarterly basis or, even better, measuring every month.

Of course, measuring and reporting on a monthly basis means there's no place to hide if no progress is being made. We don't see this as a downside, but the measure owner may beg to differ. Don't let that dissuade you!

The "Target" column

Having a measure isn't enough; you must also set a goal, or *target.* It's the desired performance in the frequency period described — your monthly target, quarterly target, or what have you. The target can be time-specific, a rolling average, a bounded or cumulative total — whatever makes the most sense for your needs.

So how do you know what that target should be? If you have some historical data to work with, just take an average of the last three or four quarters of data, bump it up by a little, and use that. If you *don't* have any data on hand, then you're taking a shot in the dark — although you can always look to your competitors for some direction. Even so, you'll want to let a few cycles go by before you set a hard target.

The target can — and likely will — vary throughout the course of the year. For example, if you're in retail, your target may be very different during the run-up to the Christmas holidays than in early summer. When setting your targets, you need to think through seasonality issues and other considerations.

The "Current Actual" column

The "Current Actual" column is pretty straightforward. This column is where you enter your most current results. If, for example, you measure on a quarterly basis, you're currently mid-quarter, and you haven't yet received data for your current quarter, you should enter the results from the *last* quarter in this column.

The "Results" column

The entries in the "Results" column describe the results — that is, your actual results relative to your target — presented in terms of a range of acceptable performance. For example, suppose your target for overall customer satisfaction is 80 percent. In that case, you might set the following performance range:

- **Acceptable:** This category may include anything that's 80 percent or higher.
- **Watch:** This category may include anything ranging from 76.5 percent to 79.9 percent.
- **Must address immediately:** This category may include anything below 76.4 percent.

TIP: Try using color indicators in this column. For example, you might use the color green for an "acceptable" rating, yellow for a "watch" rating, and red for a "must address immediately" rating. That way, users can quickly locate potential problems and concerns, even when merely scanning the dashboard.

The "Last Actual" column

The "Last Actual" column shows the last-reported results. These might be the results from the previous month or quarter, or they might show a comparative time period — for example, the same time period last year.

Under Review: Reviewing Your Customer Performance Dashboard

Creating a customer performance dashboard is only the beginning. You must also put in place a system to regularly monitor, review, and discuss each of the measures it contains. To this end, set up a formal monthly review meeting — two hours, minimum — to discuss results. The objective of this meeting is to share results and to focus on planned corrective actions to mitigate performance issues.

This meeting should occur three or so days after all customer measure results become available and are published on the dashboard. That gives measure owners time to digest their most recent scores and to work with other affected parties to develop an action plan, if needed. Attendees should include all measure owners (or, in the unlikely event they are unable to attend, someone who is empowered to act as their full surrogate). An impartial note-taker should also attend to record what's discussed and what actions will be taken. (Speaking of the note-taker, have him bring the notes from previous meetings, too. That way, you can ensure you're not rehashing the same issues over and over again.)

During the meeting, discuss the "must address immediately," or "red," items first. Then move on to the "watch," or "yellow," items. Finally, if time permits, talk about the "acceptable," or "green," items. (It's important to celebrate positive performance if you can!) Remember, though, that the "red" and "yellow" (or similar) designations should not be perceived as negative. The "red" designation simply means that the item requires immediate discussion among senior leaders, and the "yellow" mark just indicates that performance is of some concern, but may likely be rectified due to actions already in progress.

A word on accountability

If you want to improve performance, measure owners must first admit there's a problem. In many organizations, this sort of accountability is as rare as a Sasquatch sighting. You can help improve accountability by making sure the focus is on improving performance, *not* on blaming a particular measure owner for poor results. You can also promote accountability by ensuring transparency. Everyone, everywhere in the organization, should have access to information about how their peers are performing against a set of qualitative measures.

Speaking of accountability, if you find that your company has not been successful in moving the needle on its key metrics, it's probably because people haven't completely committed to the action and accountability part of the equation. Unless everyone in your organization from top to bottom — employees, supervisors, managers, and leaders — commits to improving the customer experience and is held accountable for progress (or lack thereof), nothing will change.

Here are a few do's and don'ts:

- **Don't** fire an employee for one or two bad results.
- **Don't** go bananas because performance was bad for one reporting period.
- **Don't** stop measuring just because you don't like the feedback you're getting.
- **Don't** do anything based upon a few data points. Give your measures a little time to run!
- **Do** evaluate trends over time.
- **Do** check multiple sources of data if possible when you're seeing seriously bad results.
- **Do** dig into the root causes of issues.
- **Do** watch for emerging trends.

Integrating Your Customer Experience Metrics into Your Governance Model

In addition to reviewing your customer performance dashboard with measure owners and other appropriate parties, as described in the preceding section, you must also share your findings with the organization at large. That means incorporating them into your organization's governance model to sit alongside other key metrics.

When key members of your organization gather to discuss the performance of the business — whether during weekly leadership meetings, monthly or quarterly business reviews, the annual budget planning cycle, or what have you — that discussion should include customer metrics. Ideally, these metrics should be reviewed with the same intensity and frequency as financial and other measures.

Look, it's not like you're trying to sell the C-suite some cock-and-bull story about the importance of customer metrics. These metrics *are* important. More than that: They're vital to your company's long-term success. They belong in the spotlight!

Chapter 16

Making the Most of Measures: Key Customer Experience Metrics

In This Chapter

- Choosing simple metrics to start
- Looking at loyalty and satisfaction
- Measuring customer retention
- Assessing seamlessness and ease of doing business
- Understanding the benefits of benchmarking

You've probably heard it before: "What gets measured gets improved." It's age-old wisdom. Even Galileo had something to say on the matter: "Measure what is measurable, and make measurable what is not so."

Customer experience is no exception. By measuring customer experience, you can determine what's working and what's not. Plus, when you have a good set of customer experience measures, your hard work will earn more attention and respect from internal stakeholders and, ultimately, gain traction for your customer experience program.

You have to prove that your customer experience efforts are worthwhile, and that means you need clear, concise, and easy-to-understand measures. Of course, no measures are perfect, and there's no single metric that you can use to gauge customer experience. Your best bet is to develop a series of robust metrics in a few key areas, such as loyalty, retention, portfolio, and experience.

In this chapter, you gain a working knowledge of key metrics for gauging customer satisfaction and customer experience. Don't be afraid to test different kinds of metrics in the early stages, when you're wading into the measurement business. The development and use of metrics is often an iterative process. You might try 10 or even 20 different metrics before you pinpoint the critical few that are most helpful to you!

Keeping It Simple: Opting for Simple Metrics

Once, during a visit with a Fortune 100 client, we were invited to sit in on a meeting with the senior leadership team. During the meeting, the vice president of revenue management gleefully reported that the organization's performance was vastly exceeding expectations. Profits were *skyrocketing!* The metric he was using, however, was as confusing as, well, rocket science. Looking around the boardroom table, it was clear that no one had the first clue what he was talking about. They were just too embarrassed to admit it.

The moral of this story? When it comes to metrics, you must aim for simplicity. That means everyone who comes in contact with the measure should be able to understand what's being measured — even if they don't have a degree in advanced statistics or space travel.

As noted by customer-metrics guru Richard Hanks of Mindshare/InMoment:

> If you have leanings toward the theoretical and the academic, it's fairly easy with customer metrics to find yourself sliding down the slippery slope of mental gymnastics about insignificant nuances and masterful analytics of accurate but unusable information.

Michael Hammer, a highly respected authority on process reengineering and performance measurement, agrees:

> In the real world, an organization's measurement systems typically deliver a blizzard of nearly meaningless data that quantifies practically everything in sight, no matter how unimportant; that is so voluminous as to be unusable; that is delivered so late as to be virtually useless.

Don't let that be you! If your measures don't seem immediately and obviously useful, go back to the drawing board . . . *pronto.*

Trust us: There is no end to the level of complexity that people can come up with when developing metrics. But the idea is not to bamboozle everyone into believing you're making progress with your customer experience efforts; it's to *actually measure* the factors that can help you determine whether the work you've done to redesign your touchpoints is paying off.

Make no mistake: You can measure customer experience in extremely sophisticated ways. But until you have a year or two of operating measures under your belt, it's best to avoid doing this. Complexity confuses people. Unless you want to constantly explain what a measure is and what value it has, keep things simple!

Semper Fi: Measuring Loyalty and Advocacy

If there's anything that gets customer research, data, and analytics professionals in a froth, it's this question: What is customer loyalty and what's the best way to measure it? For those of us who are interested in customer experience, loyalty — and the related advocacy — are the holy grail. If your customers love you, love your brand, *and* are itching to tell everyone in their circle of friends about it, then mission accomplished. Heck, if that's what you've achieved in your organization, you shouldn't be reading this book, you should be *writing* it!

WARNING!

Don't assume that because someone is a repeat customer, she is loyal. It could just be that buying from you is more convenient. For example, suppose you work for a bank. You have one customer who comes in every other Friday to deposit her paycheck. You assume she is loyal, but really, it's just that she lives near your branch. In fact, she doesn't particularly like your bank. She just doesn't have the time or energy to find a new one. But then, her brother tells her about *his* bank. He says their interest rates are great, and the tellers are always friendly and helpful. Plus, there's a branch right by her work! So she switches banks . . . and you're confused. You thought this customer was loyal — her behavior certainly suggested that — but in fact, the customer merely found your bank convenient.

REMEMBER

Loyalty is a high-order measure of attachment and engagement. It involves an emotional commitment or connection to your brand. It's more than mere satisfaction — although there is a link. Generally, loyal customers are satisfied. Not all satisfied customers are loyal, however. With just the slightest provocation, a customer who is merely satisfied may sniff out what your competitors have to offer. In fact, one study showed that 60 percent of lost customers reported being "satisfied" or even "very satisfied" just prior to defecting! Even so, if you're looking to drive customer loyalty, ensuring customer satisfaction is an essential first step. Remember: If your operations are awful, your customers will never be loyal (unless they're part of your immediate family).

Looking at two key measures can help you understand your customer's level of satisfaction and loyalty, or advocacy:

- Overall satisfaction (OSAT)
- Net Promoter Score (NPS)

The following sections give you the lowdown on these key measures.

Assessing overall satisfaction (OSAT)

To determine your OSAT levels, ask this question when soliciting customer feedback in a survey: "Overall, how satisfied are you with our company?"

REMEMBER

The answer to this question reflects the customer's overall satisfaction with the product or service that she has used. The greatest predictors of customer satisfaction are the customer's experiences across all touchpoints with which she has interacted.

This question can be asked in two forms:

- **As a scaled question:** A scaled question looks like this:

  On a scale of 1 to 5, with 1 being not at all satisfied and 5 being extremely satisfied, how would you rate your overall satisfaction with ABC Company?

  This is an example of a Likert scale. Named for its inventor, Rensis Likert, a Likert scale scales responses to survey research. Note that the actual scale labels may vary. Ditto the numbers used in the scale. For example, rather than using a scale of 1 to 5, you may opt for a scale of 1 to 7, 1 to 10, or whatever. Generally speaking, however, we like scales that allow for a neutral option — that is, a scale with an odd number of options, so respondents can choose a value that falls squarely in the middle. A five-point or seven-point scale works well.

- **As an open-ended question:** An open-ended question is a little different. It doesn't offer the respondent a range of options from which to choose; instead, it asks the respondent to provide feedback on her own terms. If you ask an open-ended question, you won't be able to use the responses in a quantitative way. However, if you don't plan to track trend changes in OSAT over time, then asking an open-ended question can be a good idea. You'll find the responses that your customers provide to be extremely informative!

TIP

Not sure which type of question to use? Our advice is to ask both. Start with a scaled OSAT question, and follow it with an open-ended question asking why the customer answered the way she did. You get the best of both worlds!

You can also choose when during the survey to ask the OSAT question. Our take? Ask it first. That way, you get an unbiased and unaided response. If you ask a customer to rate her overall satisfaction at the end of a survey, her answers to any previous questions will likely create a bias when she answers *this* question. That is, having answered the previous questions, she'll have already been reminded of things that went particularly well or poorly. (Some people argue that it should be the last question for precisely this reason, but we still prefer to ask it upfront.)

WARNING! Whatever you decide, stick with it. Don't move the OSAT question from the end of the survey to the beginning (or vice versa) over time. Customers will answer the question differently depending upon whether it's asked first or last (unaided or aided), which means that moving the question will invalidate your response trends.

Determining your Net Promoter Score (NPS)

Your survey can also include this question:

> On a scale of 0 to 10 (with 0 being not at all likely and 10 being extremely likely), how likely are you to refer our products/services to a friend or colleague?

If you've seen this question before (or something like it), then you're already familiar with the Net Promoter Score (NPS). Pioneered by Fred Reicheld in conjunction with Bain & Company and Satmetrix, the NPS predicts the likelihood of a customer purchasing from you again or referring your products or services to a friend. It's very widely used by corporations and organizations worldwide.

REMEMBER Although the NPS is often pitched as "the one key customer metric you need to know," this isn't really the case. Yes, it's a key metric, but it's not the only one. For one thing, by itself, the NPS tells you *nada* about why your customers answered the way they did. To find that out, you need to ask them.

One more thing: The NPS typically is used to evaluate a customer's perceptions across the entire touchpoint spectrum or journey of his experience with your organization. If you decide to use it at the touchpoint level, make sure you're also asking it at the enterprise level. That way, you'll have a baseline against which you can run correlation analysis to determine which touchpoint has the biggest impact on your overall NPS results.

Calculating the NPS

To calculate your organization's NPS, you must first divide customers into three categories, based on the answer they supply to the aforementioned question. These categories are as follows (see Figure 16-1):

- **Detractors:** Detractors rate their likeliness to refer your products/services to others anywhere from 0 to 6. These unhappy people can damage your brand, harm your reputation, and slow the growth of your business through negative word-of-mouth or other downbeat communications (on social media, online customer boards, and so on).

- **Passives:** Passives, who rate their likeliness of referral at a 7 or 8, are satisfied but unenthusiastic customers. They are more likely to be seduced away by your competitors and/or special offers.
- **Promoters:** These customers rate their likeliness of referral at a 9 or 10. They are extremely loyal and enthusiastic. You can count on them to keep buying your products and services, refer others to your firm, and serve as evangelizers. Promoters can help to fuel your growth.

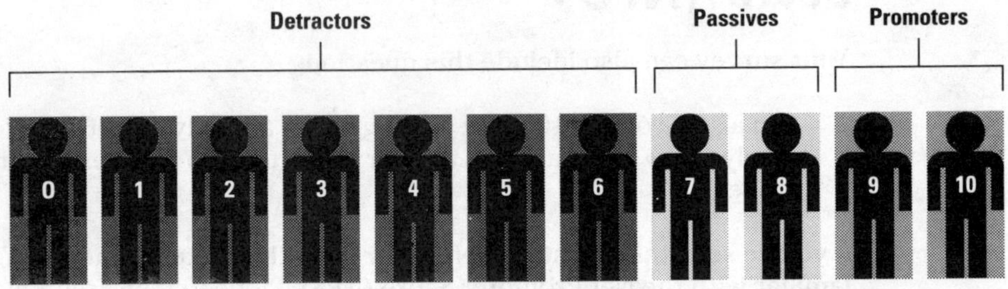

Illustration courtesy of Roy Barnes.

Figure 16-1: Divide your respondents into three categories: detractors, passives, and promoters.

Next, you calculate your NPS by subtracting the percentage of customers who are "detractors" from the percentage of customers who are "promoters," like so:

% of Promoters – % of Detractors = Your NPS

Note that your NPS can range anywhere from –100 to 100.

Here's a quick example. Suppose you send out 100 surveys, and all 100 come back. (Amazing!) Of those 100 responses:

- Twenty responses were in the 0 to 6 range (detractors).
- Forty responses were in the 7 to 8 range (passives).
- Forty responses were in the 9 to 10 range (promoters).

In other words, 20 percent of the respondents were detractors, 40 percent were passives, and 40 percent were promoters. So you subtract the detractors (20 percent) from the promoters (40 percent). The result is 20 percent, for an NPS of 20. That's all there is to it! So what can you do with your NPS? Two things. One, you can use it to compare your score with other firms in your industry or in other industries. And two, you can use it to gauge your own firm's performance over time.

Of course, it helps to know what constitutes a "good" NPS and how other companies stack up. According to Bain & Company, one of the world's leading management consulting firms, the average company has an NPS of only

5 to 10. In other words, the promoters barely outnumber the detractors. Worse, some firms have a *negative* NPS. That is, they have more detractors than promoters! An NPS that is positive — that is, higher than zero — can be considered good. An NPS of 50 or more is excellent.

Figure 16-2 shows the results of a study by the Temkin Group. It shows a comparison of Net Promoter Scores across different industry types. As you can see, auto dealers, grocery chains, hotel chains, and software firms boast the highest average scores, with NPSs of 38, 30, 29, and 29, respectively. Credit card issuers, health plans, Internet service providers, and TV service providers represent the bottom feeders; they register NPSs of 11, 9, 5, and 2, respectively.

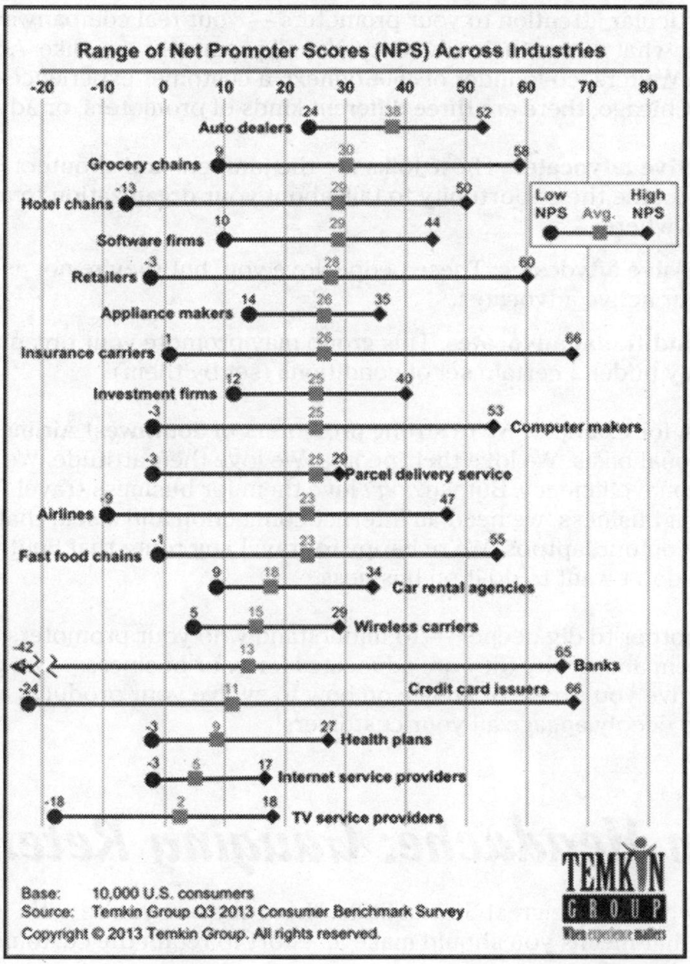

Figure 16-2: A comparison of Net Promoter Scores across different industry types.

Illustration courtesy of The Temkin Group.

The same study also revealed the Net Promoter Scores of several specific companies. Not surprisingly, USAA, which is renowned for its exemplary customer service, earned the proverbial "gold medal," earning an NPS of 66 for its insurance and credit card businesses and an NPS of 65 for its banking organization. Companies with an NPS above 50 included such well-regarded firms as Amazon.com, Chick-fil-A, Apple, Audi, Nordstrom, and others.

Following up with detractors, passives, and promoters

If you want to improve your organization's NPS, you need to follow up with your detractors, passives, and promoters to understand why they answered your question as they did and what you can do better in the future.

TIP

Pay particular attention to your promoters — your real company advocates. Find out what drives their advocacy. Not all promoters are alike. According to Jeannie Walters, co-founder of 360Connext, a customer experience consulting firm in Chicago, there are three different kinds of promoters, or advocates:

- **Active advocates:** These folks are the jumpers and shouters. They welcome the opportunity to talk about your organization to anyone, anywhere.
- **Passive advocates:** These people love you, but they're not as vocal as your active advocates.
- **Conditional advocates:** This group may promote your organization, but only under a certain set of conditions (set by them).

Take us, for example. We're strong promoters of Southwest Airlines, but on a conditional basis. We love their people. We love their attitude. We love their operational efficiency. But we *don't* love them for business travel. When we travel on business, we need an Internet connection and a seat that allows us to work on our laptops. We're happy to travel any route that Southwest flies; we just don't want to do it on business.

If you bother to dig deeper — to understand who your promoters are and talk with them about why they are advocates for your business — we guarantee they'll give you excellent advice on how to evolve your products and services to more deeply engage all your customers!

Retention Headache: Gauging Retention

In the words of the great Steven Stills, "Love the one you're with." In business terms, that means you should make an effort to retain the customers you already have.

Why? Lots of reasons. For one thing, retaining existing customers can take a lot less time and money than finding new ones. On a related note, relationships with long-term customers are more profitable. In fact, according to the results of research by Bain & Company and the Harvard Business School:

> In industry after industry . . . the high cost of acquiring customers renders many customer relationships unprofitable during their early years. Only in later years, when the cost of serving loyal customers falls and the volume of their purchases rises, do relationships generate big returns. The bottom line: Increasing customer retention rates by 5 percent increases profits by 25 percent to 95 percent.

And yet, as observed by Jim Clemmer in his book *Firing on All Cylinders: The Service/Quality System for High-Powered Corporate Performance* (published by The Clemmer Group):

> American business has developed an insane balance between customer acquisition and customer retention. Many companies will invest millions in sales and marketing costs to bring customers in the door and then throw a few thousand dollars at trying to keep them.

Those wise words were written in 1992, and they are still valid today!

So why, you might reasonably ask, don't more companies and organizations focus on retention? Simple. Because retention is a long-term effort that involves all the different entities within an organization working together to create more engaging and delightful customer experiences. Translation: It's easier to focus on new customer acquisition than to work with those nincompoops over in Departments X, Y, and Z on retention.

Here's the deal: Your organization's long-term success depends on customer retention. Sure, you may attract a slew of new customers through fantastic marketing or promotion. But if you're unable to keep them around month after month, you won't be in business long. If you want to build a sustainable and scalable business (and you do), then you need to improve your customer retention rate. Truth is, there's a lot more money to be made in customer retention than in customer acquisition!

Calculating your customer retention rate

As a first step, you must calculate your current customer retention rate — that is, the number of customers you manage to keep in a given period (for example, in a given month, quarter, or year) as compared to the number you started with. This doesn't count new customers. Think of it as being the opposite of customer churn — it's "customer keep."

Retaining versus trapping

Some industries boast high retention rates, but don't be fooled. It's not because they offer an unparalleled customer experience; it's because they make it nearly impossible for customers to move their business elsewhere. The personal banking industry is a great example. If you have your paycheck direct deposited to your bank, you're using their automated bill-pay service, you have a credit card and a debit card through them, and they hold your checking and savings accounts, then you are what they call *entwined* — although "trapped" might be a better description!

To be sure, it can be helpful to provide a one-stop shop for all your customer's needs. But don't limit yourself to merely entwining them. Don't just trap your customers. Get to the root of the problems they're experiencing and solve them!

To calculate customer retention, you need three pieces of information:

- The number of customers at the end of a given period (*P*)
- The number of new customers acquired during that period (*A*)
- The number of customers at the start of that period (*S*)

Remember, you want to know the number of customers remaining at the end of the period without counting the number of new customers acquired. So to start, you're looking for $P - A$. Next, determine the percentage of original customers retained by dividing the result of $P - A$ by the total number of customers at the start (*S*) and then multiplying by 100. For you math types out there, the equation for this is as follows:

$$((P - A) / S) \times 100 = \text{Customer Retention Rate}$$

Ideally, your retention rate would be 100 percent, meaning that you never lose a customer. But obviously, to quote Dana Carvey (quoting George H.W. Bush), "Not gonna happen." You can, however, aim for a number in the 90 percent range. Sound impossible? It's not. If you improve your customer experience, your customer retention rate will rise in kind.

Gauging switching and renewal metrics

Want a true gauge of your company's interest in delivering extraordinary customer experience? Try adding the following two questions to your customer surveys:

On a scale of 1 to 10 (with 1 being not at all likely and 10 being extremely likely), how likely are you to switch to another company?

On a scale of 1 to 10 (with 1 being not at all likely and 10 being extremely likely), how likely are you to renew your [subscription, agreement, contract] with this company?

Odds are, you'll hear a lot of marketing, sales, and account service directors howl at the inclusion of these two simple questions. No doubt they believe, given the deep and enduring nature of their profound relationships with their clients, that they have a flawless sense of whether a customer is considering quitting your company. The fact is, they don't.

Most customers simply don't tell their dedicated salesperson that they're unhappy — and they *definitely* won't mention that they're shopping around for another company with whom to do business. Most customers just quietly leave without giving any verbal clue as to their dissatisfaction.

If, however, you ask the aforementioned two questions and monitor the customer's response over time, you'll have an early warning when a storm's a-brewing. For this to work, you must make sure of two things:

- **The survey questions are sent to the right person.** If an assistant or lower-level employee, rather than the actual decision-maker, ends up answering the survey, you may never discover that the decision-maker is unhappy.
- **The questions are asked with enough frequency.** Don't just ask these questions on a quarterly basis. A lot of ill will can build up over three months! Figure out how often you need to ask this question to ensure you have a current and timely read on your customer's state of mind.

We repeat: Most customers defect without ever telling anyone why. It's not that they wouldn't be happy to share their observations and concerns; it's that no one bothers to ask! And even if someone *does* ask, the customer may not be comfortable answering. And even if the customer *does* answer, there's a good chance the organization will never get around to fixing any problems they share that caused them to want to defect in the first place. And even if . . . well, you get the idea.

Don't be afraid to ask difficult and challenging questions. If your customers know you're sincere and truly want the feedback — and that you'll respond quickly to their comments — they'll tell you what you need to know!

Assessing your portfolio

Unless your company's products and services really suck, you should find it much easier to sell additional products from your product/service line to your existing customers than to new ones. After all, your existing customers know you, they're familiar with your offerings, and they know how well you stand behind your service and commitments. In fact, research suggests that the odds of you persuading existing customers to purchase additional products or services from you is about 60 percent. In contrast, the chances of you getting a *new* customer to buy that same product or service is about 10 to 15 percent.

So why don't marketers spend more money and resources on their current customers? Why do they burn scarce budgetary dollars on attracting and persuading prospects who have no idea who your company is and why they should do business with you? Why don't they allocate those dollars to improving the relationship and experience of people who already have purchased from you?

Well, as we've said, because it's easier to focus on new clients. Also, there hasn't historically been much in the way of metrics that look closely at the penetration of new products and services into the existing customer base. But you can get a sense of the latter by adding a couple of questions to your customer surveys:

> On a scale of 1 to 10 (with 1 being not at all likely and 10 being extremely likely), how likely are you to purchase additional product and service solutions from us in the future?
>
> On a scale of 1 to 10 (with 1 being not at all likely and 10 being extremely likely), how likely are you to expand the use of our products throughout your company?

Of course, it's not enough to get the customer's 1 to 10 rating here. You also need to know *why* the customer has answered this way.

You're talking to someone who has a higher propensity to purchase from you. He's in a perfect position to tell you what's right and what's wrong with your products, processes, services, and experiences. Ask!

Are You Experienced? Assessing Customer Experience

Lately, there's been a growing body of thought that rather than wowing customers with over-the-top service, the focus should be on delivering the basics extremely well. But the way we see it, it's not an either/or proposition. You have to do both. We believe that your end game should be to delight and surprise customers with your thoughtfulness and care — but you won't delight or surprise *anyone* if you fail to do the basics well.

From the customer's perspective, there are five basic areas of customer experience:

- The service or product he wants to purchase
- The person or team delivering the service or product
- The actual process of doing business with your organization
- The atmosphere, location, or methods that encompasses the process
- The emotions the customer feels during his experience

We're not going to lie: Focusing on the basics can be kind of boring. All that attention to detail can be drudgery. But as Richard Hanks says:

> Very few people want to focus on what I call "the boring everyday" . . . But it's the "boring everyday" that will make you stand out.

So what does it mean to do the "boring everyday" well? From the standpoint of customer experience, two things:

- Offering a consistent, flowing, and smooth — in other words, seamless — customer experience
- Making it easy for customers to do business with you

Keep reading for more advice on how to achieve both of these objectives.

Ensuring seamlessness

Typically, the totality of a customer's experience is made up of individual segments, or touchpoints. For best results, you must smooth out any bumps or disturbances that may occur as the customer passes from one segment to another. Ideally, you want the customer to be completely unaware of these transitions. In other words, you want the customer's experience to be seamless. He should have no sense of being shuffled about.

To gauge how seamless your operation is, ask the following question when soliciting customer feedback via survey:

> On a scale of 1 to 10 (with 1 being not at all and 10 being always), would you describe your experience interacting with us as perfectly consistent, flowing, and smooth?

Don't be surprised if your customers score you like a Russian judge at an Olympic ice-skating competition — in other words, super low. After all, achieving seamlessness is no small feat. But the rewards in terms of customer experience, loyalty, and engagement are lasting.

As always, don't hesitate to follow up with an open-ended question to tease out more specific information about what you can do better. Remember, though, that open-ended questions generate a lot of responses. Be prepared to sift through them all and respond to any specific requests for help that may come.

Evaluating ease of doing business

Seeking feedback on how easy it is for customers to do business with an organization isn't new. Historically, however, the emphasis has been finding out how many calls it took for a customer to resolve his problem or how many hurdles he had to clear to get what he needed.

Score strength: What's a "good" score?

Clients often ask us what constitutes a "good" score. The simple answer is, any statistically significant score that's better than the last time you measured it is a good one. Yes, it's important to benchmark your performance against your competitors (see the upcoming section "Bench Warfare: The Importance of Benchmarking"). But it's even *more* important to make significant improvements to your own performance. By really understanding your own metrics, what drives them, and how they change over time, you'll be in a much better position to determine what "good" is for you.

REMEMBER

That's all well and good, but these days, we're finding that a customer's perception of the ease of doing business has more to do with accessibility, availability, and flexibility — in other words, the degree to which customers can interact with your organization however they choose. Options may include the following:

- In person
- By phone
- Via post
- By email
- Using social media (Twitter, Facebook, and so on)
- Via text
- Via live chat

Customers want ubiquitous interaction. They expect your organization to be accessible and fluent in every channel. Moreover, they expect to interact with you in the way that suits them best. That doesn't mean you can't steer them toward specific interaction channels, just that you must make yourself available on their terms. You have to be open for business when they want you to be. Translation: No bankers' hours!

In addition to accessibility, flexibility, and availability, customers expect the information you provide them to be correct — that is, accurate, timely, and integrated. Information shared by different entities across your organization must be the same, regardless of what department shared it. There should be no different versions of the truth depending on who the customer calls.

To assess how easy it is to do business with your organization, include the following question on your customer feedback surveys:

> On a scale of 1 to 10 (with 1 being not at all and 10 being always), would you describe us as easy to do business with (accessible, available, flexible, and correct)?

Bench Warfare: The Importance of Benchmarking

The great Chinese philosopher Lao Tzu once said, "When you are content to be simply yourself and don't compare or compete, everyone will respect you." Don't get us wrong: He was a great guy. *Super* wise. But when it comes to business, he was off the mark. (Sun-Tzu, a Chinese military general, strategist, and philosopher who lived around the same time as Lao Tzu, might have made a better business consultant. After all, he was the one who said, "Know the enemy and know yourself; in a hundred battles you will never be in peril.")

The truth is, if you're in business, you *do* want to compete. You also want to compare. That's where benchmarking comes in. *Benchmarking* is the process of measuring your organization's performance (in this case, your performance with respect to customer experience) and comparing it with that of other organizations.

Benchmarking requires more than a little humility. It requires you to admit that there are other organizations whose performance surpasses your own. But if you want to improve, you must seek out comparative measures from multiple sources. If you find you're outclassed, it's time to explore the different philosophies and operating practices of your competitors.

Before you start benchmarking your business against others in your industry, ask yourself: Which customer experience metrics should we benchmark? The answer is that you should benchmark those metrics that measure areas where you need — and want — to significantly improve.

Here's an example of some metrics that are regularly benchmarked by call-center clients.

- **Average speed to answer a call:** On average, 68 percent of calls are answered within 30 seconds, while 7 percent take more than a minute.
- **Average time on hold:** Most call centers report hold times of less than 1 minute and 45 seconds. Less than a quarter of companies report no hold time at all.
- **Average time to answer email:** A third of companies respond to emails within one hour. This may be misleading, however, as it could simply refer to an acknowledgement of receipt, not an actual response. As with all metrics, look under the covers to really understand exactly what's being measured!
- **First call resolution (FCR):** One of our favorite metrics, FCR tracks the efficiency with which your representatives are able to resolve customer issues (account status, assistance, product information, billing, and so forth). Basic issues can be resolved on a customer's first call. Other more-complex issues may require more research, in which case they may not be able to be resolved on the spot.

Whatever metrics you choose to measure and benchmark, they should be perfectly aligned with your organization's strategic objectives and measures. To quote the Greeks, "Know thyself." Before choosing which metrics to benchmark, be sure you have a thorough understanding of your customer experience intent and your touchpoint and journey maps. In addition, you should already have codified your key customer business processes and should be clear on your key customer performance metrics. A deep understanding of your own metrics and their drivers enables you to understand your operational performance relative to external benchmarks (such as the industry average and top performers) and to assess your own internal progress over time.

TIP

To ensure comparability, metrics should be normalized (in other words, put on a common unit basis) to reduce issues of operational scale.

There are dozens of global and local market-research firms that provide benchmarking data for all sorts of industries, including automotive, consumer packaged goods, electronics, energy, financial services, healthcare, insurance, real estate, telecommunications, and more. Typically available on a subscription basis, this type of benchmarking information aggregates common measures, issues, and performance parameters within particular industry segments. These firms make comparative information available to those subscribers who are willing to share their own information with others. Here are a few examples of firms that supply this type of data:

- **J.D. Power (`www.jdpower.com`):** This firm offers information spanning multiple industry types on customer experience.
- **STR Global (`www.strglobal.com`):** This organization specializes in data from the hospitality industry.
- **Institute of Customer Service (`www.instituteofcustomerservice.com`):** This Britain-based not-for-profit offers customer service benchmarking data on a variety of industries.
- **Customer Service Benchmarking Association (`csbenchmarking.com`):** This is an association of companies that conduct benchmarking studies to identify best practices in customer service.

The challenge with this type of data is making sure that the competitive set into which your company is grouped is accurate and fair. You don't want to sign up for a benchmarking comparison with companies that aren't similar in terms of scope, issues, or geographic reach, or that have substantially different regulatory or political environments! To avoid this, you simply need to ask some detailed questions about what kinds of companies are in the benchmarking database to determine whether they are a fair comparison.

Chapter 17

Initiatives, Projects, and Programs . . . Oh My!

In This Chapter

- Looking at the initiative-launching addiction
- Understanding how to prioritize initiatives
- Taking the STRATEX approach

Here's a riddle for you: One hot Monday morning, five frogs were sitting on a log that was floating in the middle of a pond. The frogs, who were close friends, were discussing the appeal of going for a swim in the cool, sparkling water. After much debate, four of the frogs decided to jump off and enjoy a swim. How many frogs were left on the log?

If you answered "one," you're not alone. Most people do. But the real answer is "five." Why? Because in ponds, as in business, *deciding* to do something (like jumping off a log) and actually *doing* it are two entirely different things.

We've been part of all too many meetings where the conversation goes something like this:

> **President of the company:** Where are we on the XYZ project?
>
> **Collective executive team:** [silence]
>
> **President of the company:** Anyone?
>
> **Brave executive team member:** Uh, I don't think we've done anything about the XYZ project.
>
> **Exasperated president of the company:** *What?!* We talked at length about this last month. We decided we were going to go ahead with Option A. We decided that, didn't we? I *was* part of that decision, wasn't I?!
>
> **Really brave executive team member:** Um, Boss, we decided we were going to do that, but we didn't actually assign anyone to the task of actually doing anything, so nothing has actually been done.

In fact, this type of senior-level frog talk happens all the time. Why? Because planning is not doing. Deciding is not doing. Only *doing* is doing.

This lack of follow-through — execution — is the root cause of a lot of what's wrong in many organizations around the world. Businesses are great at planning. They have initiatives, projects, and programs out the wazoo. They just don't execute them well. In this chapter, you discover that what *really* moves metrics — including ones that pertain to customer experience — is targeted action, not random initiatives.

Might as Well Face It: You're Addicted to Launching Initiatives

Coauthor Roy tells about witnessing a particularly memorable launch:

> When my family and I moved to Orlando, one of the first things we did was drive to Cape Canaveral to watch the launch of one of the space shuttles. We, along with several thousand other people, arrived plenty early and found a close spot from which to watch the launch. As the clock counted down from T-minus 120 minutes to less than 5 minutes, our excitement grew.
>
> Soon, we heard the voice of the announcer at Mission Control over the loudspeakers: "T-minus 10, nine, eight . . ." The massive engines fired. "Seven, six, five . . ." The earth began to shake. "Four, three, two, one, zero. We have lift off." My eyes teared up as we watched the space shuttle, with seven astronauts on board, accelerate from 0 to 1,000 miles per hour in just one minute, appearing smaller by the second. Just after two minutes, we saw the shuttle jettison its two solid rocket boosters as it roared away at 3,000 miles per hour and disappeared from site. *"Holy cow!"* I said to a complete stranger behind me. *"That was amazing!"*
>
> With nothing else to see except the rocket contrails dissipating in the breeze, we packed up our stuff and headed home. For the first half hour of the drive, all we talked about was how unbelievable the launch was. But soon, the conversation turned to other things, and the kids pulled out their iPhones. By the next morning, the launch was all but forgotten.
>
> I didn't think much about the space shuttle until it was scheduled to return a week later. Normally, when a space shuttle reenters the atmosphere on its way back to Cape Canaveral, we can hear the sonic boom. So that afternoon, I was half-listening for it as I worked in the yard. I never heard it. The space shuttle Columbia broke apart and burned up on

reentry, splintering into pieces over Texas and killing all seven astronauts on board. It was a staggering tragedy that put a scar on the hearts of all of us who watched that team of astronauts launch.

A few months later, I was working with a client, and he mentioned all the different customer initiatives they had going on. "We've launched so many rockets lately, we can't even keep track of them all!" He continued: "We're addicted to the excitement of starting something new." His comments took my mind right back to the space shuttle launch and how, almost immediately — within a day — we had forgotten all about it.

I knew exactly what he was talking about. In my corporate career, I've been through more than my share of launches of new initiatives, and you probably have, too. Odds are, these initiatives launched with enormous fanfare, complete with posters, coffee mugs, ball caps, and tote bags, all emblazoned with the name of the critically important new initiative du jour.

Looking at a typical launch

Here's how a typical launch works in most organizations. First, someone has a "great new idea" to solve some problem. (See Figure 17-1.) The idea may originate with a corporate executive, a department head, or some group in the company. It doesn't really matter. What matters is that they've sold somebody higher up on their vision, which is usually just some vague objective that they want to accomplish.

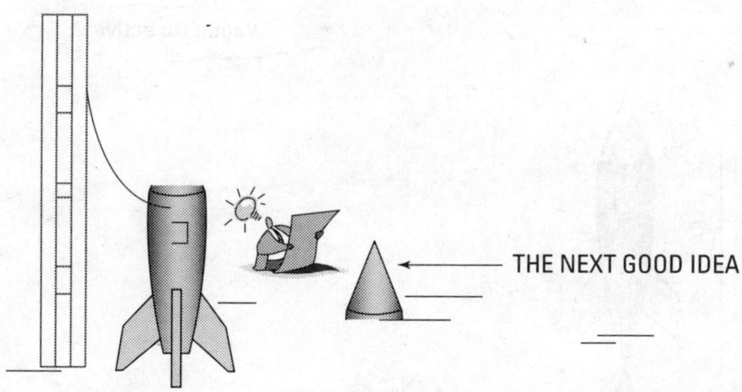

Figure 17-1: Someone has a "great new idea."

Illustration courtesy of Roy Barnes.

After getting the right approvals to proceed, those responsible for the idea start gathering the necessary human and financial resources to launch their idea. (See Figure 17-2.)

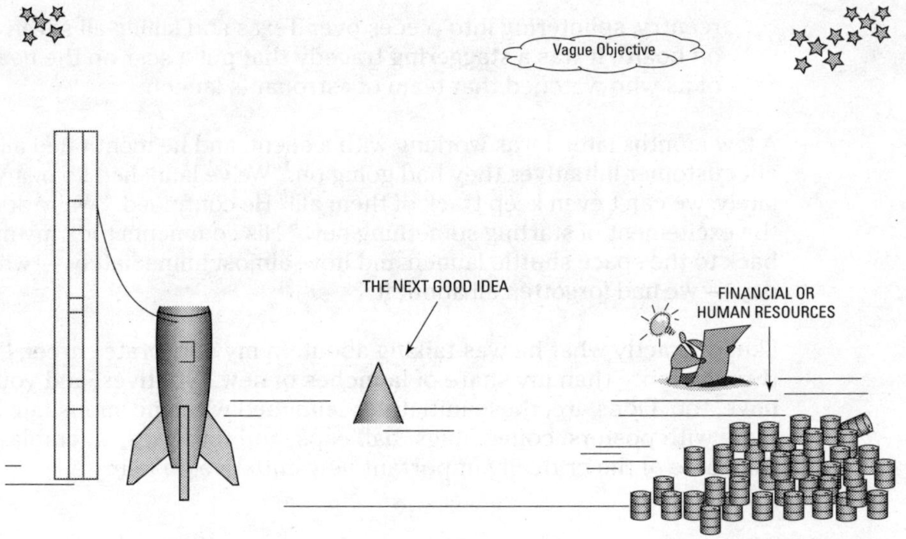

Illustration courtesy of Roy Barnes.

Figure 17-2: The necessary approvals and resources are gathered.

Next comes the exciting rollout and launch party. Blast off! Very exciting!

But before the just-launched initiative is even out of sight, they (or others in the company) dream up another new initiative, and the cycle starts all over again. (See Figure 17-3.)

Illustration courtesy of Roy Barnes.

Figure 17-3: Even as this initiative is launched, folks in the company are dreaming up new initiatives.

Lacking focus

Often, after we launch something new (customer related or not), we forget all about it. We all attend the launch, we get excited about the vague objective the initiative is supposed to meet, and then we get on with our normal work. Out of sight, out of mind. As a result of this lack of focus, the initiative is quickly submerged in the great ocean of started but not completed corporate initiatives.

It gets worse: Many companies become addicted to launching new stuff, usually before the old stuff has had any chance to make any significant headway. Rocket launch after rocket launch leads employees to believe (rightfully) that their organization's leaders have no focus and no stick-to-itiveness. This state of affairs leads to an increase in what we call *organizational gravity,* where every new initiative is looked upon by employees with legitimate skepticism. Leaders are the only ones to blame as initiatives slowly fade away and die of neglect. (See Figure 17-4.)

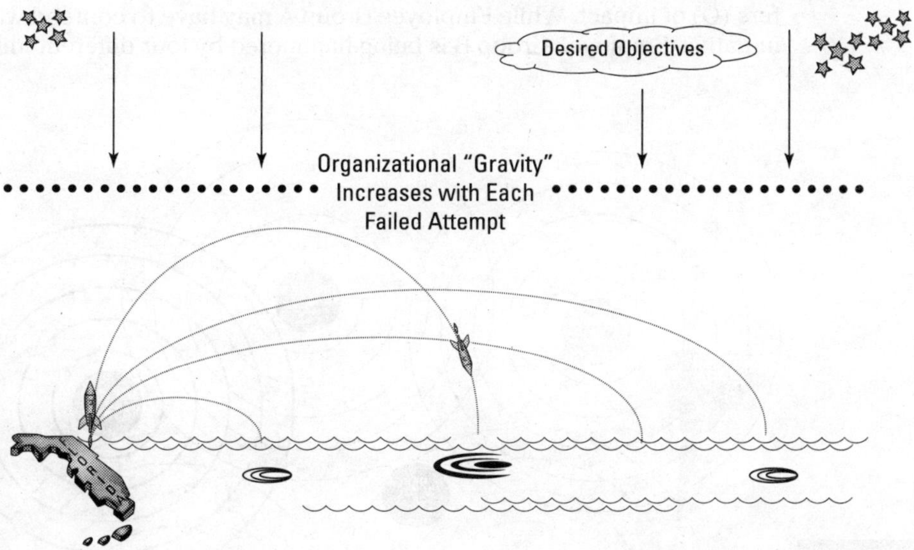

Figure 17-4: Organizational gravity dooms subsequent initiatives.

Illustration courtesy of Roy Barnes.

REMEMBER

It's not enough to launch an initiative. You have to fulfill its mission completely. You have to *execute*. You have to hammer away at it, giving no ground. You have to speak about it at every meeting and sell it every chance you get. And the powers that be have to call you into account if you don't meet your objective.

Getting Your Priorities Straight: The Importance of Prioritizing Initiatives

The financial and human resources needed to fulfill the mission of any initiative — be it one that pertains to customer experience or to some other area of the organization — are always in short supply. Even if they aren't, the problems of time and attention still remain. For example, just because you have the money to do something doesn't mean you have the time or the organizational "bandwidth" to do it.

Attempting to juggle multiple initiatives — even just a few — significantly affects employees throughout the organization. This fact was brought to life during a conference hosted by Bain and Company, which featured a graphic similar to the one shown in Figure 17-5. As you can see from the graphic, different initiatives affect different populations of employees at different times. In this example, there are six different initiatives, with the concentric rings around each initiative representing the likely weeks (W), months (M), or quarters (Q) of impact. While Employee Group A may have to contend with just one initiative, Employee Group B is being hammered by four different initiatives.

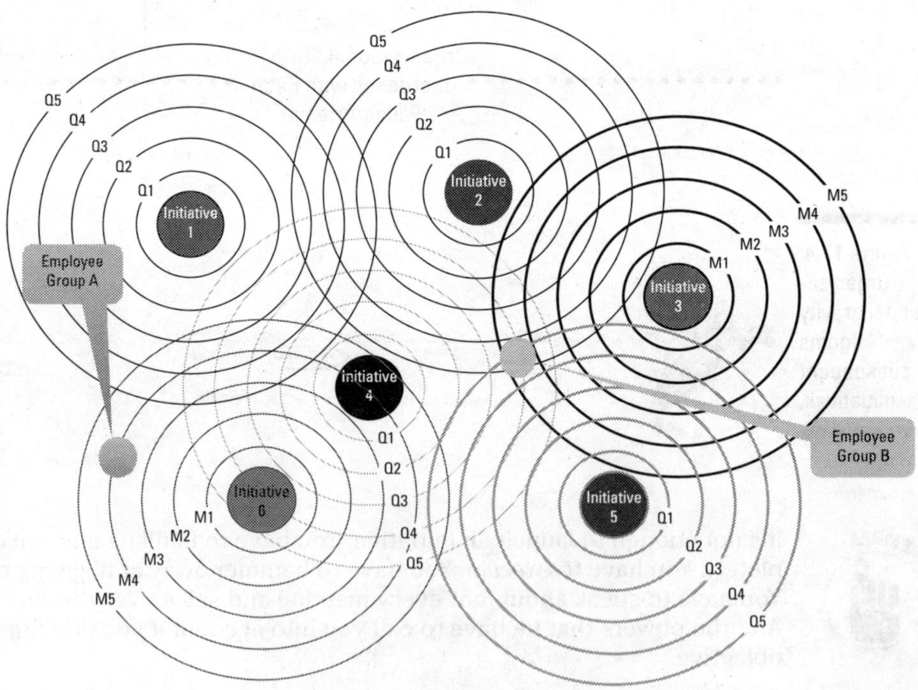

Figure 17-5: Multiple initiatives can have a significant impact on teams.

Illustration courtesy of Bain and Company.

It's imperative that senior leaders, strategic planners, project managers, and others conduct due diligence to understand not only how multiple initiatives will affect specific teams of employees but also which initiatives are really needed. In other words, you need to prioritize.

So how do you choose what to work on?

Because of the complexity and risk involved in deciding which initiatives to pursue, we recommend establishing a formal evaluation process. This process can be fairly basic or somewhat complex — something we call the *strategic initiative selection process* (SISP). We cover both approaches here.

The "basic" process

Chapter 15 talks about creating a balanced scorecard for your organization that contains all of your organization's strategies, measures, and performance ranges. This scorecard should include just those critical few financial, customer, process/technology, and people strategies that are critical to the organization's short- and long-term success.

What does this have to do with prioritizing initiatives? Simple. You should give precedence to those initiatives that mesh with the strategies outlined on your balanced scorecard.

To determine which initiatives line up with these strategies, you want to build a decision matrix. To do so, follow these steps. (Note that this process may take a few weeks.)

1. **List all the company's strategies from your balanced scorecard along the left side of the matrix.**
2. **List all your initiatives along the top.**

   Include those initiatives that are currently underway as well as those you've planned for the near term (within the next year).
3. **Have the owner of each initiative indicate which strategy her initiative will affect.**

Check out Figure 17-6 to see how this works.

	Initiative A	Initiative B	Initiative C	Initiative D	Initiative E	Initiative F	Initiative G	Initiative H
Financial Strategy #1	✓		✓			✓		
Financial Strategy #2	✓		✓			✓	✓	
Customer Strategy #1								
Customer Strategy #2		✓		✓				✓
Customer Strategy #3			✓			✓		✓
Process Strategy #1	✓	✓				✓		✓
Process Strategy #2	✓					✓		✓
People Strategy #1		✓		✓				✓
People Strategy #2				✓				

Figure 17-6: Aligning initiatives to strategy.

Illustration courtesy of Roy Barnes.

TIP

It's a good idea to ask the owner of each strategy whether she agrees that a particular initiative will have a substantial effect on said strategy. Often, the initiative owner will insist that her initiative will affect every critical strategy and measure in the company *and* solve world hunger. It's best to check the initiative owner's unbridled enthusiasm by having the strategy owner verify the accuracy of this claim. Both parties — the initiative owner and the strategy owner — should be completely aligned in terms of what the initiative will contribute to the strategy.

With your decision matrix complete, your next step is to see whether any of the listed initiatives have no effect on your corporate-level strategies. In our example, Initiative E is one such initiative. (See Figure 17-7.) Although it may seem ridiculous to think that your organization could be supporting initiatives that have zero impact on your key strategies, the sad truth is, this is surprisingly common.

REAL WORLD EXAMPLE

When I (coauthor Roy) was senior vice president of strategic planning for Marriott's leisure division, we unearthed a dozen such initiatives — some of which had been kept alive for years. I was terribly embarrassed by this until I talked to a counterpart of mine at one of the big three U.S. automakers. When he and his team had conducted this exercise, they discovered that close to one-third of his organization's non-production-line initiatives were in no way tied to the company's strategic goals and measures. Scary!

	Initiative A	Initiative B	Initiative C	Initiative D	Initiative E	Initiative F	Initiative G	Initiative H
Financial Strategy #1	✓		✓			✓		
Financial Strategy #2	✓		✓			✓	✓	
Customer Strategy #1								
Customer Strategy #2		✓	✓	✓				✓
Customer Strategy #3			✓			✓		✓
Process Strategy #1	✓	✓				✓		✓
Process Strategy #2	✓					✓		✓
People Strategy #1		✓		✓				✓
People Strategy #2				✓				

Illustration courtesy of Roy Barnes.

Figure 17-7: An initiative with no strategic purpose.

REMEMBER

An initiative that serves no strategic purpose must be killed. You must hold it underwater until its last breath is gone, dig a hole, and throw it in. You can say a few kind words if you must — after all, somebody loved that initiative once, and fed it, and kept it alive — but after you do, quickly fill the hole with as much wet concrete as you can afford. Why? Because like zombies, these initiatives have a way of resurrecting themselves. You think an initiative is dead and gone, but come budget time, it's amazing how many of them reappear!

If you look at the example decision matrix, you'll notice another problem: One of the company's key strategies, Customer Strategy #1, is supported by no initiatives of any kind. (See Figure 17-8.) Unless you believe in the power of prayer, you can assume that not much progress will be made on that particular strategy if absolutely no work is being undertaken on its behalf. Obviously, the organization needs to start some initiatives to help move the needle on this strategy!

Figure 17-9 illustrates a third concern — what we call the "all eggs in one basket" problem. Here, you can see that People Strategy #2 is supported by only one initiative. That may be all fine and good, but if that particular initiative doesn't yield the expected results, it puts the strategy itself at risk.

	Initiative A	Initiative B	Initiative C	Initiative D	Initiative E	Initiative F	Initiative G	Initiative H
Financial Strategy #1	✓		✓			✓		
Financial Strategy #2	✓		✓			✓	✓	
Customer Strategy #1								
Customer Strategy #2		✓	✓	✓				✓
Customer Strategy #3			✓			✓		✓
Process Strategy #1	✓	✓				✓		✓
Process Strategy #2	✓					✓		✓
People Strategy #1		✓		✓				✓
People Strategy #2				✓				

Figure 17-8: A strategy with no corresponding initiatives.

Illustration courtesy of Roy Barnes.

	Initiative A	Initiative B	Initiative C	Initiative D	Initiative E	Initiative F	Initiative G	Initiative H
Financial Strategy #1	✓		✓			✓		
Financial Strategy #2	✓		✓			✓	✓	
Customer Strategy #1								
Customer Strategy #2		✓	✓	✓				✓
Customer Strategy #3			✓			✓		✓
Process Strategy #1	✓	✓				✓		✓
Process Strategy #2	✓					✓		✓
People Strategy #1		✓		✓				✓
People Strategy #2				✓				

Figure 17-9: The "all eggs in one basket" problem.

Illustration courtesy of Roy Barnes.

Using your decision matrix, you can quickly identify which initiatives will likely have the greatest impact on all the stated strategies of the organization. Even conducting this simple prioritization exercise will take you and your organization a long way toward rationalizing which initiatives should get funding, keep receiving funding, or be drowned! The more measures an initiative legitimately affects, the higher its value and the more support it should receive.

The strategic initiative selection process

The strategic initiative selection process (SISP) is a more involved selection process. It builds on the "basic" model, but adds a bit more detail work. SISP involves the following four steps:

1. Developing more robust strategic prioritization filters
2. Gathering more detailed information on each initiative
3. Making prioritization decisions
4. Creating an ongoing initiative performance review and reprioritization process

Developing more robust strategic prioritization filters

In the "basic" process, you use one filter to gauge an initiative: whether it aligns with your corporate strategies. But you can use lots of different kinds of filters and even weight them differently depending on your needs. For example, in addition to strategic alignment, you can choose additional filters that consider the following:

- Relative impact on company growth
- Relative complexity to implement
- Relative financial investment required
- Relative impact on overall cost reduction
- Relative improvements to process efficiency or effectiveness
- Relative improvements to product or service quality
- Requirements for audit reconciliation or regulatory compliance
- Relative human asset investment required (that is, how many employees × how much time)
- Overall time to implement

- Relative impact on already stressed employees or work groups within your organization
- Relative need to mess with legacy technology systems or develop new technological interfaces

The list can go on and on. Just remember that the filters you use to evaluate an initiative should reflect all the considerations that you think apply to your organization's unique strategic situation.

TIP

Determining how many initiatives is the right number is a delicate balance between biting off more than you can chew and underestimating the work that needs to be done to significantly move your important strategic measures. To gauge this, measure your resource capacity — not just the number of available person-hours by organization unit but also the availability of machinery, facilities, and materials.

Gathering more detailed information on each initiative

If they're well thought out, most initiatives can be quite complex in terms of their timing, impact, phases, scope, and so forth. It's critical that you (and the broader team) take the time to *really* understand what the initiative is and what impact it will bring about. Time for a little more detective work, Sherlock!

Here are some questions to ask:

- How many initiatives are currently underway?
- In what phase of implementation are they currently?
- Who is the owner/advocate of each initiative?
- What is the stated scope of each initiative?
- What are the specific deliverables and/or metric movement commitments?
- What is the overall time frame associated with each initiative and its deliverables (short, medium, multi-year)?
- Can any of these initiatives be reduced in scope without completely sacrificing deliverables?
- What is the burn rate (in other words, how many employee hours or financial resources does the initiative consume) on a weekly/monthly basis?
- Are there any initiatives that should be killed immediately?

TIP

You may want to have each initiative owner fill out a common template that allows you to quickly scan for common information across many different initiatives. For a sample template, see Figure 17-10.

Initiative Information Template

Initiative Name: ____________

Sponsor/Owner: ____________

Strategy Connection:

Initiative Objective: ____________

Specific Strategic Measures Impacted: ____________

Key Deliverables: ____________ Start/End Dates: ____________

Key Phases: ____________ Key phase completion dates: ____________

Workgroups Impacted by Phase: ____________

Key Dependencies: ____________

Technology/Systems Dependencies: ____________

Approved Budget: ____________

Requested Budget: ____________

Approved Human Resources: ____________

Requested Human Resources: ____________

Last Status Update: ____________

Current Status Update: ____________

Recommended Next Steps and Actions: ____________

Illustration courtesy of Roy Barnes.

Figure 17-10: Initiative information template.

Making prioritization decisions

Making prioritization decisions is where things get hard. Using all the information you've gathered, you can populate a more detailed decision matrix to capture your key decision filters. When the template is populated, you and a team of appropriate senior leaders (as well as owners of each relevant measure and initiative) must meet to answer each of these questions:

- Which new initiatives should not be launched and which existing initiatives should be stopped due to a lack of strategic alignment?
- Which initiatives could be combined?
- Which initiatives will receive full funding?
- Which initiatives will not be funded?
- Which initiatives will be put off until a later date?
- What is the appropriate sequencing (order of attack) for all initiatives?
- Which initiatives will be cut back or eliminated based on future budgetary cutbacks or constraints?

Creating an ongoing initiative performance review and reprioritization process

Evaluating initiatives is not a one-and-done activity. As strategies and market conditions change, smart companies must readjust their focus, priorities, and resource allocation in kind. And of course, smart people will always think up new programs, projects, and initiatives to help the organization. New ideas come along every day.

To deal with these realities, you must develop a disciplined and formal process by which you review your existing initiatives, as well as a process to collect and review emerging ideas. To achieve this, schedule a standing meeting to assess the performance of your existing initiatives, evaluate ideas for new initiatives, and reprioritize as needed. In this way, you can prevent the organization from slipping back into the habit of launching more initiatives than it can successfully support. In addition, you can ensure that the initiatives that *are* launched are those that will likely have the greatest positive impact on the organization.

At each of these quarterly meetings, you want to do the following:

- Review the notes from the previous meeting to identify any open issues.
- For each initiative, report the projected performance and the actual performance.

- Discuss any modifications to initiative scope, budget, or timing.
- Discuss any proposed new initiatives. (Consider setting a resource/monetary threshold for proposed initiatives. That way, the team won't get bogged down reviewing small initiatives. For example, you might only review initiatives with spending over $100,000 or requiring 1,000 or more work hours.)
- Decide which, if any, new initiatives will receive approval and funding.
- Take notes on all decisions and publish those meeting notes widely throughout the organization. That way, everyone will know which initiatives are officially approved (and sanctioned) and which ones are not.

Putting Your Money Where Your Mouth Is: Budgeting for STRATEX

Unfortunately, most organizations have no solid synergy between their strategy development process and their budgeting process. But according to Bill Kaplan and Dave Norton, who invented the balanced scorecard (and with whom Roy worked during his tenure at Marriott), these two processes must be in close alignment. Otherwise, the organization simply won't achieve sound, predictable, or dependable strategic execution. Put more simply, the best strategic plan in the world won't work if it never gets funded.

Along these lines, Kaplan and Norton have developed an idea that builds on the financial concepts of operating expense (OPEX) and capital expenditure (CAPEX) — something they call STRATEX, short for *strategy execution expense*. In a budgeting model that includes STRATEX, the initiatives and investments required to implement the organization's strategy are funded separately from all the other ongoing operational and capital costs. In other words, all funding decisions pertaining to the pursuit of the organization's strategic goals are separated out and invested for separately. The idea is to isolate those specific activities that are linked to strategic results and manage the budgeting for them as an entirely discrete exercise.

What kinds of customer initiatives might you want to include in a customer STRATEX budget? Here are a few ideas:

- Funding for employees to participate on a touchpoint redesign team
- Funding for ideas, process changes, or additional customer communication collateral that the touchpoint redesign team may suggest

- Funding for deeper and more robust customer feedback and dialogue capabilities (surveys)
- Funding for additional internal (employee-centered) communications
- Funding for additional variable compensation/bonuses for improved customer result performance
- Funding to hire a top-notch customer experience expert to help you through the process (hint-hint)

Using the STRATEX approach enables most organizations to reap enormous benefits, including the following:

- It enables them to pull back from a widely distributed, often untraceable, and unwieldy funding model for strategic initiatives.
- It allows them to make strategic investments much more visible.
- It allows STRATEX investments to be examined with the same level of scrutiny as other investments. This leads to greater transparency and necessary performance accountability for initiative owners and supporters. They have to prove the value of their investments!

Why is STRATEX important? Because if you are serious about improving customer experience, you need to fund a significant amount of new activity. This includes touchpoint redesign teams, process improvements, and other customer-focused initiatives. And these funding requests have to go toe-to-toe with other similar requests from across the organization.

If you can convince the powers that be to isolate specific strategy budget funds using a STRATEX-like model, you'll give your strategic customer initiatives a fighting chance. If you don't, there's a strong likelihood they'll get lost in all the other day-to-day operational budget line items. Bring visibility to customer strategy items any way you can!

Part V
The Part of Tens

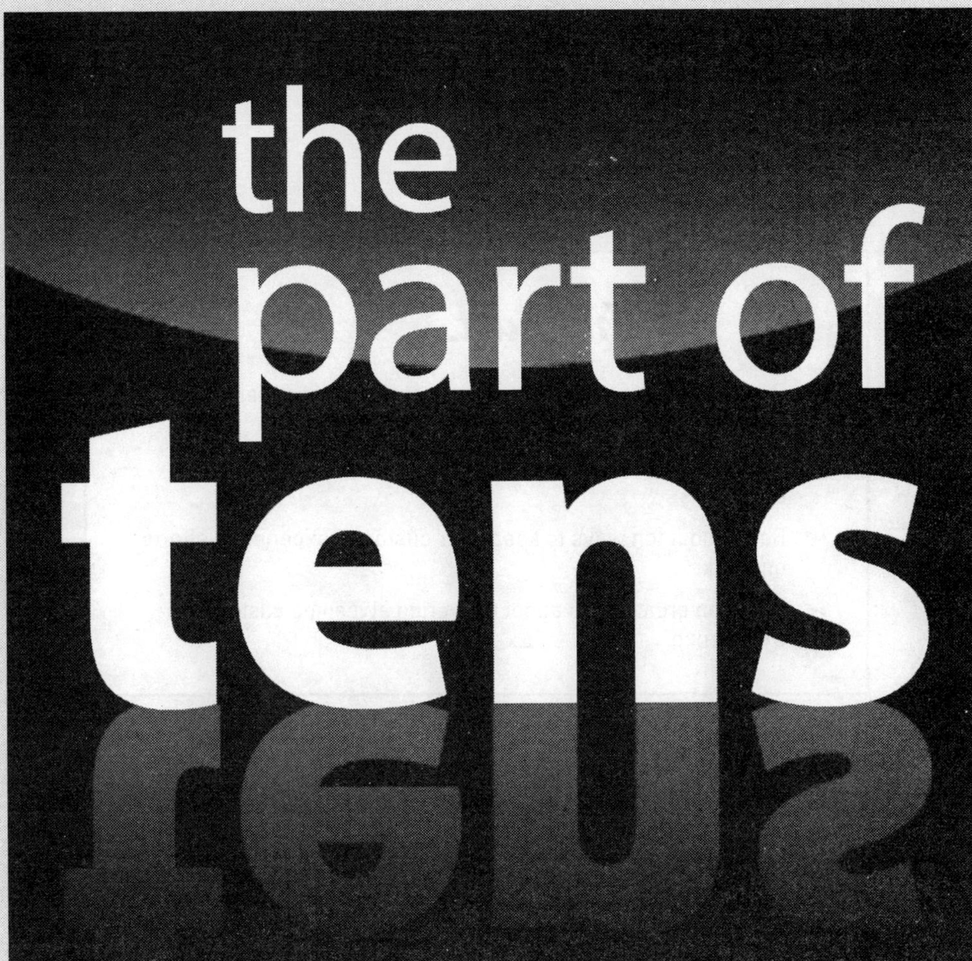

For ten tips on how to find more information about improving customer experience, head to a free article on `www.dummies.com/extras/customerexperience`.

In this part...

- Discover ten ways to improve your customer experience delivery.
- Find ten key qualities of awesome customer experience advocates.
- Read about ten ways to keep your customer experience efforts on track.
- Read ten great books about delivering awesome customer experience.

Chapter 18

Ten Ways to Improve Your Experience Delivery

In This Chapter

- Exercising patience and listening
- Becoming an expert in your area
- Being proactive, following through, and persevering
- Triaging customers
- Understanding the importance of smiling and body language

Want to improve your own customer experience delivery in a hurry? Here are ten things you can change *today* that will make an instantaneous impact on your customer interactions.

Be Patient

Patience, as they say, is a virtue — and it's one that people who deal with customers must have in buckets. Here are some tips for dipping into your inner well of patience when dealing with a difficult customer (or other work frustrations):

- Take a deep breath and let it out slowly.
- If you're dealing with a customer on the phone, ask her to hold for just one moment. Then consciously focus on relaxing your body.
- If you're dealing with a customer face-to-face, remove yourself from his presence for a moment. Step into a back-office area and slap a coworker if need be. (Kidding!)
- Slow down your speech. Sometimes by acting patient, you can feel patient.

- Try to remember that it's not personal. The customer isn't mad at *you* — at least, she shouldn't be.

It also helps to pinpoint what's triggering your loss of patience. Could it be something *other* than the customer — say, lack of sleep, a too-long shift, or stress at home? Regardless of the cause, can you do something to interrupt this pattern? Try standing up and walking around, taking some deep breaths, or squeezing a stress ball.

Really Listen

It simply isn't possible to truly help a customer if you don't listen to her needs. Moreover, customers know when you're not listening to them, and their frustration level rises accordingly.

Listening requires more than just hearing. To listen, you must *really focus* on what another person is saying. That means staying quiet and working hard to understand the message behind the other person's words. Here are some tips to help you improve your listening skills:

- Don't be distracted by whatever else is going on around you. Focus on the customer.
- Don't think about what your response is going to be. Hear the customer out before you begin formulating your response.
- Show that you're listening by acknowledging what the person is saying. A simple nod of the head or a "Yes, I understand" does the trick.
- Repeating back what the customer said verifies that you're hearing her correctly. This is important!
- If you're face-to-face with the customer, pay attention to both his verbal and nonverbal communication, as well as his body language.
- Don't be afraid to say, "Tell me more about that." Sometimes customers need a little prodding to get to the root of what's really bothering them.

Know Your Stuff

You may have a winning smile, a personality without peer, and an uncanny ability to connect with customers. But if you're not an expert on your company's product or service, you are of absolutely no help to a customer who is in need of expertise. You are, as we like to say, "delightfully clueless."

Some organizations feel that it's perfectly reasonable to let new, customer-facing employees loose after a shift or two shadowing someone who theoretically "knows the ropes." Bad idea! All employees — especially customer-facing staff — need time to grasp the details and nuances of the business before they are put in contact with customers. Really, no one should interface with the customer unless she has the requisite knowledge to answer at least 80 percent of the questions customers are likely to ask her. That's why the Ritz-Carlton Hotel Group reportedly trains its staff for more than four weeks before allowing them to deal directly with its guests!

So be an expert. Make it your mission to know your product and service line inside and out, so you'll be able to answer just about any question a customer throws at you. Knowing your stuff enables you to move quickly, make the right decisions, and find workable solutions for your customers.

If you find yourself stumped by a customer's question, simply admit that you don't know the answer. (It turns out, "I don't know" is a trust-building statement! It lends credibility to the answers you *are* able to provide.) Then vow to find out and report back.

Show a Yearn to Learn

Yes, you should strive to become an expert in your area (see the preceding section). But you'll quickly find that the more you know about your area of expertise, the more there is to learn.

You must *own* your personal learning and development. Don't wait for someone else to identify what you need to know. Seek feedback from lots of different sources on how to improve and develop. When training is offered, participate fully. Finally, integrate and apply what you learn into your everyday existing work style and flow.

Be Proactive

If you're looking to provide a great experience, you cannot be passive. You must take charge and control the experience the customer is going to receive. You must be proactive.

As soon as you understand a customer's problem, work to offer a solution. If others need to be involved in the solution-making, reach out to them quickly. Gather all relevant information from whatever sources are available. Ideally, you'll be able to solve the customer's problem right away. If you can't, tell the customer exactly how long it will be before you can, and then deliver on that timeline.

As you're working to solve the problem, be decisive. Your ability to be decisive stems from your understanding of the nuances of your business. Don't wait longer than is absolutely necessary to develop a plan of resolution and execute on it.

Follow Through

If you tell a customer you're going to do something, do it. Keep your word. Your promise is a commitment. It's a bond. Nothing is more frustrating for a customer than being told "Let me look into this and I'll get back to you" and then never hearing from the company representative again. It destroys trust, confidence, and the relationship you've worked so hard to create with your customers. And if you don't have an answer just yet, let them know. Bad news is better than no news!

Persevere

> *In the confrontation between the stream and the rock, the stream always wins, not through strength but by perseverance.*
>
> *—H. Jackson Brown*

Look, dealing with customers can be tough. No matter how patient, proactive, or engaging you are, every so often, somebody is just going to let you have it. Fairly or not, he's going to direct all his pent-up anger and frustration at you. That's where perseverance comes in.

Letting all those negative emotions roll off your back like water off a duck isn't easy, but let them you must. You simply cannot permit yourself to wallow in the negativity. You must pick yourself up, dust yourself off, and let it go. Here are some tips to help you:

- **Review your company's customer experience intent statement.** It will help to remind you of why it is you're doing what you're doing.
- **Set small, discrete goals for a call or customer interaction.** Anything broken up into smaller steps is more easily achieved — even dealing with a particularly obnoxious customer. For example, your goal might be to get the customer to say "yes" twice in a row or to get her to ask you a question.

- **Try something new.** Use a different story, analogy, or script than you normally use. Sometimes, changing things up a little can foster a different type of interaction between you and your customers.
- **Try and try again.** Babe Ruth once said, "Every time I strike out, I get closer to hitting a home run." The issue isn't failing; it's getting up and trying again. Learn from your mistakes.
- **Get support.** No one who's really great at delivering awesome customer experience is a solo act. Build your support system. Find people who persevere and overcome. Hang out with them and learn their tricks.

Be Fast on Your Feet

Those who interact with customers on a regular basis must be fast on their feet. That is, they must be able to triage a situation without really thinking. Think about how first responders such as EMTs or ER nurses react when faced with several badly injured accident victims: They quickly determine who needs their attention first, and then prioritize from there. As someone who deals with customers, you must do the same.

To help yourself prepare for this, establish a set of triage guidelines. Do this *before* you're confronted with an unhappy customer. In these guidelines, include the name of your go-to person (or people) — that is, the person you'll contact when you don't know what to do. Be sure to have his or her (or their) contact info handy. Also, decide what information you'll send up the chain of command if you're confronted with a customer challenge that is above your pay grade. Will you need to pass on verbatim recordings of an interaction? Will you need to share the customer's purchase history with the company? Whatever it is, try to be ready to communicate the whole story.

Smile

Like yawning, smiling is contagious. Unless you're super creepy, when you smile at somebody, that person will probably smile back. A sincere smile works wonders! If you can keep smiling even when everything around you is going to heck in a hand basket, you'll find that others will smile, too.

A smile is so powerful, people can *hear* it. Your voice sounds different when you smile! Even people who are speaking with you on the phone will be able to detect it. Don't believe us? Put a small mirror right by your work telephone. Right before you pick up your next call, stop, look, and smile. You'll be amazed at the different reception you get from your customers!

Manage Your Body Language

When it comes to how people perceive you, nonverbal communication — that is, body language — is extremely influential. In fact, some reports suggest that up to 50 percent of the meaning that people take from an interaction with another is based on this type of communication. That means when you're dealing with customers, you need to be aware of what signals your body may be sending! Here are a few points to keep in mind:

- **Don't shield your body.** Holding a notebook, a clipboard, or even a coffee cup in front of you may send the message that you are shy or uncomfortable.
- **Keep your hands away from your face.** This is a common "tell" when someone is being deceptive. (Are you listening, all you Poker players?) Also, avoid stroking your chin while looking at someone; it may be interpreted as you being judgmental.
- **Don't fake-smile.** A fake smile is easy to spot and sends entirely the wrong message. Whereas a real smile causes the corners of your eyes to wrinkle and changes the expression of your entire face, a fake smile involves only the mouth and lips. If you're dealing with a customer face-to-face, look him directly in the eye and smile naturally.
- **Watch where you stand.** Don't be a "close talker," like that guy on *Seinfeld.* That is, don't stand 4 inches away from the customer while speaking to him. Most people consider the 2 or 3 feet surrounding their body to be their "personal space." You may come closer if you're invited, but otherwise, keep your distance. If you notice people backing away from you, this may be why (or maybe a breath mint would help).
- **Keep your hands out of your pockets.** Although humans have used spoken language for millions of years, they still employ their hands to communicate. Don't hide them! It just seems weird.
- **Don't fidget.** I (coauthor Roy) once flew cross-country next to a guy who clicked and unclicked his ballpoint pen *the entire time.* Trust me: If you do that around your customers, they will go insane.
- **Stand up straight.** Posture is one of the first things people notice. It instantly relays how you feel about yourself, whether it's confident and alert or shy and retiring.
- **Face the person you're talking to.** Turning away from someone while speaking to them suggests a certain level of disinterest or discomfort. Ever tried talking to a teenager texting on her phone? Give them your full attention.
- **Stand still.** This isn't *Dancing with the Stars!* Constant movement — for example, shifting your weight from side to side — suggests that you are uncomfortable, either physically or mentally, or that you want to abandon the conversation.

Chapter 19

Ten Key Qualities of Awesome Customer Experience Advocates

In This Chapter

- Knowing the enemy
- Partaking in a "commitment culture"
- Communicating powerfully and dealing with bureaucracy
- Finding like-minded souls
- Being courageous, going the distance, and staying engaged

What do we mean by *customer experience advocates?* Simple. We're talking about those employees who lead, direct, and foster change in the area of building and sustaining a customer-centric culture. This chapter discusses ten key qualities of awesome customer advocates.

They Know Their Corporate Culture May Be the Enemy

The great military strategist Sun T'zu once said:

> If you know your enemies and know yourself, you will not be imperiled in a hundred battles; if you do not know your enemies nor yourself, you will be imperiled in every single battle.

So what is the enemy of the customer advocate? Perhaps, it's your company's current culture.

As you confront the realities of an intransigent corporate culture, an understanding of Newton's Laws of Motion (albeit slightly modified) will serve you well:

- A body in motion (your company) tends to stay in motion unless an external force (your efforts) is applied to it.
- Movement is produced when a force acts on a mass. The greater (the larger and more entrenched) the mass of the object (the organization being moved), the greater the amount of force (by you) needed.
- For every action, there's an equal and opposite reaction. (Be careful not to get your butt kicked in the midst of trying to change the organization.)

Moving your organization takes substantial effort. You need to apply all the cultural change tools available to you. For more on these, see Chapter 14.

Moreover, it requires tremendous personal courage. Often, being a strong customer advocate means taking on the existing organizational establishment. Don't underestimate the challenge before you!

They're Part of the "Commitment Culture"

As noted by transformational leadership experts Carol and Jack Weber of the University of Virginia Darden School of Business, many organizations have a *compliance* culture rather than a *commitment* culture. The difference between these two cultures is spelled out here:

Compliance Culture	***Commitment Culture***
Business as usual	Want to really believe it
Have to go through the motions	Understand the "why"
Do what we're told	Self-motivated
Feel burdened	Feel excited
Feel constrained	Think for yourself
Stay out of trouble	Want to excel
Do the bare minimum	Go beyond requirements
Wait for instructions	Take action
Need more supervision	Intent directed
Quickly yield to pressure	Emotionally compelled and engaged

It's the job of the customer experience advocate to help transition employees from a compliance culture to a commitment culture. Just be warned: It isn't easy. As noted by Italian historian, politician, diplomat, and writer Niccolo Machiavelli more than 500 years ago:

> There is nothing more perilous to conduct, or more uncertain in its success, than to take the lead in the introduction of a new order of things, because the innovator has for enemies all those who have done well under the old conditions, and lukewarm defenders in those who may do well under the new.

They Declare Themselves

To be an awesome customer experience advocate, you must take a stand. You must make your opinions known. You must draw your line in the sand to let people know what's important to you. You must *declare* yourself.

Most of the time, when people communicate, they make assertions. *Assertions* are statements about the past, present, or future for which one can provide evidence or rely on previously known facts. Making assertions is "safe" talk. When you make assertions, you *talk about* things rather than *speak for* things.

A more impactful way to communicate is to make declarations. A *declaration* is a statement about a future to which one is committed, but for which there is little or no current evidence. When you make a declaration, you speak for something rather than talk about it.

They're Believable

To communicate your views on customer experience, whether in public or in private, you must forge an emotional connection with your audience. You must be *believable.*

Believability is overwhelmingly determined at the preconscious level — in other words, in the first brain. The *first brain* is the part of the human brain that is ancient and primitive. It's the source of instinctual survival responses like hunger, thirst, and the sensing of danger. Our first brain is similar to that of many animals. (This stands in contrast to our *new brain.* Intellectual and advanced, it gets all the attention. Our new brain is uniquely human. It's the source of rational thought, consciousness, memory, language, creativity, planning, and decision-making.)

To reach your audience's new brain, you must get past the gatekeeper — their first brain. And to do that, you must be believable.

Believability comes from your core, and it can't be faked. It is best created by establishing trust. For its part, trust comes from you consistently behaving a certain way — in what you say and in what you do. It also comes from being personally committed to what you're advocating.

They Say Thanks

Excellent customer experience advocates say thanks — and they say it often, regardless of whether the "thank-ee's" contribution was big or small.

So what's the best way to say thanks? Ask your grandmother. She'll tell you that sending a handwritten note is the way to go. When you take the time to send a handwritten note, it will *never* be forgotten.

Your note can be straight and to the point or can reflect your unique style and sensibility. Look at two thank you notes that follow. The first is from late-night TV host Conan O'Brien to a girl who asked him to her prom. The second is from Audrey Hepburn to Henry Mancini, who wrote the Academy Award–winning musical score for her movie, *Breakfast at Tiffany's.* Both notes reflect the writer's personality, and both are unforgettable.

> Dear Nikki,
>
> Thanks for your very flattering offer. It's great to know I have such a devoted fan out there, and I'm sure you would make a great prom date (I didn't go to mine — it's a very *sad* story). Unfortunately, I got married recently and my wife doesn't allow me to go to proms anymore with cute 16-year-old girls. Still, it was very cool of you to ask me. Thanks and have a great evening.
>
> Your Friend, Conan

> Dear Henry,
>
> I have just seen our picture — Breakfast at Tiffany's — this time with your musical score. A movie without music is a little bit like an aeroplane without fuel. However beautifully the job is done, we are still on the ground and in a world of reality. Your music has lifted us all up and sent us soaring. Everything we cannot say with words or show with action you have expressed for us. You have done this with so much imagination, fun and beauty. You are the hippest of cats — and the most sensitive of composers! Thank you, dear Hank.
>
> Lots of love, Audrey

They Can Deal with Bureaucracy

Trust us: In your efforts to improve customer experience, you will eventually run head-on into your organization's bureaucracy. If you don't deal with it the right way, this red tape will leave you exhausted and frustrated.

Here are a few tips for effectively navigating the bureaucracy in your organization:

- **Know exactly what you are trying to accomplish.** To the extent that you can, be clear about the resources you need, the process you want to implement, and/or the benefit(s) you're trying to create.
- **Learn how the bureaucracy operates.** Break it down into its component parts. That way, what looks like a tangled, impassable system will appear more manageable.
- **Understand the approval process.** Nothing is more frustrating than getting to what you thought was the end of the approval process and discovering that you're missing some critical step or additional sign-off!
- **Ask questions.** Not clear on some bureaucratic procedure? Ask someone to explain it to you. It's also usually okay to question why a certain rule or policy exists — just try not to sound too argumentative if you do.
- **Identify the gatekeepers.** Most bureaucratic approval processes involve two kinds of people: the ultimate decision-makers and the *gatekeepers.* The latter of these filter and pass along information used in the decision-making process. Keep the gatekeepers involved as much as you can in every step of your thinking and planning.
- **Do it in person.** The likelihood of you moving contentious issues to resolution depends on your ability to understand the specific needs and issues of the people who will be affected by the change. That means you need to make every sale personally. In other words, no email, no texting, and no memos!

  To the extent that it's possible, every communication you have when navigating bureaucracy should be in person. Yes, simple questions can be answered over the phone. But if your request is a complicated one, make it in person. A face-to-face encounter reduces the chances of a miscommunication and exponentially increases the likelihood of adoption.
- **Be friendly and courteous.** Odds are, the person you want to help you is already being pulled in a million different directions by other people with requests of their own. And there's a good chance those other people were rude or impatient. By being friendly and courteous, you

make a good impression, and you increase the likelihood that the person will help you. And besides, you never know when you may need this person's help again!

- **Remember that a bureaucracy is made up of individuals just like you.** Well, maybe they're not as smart or good-looking as you are, but they are still people nonetheless. (At least, most of them are.) The trick is to view a bureaucracy as a group of people to cooperate with rather than an adversary to fight against.

They Find Customer Experience Co-Conspirators

You are not alone! The secret is to find people who share your views. If the online world has proven anything, it's that you are not alone. These days, you can find any number of people around the world whose perspectives and interests closely align with yours. In the online world, people interact anonymously. This can lead to a wide-open environment where people are very comfortable with expressing who they truly are.

But when we unplug from this online world, human interactions quickly change. All of a sudden, everyone becomes much more careful about revealing his true interests and points of view. To fit in, people dress alike, act alike, and only express their opinions when they know the group is likely to agree with them.

As a customer experience advocate, your job is to persuade these people to once again reveal their true selves — even if they aren't online. Think of yourself as a great liberator of souls. Yes, we know: When everyone is pretending to be "normal," it's hard to find people who share your passion for customer experience. But they are out there. We promise. Reveal yourself and your point of view, and so will they.

They're Courageous

Anytime you try to break the mold — anytime you try to do something different, like change the customer experience at your organization — you need courage. But of course, courage isn't always easy to come by.

Fortunately, American essayist and lecturer Ralph Waldo Emerson wrote a little something that should give you a boost:

> Whatever you do, you need courage. Whatever course you decide upon, there is always someone to tell you that you are wrong. There are always difficulties arising that tempt you to believe your critics are right. To map out a course of action and follow it to an end requires some of the same courage that a soldier needs. Our greatest glory is not in never failing, but in rising up every time we fail.

They Go the Distance

Fixing customer experience is a marathon, not a sprint. In endurance activities of any kind, the objective is to hang in there until the end. You have to pace yourself. It's a big risk to push yourself too hard in the beginning. As Tom Holland, a sport-performance coach and the author of *The Marathon Method* and *The 12-Week Triathlete,* notes, "It's not who goes the fastest but who slows down the least."

Mental stamina is also called for. At the most basic level, you can build stamina by taking care of yourself. Manage your stress and get enough sleep. Then make sure you plan for setbacks. Somewhere along the line, you're going to get knocked down by some intransigent bureaucrat. Have a plan for how you're going to pick yourself back up. Every marathon runner hits the wall eventually. Prepare for it now.

Finally, think positively. Nothing builds mental toughness and resilience better than self-confidence. Listen to the internal words that you are saying to yourself. If they're negative, shut them down. Consciously give yourself more positive messages.

They're Engaged

Are you wondering what the top quality of awesome customer experience advocates is? In a word: Engagement! You want employees who are fully involved and enthusiastic about their work. The best customer experience advocates are those who are inspired and deeply committed not only to their specific jobs but to the company's mission overall.

Engaged employees talk about the future with energy and excitement. They give extra discretionary effort to ensure that the right results happen. It's not just about employees who are willing to put in the extra hours, it's about ones who are enamored with the end result — the ones who just can't wait to see how it all turns out.

Engaged employees are out there, but they are likely to be in pretty short supply. According to Gallup's "State of the Global Workplace" report, only 13 percent of employees worldwide are engaged at work. It's better news in the United States, but even here, just 30 percent are engaged at work.

If you'd like to find out how to boost engagement in your workforce, check out *Employee Engagement for Dummies* (published by Wiley) by Bob Kelleher, coauthor of this book!

Chapter 20

Ten Tools to Track Your Customer Experience Program's Performance

In This Chapter

- Exploring tools to track your progress on each step of your customer engagement program
- Looking at a tool to gauge your progress overall
- Recognizing the role of your customer experience dashboard — the ultimate tool

This book focuses on eight primary steps to improve customer experience:

1. Developing and deploying your customer experience intent statement
2. Building journey maps
3. Redesigning customer touchpoints
4. Getting feedback from customers and creating dialogue
5. Building customer experience knowledge in the workforce
6. Recognizing and rewarding a job well done
7. Executing an integrated internal communications plan
8. Building a customer performance dashboard

This chapter provides tools you can use to gauge your progress on each of these steps, enabling you to see what you've done so far and get a handle on what still needs to be accomplished. Feel free to copy these tools and use them in your efforts to improve customer experience in your own organization!

These tools are, in effect, questionnaires. Each one includes a list of tasks; your job is to indicate your status on each one. Rate your status as follows:

- **Thinking about doing:** 1 point
- **Plan to do:** 2 points
- **Initiated:** 3 points
- **50 percent complete:** 4 points
- **100 percent complete:** 5 points

Then, add the total number of points and divide that sum by two to determine your score.

In addition to providing tools to help you gauge your progress on each step, this chapter provides one to help you gauge your progress on implementing your customer experience program as a whole. Finally, you revisit the customer experience dashboard, discussed in Chapter 15.

Developing and Deploying Your Customer Experience Intent Statement

The customer experience intent statement is a descriptive paragraph that outlines two things:

- The experience that your organization wants to deliver
- The emotions that you want to elicit in your customers when they interact with you

Use Figure 20-1 to gauge your progress on developing and deploying your customer experience intent statement. For more on the customer experience intent statement, see Chapter 6.

Activity	Thinking About: 1 Point	Plan to Do: 2 Points	Initiated: 3 Points	50% Complete: 4 Points	100% Complete: 5 Points
Develop the intent statement					
Circulate final draft to senior leaders					
Finalize the intent statement					
Publicize the intent statement					
Scoring					
					Total Step Score ÷ 5

Figure 20-1: Gauge your progress on your customer experience intent statement.

Illustration courtesy of Roy Barnes.

Building Touchpoint/Journey Maps

A customer journey map visually represents all the different points of interaction between your organization and its customers. As you build your own customer journey maps, remember to think enterprise-wide, across all possible customer interactions. Figure 20-2 contains key markers that you can use to track your efforts in this arena. (For more on building journey maps, see Chapter 7.)

Activity	Thinking About: 1 Point	Plan to Do: 2 Points	Initiated: 3 Points	50% Complete: 4 Points	100% Complete: 5 Points
Describe the major "buckets" of customer interaction					
Describe all customer touchpoints					
Socialize and review touchpoint map across organization for completeness					
Publicize the customer journey map					
Scoring					
					Total Step Score ÷ 5

Figure 20-2: Track your efforts in building touchpoint maps.

Illustration courtesy of Roy Barnes.

Redesigning Touchpoints

As we discuss in Chapter 10, redesigning a customer touchpoint is a four-week (20 workday) effort that involves brainstorming, proposing change, and, most importantly, executing that change. To keep your redesign efforts on track, use the questionnaire in Figure 20-3.

Activity	Thinking About: 1 Point	Plan to Do: 2 Points	Initiated: 3 Points	50% Complete: 4 Points	100% Complete: 5 Points
Determine "ideal" customer behaviors					
Prioritize "high-value" touchpoints					
Baseline current touchpoint performance and build metrics					
Select redesign team members					
Field touchpoint redesign teams					
Scoring					
					Total Step Score ÷ 5

Figure 20-3: Get a handle on your progress redesigning touchpoints.

Illustration courtesy of Roy Barnes.

Getting Feedback from Customers and Establishing Dialogue

Real-time customer feedback is available at all major customer touchpoints. In addition, current performance is attributable and visible for all customer-facing employees. To stay abreast of customer feedback, use the questionnaire in Figure 20-4. (Chapter 11 discusses managing customer feedback.)

Activity	Thinking About: 1 Point	Plan to Do: 2 Points	Initiated: 3 Points	50% Complete: 4 Points	100% Complete: 5 Points
Inventory current listening today					
Prioritize high-value listening touchpoints					
Create baseline touchpoint performance metrics					
Set governance model for managing VOC					
Communicate customer response standards					
Scoring					
					Total Step Score ÷ 5

Figure 20-4: Keeping abreast of customer feedback.

Illustration courtesy of Roy Barnes.

Building Customer Experience Knowledge in the Workforce

Employees who interact with customers on a regular basis must understand not only your organization's customer experience intent, but also how to deliver that experience. That means ensuring they receive the right training. The questionnaire in Figure 20-5 is designed to help you get a handle on what training has been delivered and what still needs to be done. (For more on building customer experience knowledge in the workforce, see Chapter 12.)

Activity	Thinking About: 1 Point	Plan to Do: 2 Points	Initiated: 3 Points	50% Complete: 4 Points	100% Complete: 5 Points
Foundational customer experience training (all employees)					
Role-specific skills training for customer-facing employees					
Skills training for touchpoint redesigners					
Conflict management and problem-resolution training					
Scoring					
					Total Step Score ÷ 5

Figure 20-5: Track your training efforts.

Illustration courtesy of Roy Barnes.

Recognizing and Rewarding a Job Well Done

Your compensation system informs your entire organization of what's really important and what isn't. Unless this system, as well as other rewards and recognition programs, support customer focus, your best efforts to make your culture customer-centric will ultimately fail. The same is true if individuals who "make their numbers" but ignore or injure customer experience are allowed to achieve success in your organization. To assess the degree to which your compensation system and other rewards and recognition programs promote excellent customer experience, use the questionnaire in Figure 20-6. For more on recognition and rewards, see Chapter 13.

Activity	Thinking About: 1 Point	Plan to Do: 2 Points	Initiated: 3 Points	50% Complete: 4 Points	100% Complete: 5 Points
Inventory existing monetary incentives					
Move variable compensation to include customer results					
Inventory existing recognition programs and include customer performance					
Exact consequences for non-performance					
Scoring					
					Total Step Score ÷ 5

Figure 20-6: Assess your compensation system and other rewards and recognition programs with regard to customer experience.

Illustration courtesy of Roy Barnes.

Executing an Integrated Internal Communications Plan

If organizational leaders rarely mention customer concerns, issues, or opportunities, all the best internal marketing will fall short of creating significant culture change. To help change the culture, you need a tightly focused communications plan. Figure 20-7 outlines the key steps and enables you to track your progress on them. (Chapter 14 discusses the development of a communications plan in more detail.)

Activity	Thinking About: 1 Point	Plan to Do: 2 Points	Initiated: 3 Points	50% Complete: 4 Points	100% Complete: 5 Points
Inventory existing internal communication channels and messaging					
Create messaging and channel content					
Distribute customer survey data and touchpoint redesign results					
Measure "adoption" in employee 2x yearly opinion surveys					
Scoring					
					Total Step Score ÷ 5

Figure 20-7: Track your progress on your internal communications plan.

Illustration courtesy of Roy Barnes.

Building a Customer Performance Dashboard

Feel-good customer initiatives are not the way to go. These must be replaced with laser-guided projects that feature clear and formal performance metrics and owned commitments. And of course, you must carefully track those metrics to drive accountability and improvement. To do so, you'll want to build a customer performance dashboard, as discussed in Chapter 15. For help, refer to the questionnaire in Figure 20-8.

Activity	Thinking About: 1 Point	Plan to Do: 2 Points	Initiated: 3 Points	50% Complete: 4 Points	100% Complete: 5 Points
Set enterprise customer strategies					
Determine leading and lagging customer metrics					
Assign measure ownership					
Align initiatives to ensure measure contribution					
Conduct monthly reviews of customer metrics					
Scoring					
					Total Step Score ÷ 5

Illustration courtesy of Roy Barnes.

Figure 20-8: Keep abreast of key metrics.

The Customer Experience Progress Tracking Tool

In Figure 20-9, each of the eight customer experience implementation steps appears around the edges of the diagram. To utilize this customer experience progress tracking tool, transfer your step scores onto each ring of the diagram to see how you're doing. For an example of what your plot line may look like, see Figure 20-10.

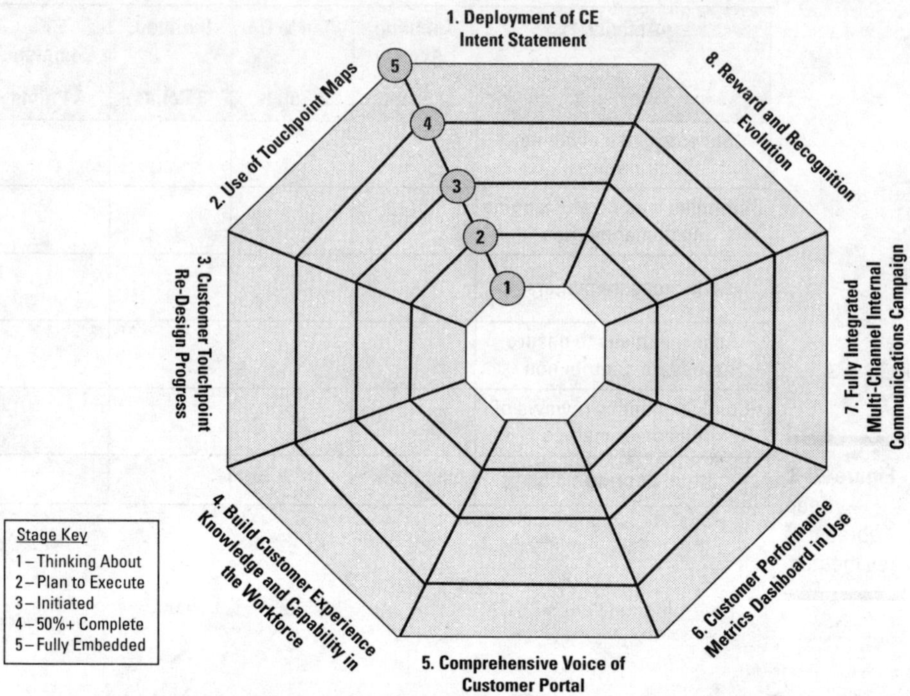

Figure 20-9: Transfer your step scores onto each ring of the diagram.

Illustration courtesy of Roy Barnes.

We strongly suggest that you conduct this exercise every six months. You can overlay each line over the previous one to see your progress. The goal, of course, is to move every step to Ring 5.

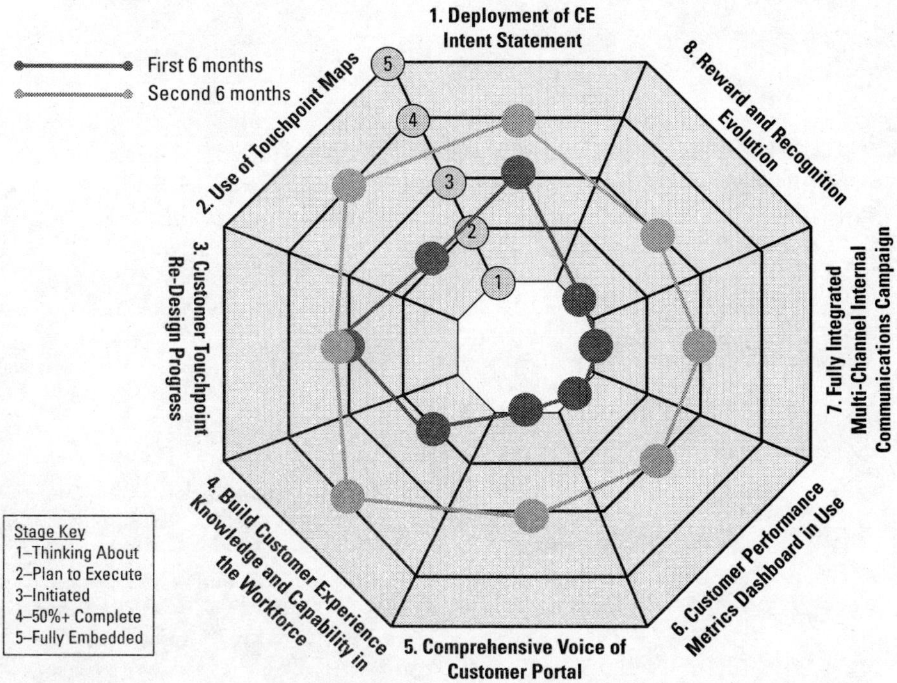

Figure 20-10: Your plot line might look something like this.

Illustration courtesy Roy Barnes.

Understanding the Importance of the Customer Performance Dashboard

In the end, customer experience must be quantifiable. You must do everything you can to build and monitor a set of easy-to-understand performance metrics that focuses both on customer results and the impact those results have on the business. Chapter 15 lays out the format for doing just that by creating a dashboard, or scorecard. Your customer experience dashboard is the ultimate tool for keeping track of your progress, organization-wide.

Chapter 21

Ten(ish) Great Books for Boosting Customer Experience

In This Chapter

- Knowing where to look to delve deeper into specific topics
- Exploring other aspects of customer experience

Customer experience management is a budding, dynamic discipline. Like most new disciplines, the field of customer experience management is evolving in both sophistication and depth. Emerging sub-fields include customer research, analytics, experience and user design, customer experience marketing, journey mapping, touchpoint management, and emotion management. This chapter lists ten great books, in no particular order, to help you find your bearings in this exciting field.

The Experience Economy

Consumers face a torrent of brands, attacking from all sides. How can you make yours stand out? By staging customer experiences that leave a memorable impression, according to *The Experience Economy* by B. Joseph Pine II and James H. Gilmore (published by Harper Business Review Press). Indeed, for Pine and Gilmore, these experiences are the missing link between a company and its potential audience. For even more insight from this dynamic duo, check out their book *Authenticity: What Consumers Really Want* (also from Harvard Business Review Press). It can help you determine whether your customer experience intent statement is authentic.

Building Great Customer Experiences

In *Building Great Customer Experiences* (published by Palgrave Macmillan), one of the early books on building and delivering great customer experiences, authors Colin Shaw and John Ivens demonstrate that the emotional impact of customer experiences ultimately determines customer satisfaction and loyalty. And *that*, in turn, drives the commercial success of both companies and brands. Still not sold on the importance of customer experience? This book, which features compelling examples and case studies, should change your mind!

Delivering Happiness: A Path to Profits, Passion, and Purpose

Zappos, an online retailer that boasts more than $1 billion (with a "B") in annual gross merchandise sales, is known for its progressive policies and corporate culture. In *Delivering Happiness: A Path to Profits, Passion, and Purpose*, the hip, iconoclastic CEO of Zappos, Tony Hsieh, shares the lessons he has learned in business and life. According to Hsieh, the key to success is focusing on the happiness of those around you — your customers *and* your employees. Of particular note here is how Hsieh integrates customer experience values into every aspect of his business.

The Nordstrom Way: The Inside Story of America's #1 Customer Service Company

If you've ever visited a Nordstrom store, you've probably noticed that their customer service is second to none. And believe me, you aren't the only one! If you want to become the Nordstrom of your market niche — and believe us, you do — then *The Nordstrom Way: The Inside Story of America's #1 Customer Service Company,* by Robert Spector and Patrick D. McCarthy (published by Wiley), is for you. As noted by J. Willard Marriott, Jr., of hotel-chain fame: "Nordstrom is a national model for outstanding customer service. American business should use this book as a primer to learn how to make and keep happy, satisfied customers." Coauthored by one of the chain's top sales associates, it outlines just how Nordstrom earned its fine reputation.

The Starbucks Experience: 5 Principles for Turning Ordinary into Extraordinary

No doubt, you've visited a Starbucks. And odds are, when you did, you enjoyed a personalized customer experience with turned-on employees. Indeed, this is at the very core of Starbucks' astounding success! In *The Starbucks Experience: 5 Principles for Turning Ordinary into Extraordinary*, authored by Joseph Michelli (published by McGraw Hill), you can read real-life insider stories, eye-opening anecdotes, and solid step-by-step strategies that reveal how this coffee juggernaut has aggressively defined and managed customer experience. The secret? Listening to individual consumers and employees and reaching out to entire communities, resulting in a custom-designed, satisfying experience that benefits all involved.

Exceptional Service, Exceptional Profit: The Secrets of Building a Five-Star Customer Service Organization

The premise of *Exceptional Service, Exceptional Profit: The Secrets of Building a Five-Star Customer Service Organization* by Leonardo Inghilleri and Micah Solomon (published by AMACOM) is that customer loyalty is key. Loyal customers, the authors say, are less sensitive to price competition, more forgiving of small glitches, and, ultimately, become walking billboards for your company, happily promoting your brand. So how do you cultivate loyalty? Through excellent customer service and an exceptional customer experience. According to Inghilleri and Solomon, of particular importance is "anticipatory customer service" — that is, anticipating the unexpressed wishes of your customers. Numerous organizations in several sectors have embraced this approach, including The Ritz-Carlton, BVLGARI, CarQuest, and more. The authors' discussion of this topic can revolutionize your thinking on delivering customer experience both online and face to face!

What's the Secret? To Providing a World-Class Customer Experience

You know it and we know it: Business is *tough.* Your organization just isn't going to make it if it fails to differentiate itself through the customer experience it delivers. In *What's the Secret? To Providing a World-Class Customer Experience* (published by Wiley), author John DiJulius III, a top customer-service consultant, presents an in-depth look at the customer-service strategies used by top companies worldwide, including Nordstrom, the Ritz-Carlton, Disney, and more. The best practices outlined in this book can change the way you serve your customers! It's simple: If you want to dominate your market, you need to provide a world-class customer experience!

Managing Customer Relationships: A Strategic Framework

As noted by authors Martha Rogers and Don Peppers, the originators of customer relationship management, "No company can succeed without customers. If you don't have customers, you don't have a business. You have a hobby." In their book *Managing Customer Relationships: A Strategic Framework* (published by Wiley), they lay out a clear and thoughtful approach for creating a customer relationship that integrates the diverse realities of technology, interactivity and customization, privacy, customer feedback, insight, dialogue, social media, and networking. With contributions from academic and industry leaders, Peppers and Rogers share techniques that every company can use to sharpen its competitive advantage. The useful concepts and case studies revealed in this book remove any excuse for those responsible for actually delivering one-to-one customer results. Trust us: It's a great read!

Story: Substance, Structure, Style, and the Principles of Screenwriting

Yes, we know. You're not looking to make it as a screenwriter in Hollywood. But we encourage you to read *Story: Substance, Structure, Style, and the Principles of Screenwriting* (published by ReganBooks) because it can help you understand how to construct a cohesive story — something you'll need as you ponder customer journeys. Nobody — and we mean *nobody* — has a better grasp of how all the elements of a story fit together than author Robert McKee, who has worked with such luminaries as Quincy Jones, Diane Keaton, Gloria Steinem, Julia Roberts, John Cleese, David Bowie, and more.

The Design of Everyday Things, Living with Complexity, and Emotional Design

Yes, we know. This entry refers to *three* books by Don Norman, not one. But Norman, a cognitive scientist, is seen by many as the godfather of design. He makes design accessible for those who aren't trained in that field. If you find yourself involved in a touchpoint redesign, *The Design of Everyday Things* (published by Basic Books), *Living with Complexity* (published by The MIT Press), and *Emotional Design: Why We Love (or Hate) Everyday Things* (published by Basic Books) can help you expand your thinking. They provide a working knowledge of how and why some products and services engage customers, while others merely frustrate them.

Index

• Numerics •

• A •

• B •

• F •

• G •

• H •

• I •

• N •

• O •

• P •

• R •

• S •

• T •

• U •

• V •

• W •

• Y •

• Z •

About the Authors

Roy Barnes is one of the leading authorities on customer experience design and performance management. Roy brings humor, focus, and unusual passion to the need for creating greater, truly differentiated customer service, experience, and creativity. Roy brings the unique perspective of not just talking about customer experience and performance management but having delivered it as well. He has more than 25 years of experience leading work teams and delivering world-class results in both the profit and nonprofit sectors.

As senior vice president for strategic planning and later as senior vice president for customer experience development within the leisure division of Marriott International, Roy managed the introduction and execution of process and strategy management tools that focused Marriott Vacation Club on building a sustainable and strategic operating infrastructure.

Roy Barnes experienced it all as he worked his way up through the ranks. Starting as a front desk manager, he led his hotel to the highest guest satisfaction scores in the Marriott system worldwide for two years in a row.

Bob Kelleher is an award-winning author, thought leader, keynote speaker, and consultant. He travels the globe sharing his insights on employee engagement, leadership, and workforce trends. Bob is the author of the bestseller *Louder Than Words: 10 Practical Employee Engagement Steps That Drive Results* and *Creativeship: A Novel for Evolving Leaders* (both from BLKB Publishing), and *Employee Engagement For Dummies* (published by John Wiley and Sons).

Bob is the founder of The Employee Engagement Group, a global consulting firm that works with leadership teams to implement best-in-class leadership and employee engagement programs, workshops, and surveys. Bob's website, `www.employeeengagement.com`, is one of the world's most visited employee engagement websites and is a terrific source for articles, best practices, tools, and resources on the topic.

Bob can be seen or heard on national media (most recently on CNBC, CBS Radio, and NBC News, as well as in *Bloomberg Businessweek, Forbes, Training,* Yahoo!, and *Fortune*), and is a frequent guest writer and contributing editor for many national publications.

Dedication

For Paul Barnes (who taught me to be of service) and Helen Barnes (who loved it when I called her that). – Roy Barnes

Author's Acknowledgments

I owe more thanks than I could possibly say to Evan and Casey, who are a constant source of inspiration, and to Jill, for whom I waited so long.

A very sincere debt of gratitude is owed my fantastic clients who have taken my ranting, ideas, and passion and turned them into astonishing operational results.

If you find this book helpful, grammatically correct, and only occasionally offensive, that outcome is entirely due to the skill of Kate Shoup (she's magic) and the team at Wiley. I'd like to especially acknowledge Bob Kelleher for getting me into this fine mess. Let's do it again. –Ray Barnes

Publisher's Acknowledgments

Executive Editor: Lindsay Lefevere

Assistant Editor: David Lutton

Project Editor: Tracy Brown Hamilton

Copy Editor: Christine Pingleton

Technical Editor: Aline Geike

Art Coordinator: Alicia B. South

Project Coordinator: Lauren Buroker

Cover Photos: © iStock.com/kay

ISBN	Name	Author	Price
9788126544974	Training Your Brain For Dummies	Dr Tracy Packiam, Alloway	299.00
9788126544981	Personal Development All-in-One For Dummies, 2nd Edition	Edited by: Gillian Burn	499.00
9788126545346	Counselling Skills For Dummies	Gail Evans	399.00
9788126545353	Passing Exam For Dummies	Patrick Sherratt	299.00
9788126545810	Data Driven Marketing For Dummies	David Semmelroth	499.00
9788126545827	Starting an Online Business For Dummies 7th Edition	Greg Holden	499.00
9788126545964	Java Programming For Android Developers For Dummies	Barry Burd	449.00
9788126545971	Social Collaboration For Dummies	David F. Carr	449.00
9788126546183	Oracle 12c For Dummies	Chris Ruel, Michael Wessler	499.00
9788126546268	Playing Keyboard For Dummies	Jerry Kovarsky	499.00
9788126546442	Success as an Introvert For Dummies	Joan Pastor, PhD	399.00
9788126546640	Blogging For Dummies, 5th Edition	Amy Lupold Bair, Susannah Gardner	499.00
9788126546657	Business Storytelling For Dummies	Karen Dietz, PhD, Lori L. Silverman	499.00
9788126524877	Cloud Computing For Dummies	Judith Hurwitz, Robin Bloor, Marcia Kaufman, Fern Halper	499.00
9788126547128	Networking All-in-One For Dummies, 5th Ed.	Doug Lowe	599.00
9788126547548	Russian For Dummies	Andrew Kaufman, PhD, and Serafima Gettys, PhD	499.00 w/CD
9788126547555	Arabic For Dummies	Amine Bouchentouf	499.00 w/CD
9788126548590	Visual Social Marketing For Dummies	Krista Neher	499.00
9788126548972	Java All-in-One For Dummies, 4th Edition	Doug Lowe	599.00
9788126548965	Predictive Analytics For Dummies	Anasse Bari,PhD, Mohamed Chaouchi, Tommy Jung	549.00
9788126549177	Excel Dashboards & Reports For Dummies®, 2nd Edition	Michael Alexander	449.00
9788126549184	Lead Generation For Dummies	Dayna Rothman	449.00
9788126549276	3D Printing For Dummies	Kalani Kirk Hausman Richard Horne	499.00
9788126549467	Hinduism For Dummies	Dr. Amrutur V. Srinivasan	499.00
9788126550449	Mindfulness at Work For Dummies	Shamash Alidina and Juliet Adams	499.00
9788126550418	Salesforce.com For Dummies, 5th Edition	Liz Kao and Matt Kaufman	499.00
9788126550432	Marketing Automation For Dummies	Mathew Sweezey	499.00
9788126550425	Piano & Keyboard All-in-One For Dummies	Holly Day, Jerry Kovarsky, Blake Neely, David Pearl, and Michael Pilhofer	599.00
9788126550470	Running Great Meetings & Workshops For Dummies	Jessica Pryce-Jones Julia Lindsay	299.00
9788126550487	Business Networking For Dummies	Stefan Thomas	299.00
9788126550500	Facebook All-in-One For Dummies, 2nd Edition	Jamie Crager, Scott Ayres, Melanie Nelson, and Daniel Herndon	599.00

ISBN	Name	Author	Price
9788126550517	**Hadoop For Dummies**	Dirk deRoos, Paul c. Zikopoulos, Roman B. Melnyk, PhD Bruce Brown Rafael Coss	499.00
9788126550524	**Excel Data Analysis For Dummies, 2nd Edition**	Stephen L. Nelson	499.00
9788126550531	**Beginning iOS Programming For Dummies**	Rajiv Ramnath, PhD	499.00
9788126550548	**iOS App Development For Dummies**	Jesse Feiler	499.00
9788126551002	**Lean Six Sigma for Dummies, 2nd Edition**	John Morgan, Martin Brening-Jones	499.00
9788126551286	**Social Media Design For Dummies**	Janine Warner and David LaFontaine	499.00
9788126551279	**Innovative Presentations For Dummies**	Ray Anthony and Barbara Boyd	449.00
9788126552016	**R For Dummies**	Andrie de Vries Joris Meys	499.00
9788126552184	**Windows 8.1 For Dummies**	Andy Rathbone	449.00
9788126552191	**Willpower For Dummies**	Frank Ryan	149.00
9788126552252	**UX For Dummies**	Donald Chesnut, Kevin P. Nichols	499.00
9788126552269	**Lean Six Sigma Business Transformation For Dummies**	Roger Burghall, Vince Grant & John Morgan	499.00
9788126552290	**Facebook Marketing For Dummies, 4th Edition**	John Haydon	499.00
9788126552306	**Chinese For Dummies, 2nd Edition**	Wendy Abraham	499.00 w/CD
9788126552801	**Webinars For Dummies**	John Carucci & Sharat Sharan	499.00
9788126552818	**Guitar All-In-One For Dummies, 2nd Edition**	Jon chappell, Mark Phillips, and Desi Serna	599.00
9788126552825	**Beginning Programming with Java For Dummies**	Barry Burd, PhD	499.00
9788126553297	**Teachers' Skills Tests For Dummies**	Colin Beveridge, Andrew Green	299.00
9788126553419	**DJing For Dummies, 3rd Edition**	John Steventon	499.00
9788126554355	**Customer Experience For Dummies**	Roy Barnes & Bob Kelleher	499.00
9788126554362	**Chess For Dummies, 3rd Edition**	James Eade	499.00
9788126554379	**Guerrilla Marketing For Dummies**	Jonathan Margolis & Patrick Garrigan	499.00
9788126554386	**Location-Based Marketing For Dummies**	Aaron Strout & Mike Schneider	499.00
9788126554393	**Customer Analytics For Dummies**	Jeff Sauro	499.00
9788126554409	**Twitter® For Dummies, 3rd Edition**	Laura Fitton, Anum Hussain, & Brittany Leaning	399.00
9788126554416	**Decision Making For Dummies**	Dawna Jones	499.00
9788126554485	**Creating a Business Plan For Dummies**	Veechi Curtis	499.00
9788126554584	**Getting a Web Development Job For Dummies**	Kathleen Taylor, Bud E. Smith	299.00
9788126554591	**Getting a Big Data Job For Dummies**	Jason Williamson	299.00
9788126554683	**Key Performance Indicators For Dummies**	Bernard Marr	499.00
9788126554690	**Film Studies For Dummies**	James Cateridge	599.00

ISBN	Name	Author	Price
9788126533732	**Boosting Self-Esteem For Dummies**	Rhena Branch, Rob Willson	349.00
9788126533756	**Linkedin For Dummies, 2nd Edition**	Joel Elad	349.00
9788126533770	**Twitter Marketing For Dummies**	Kyle Lacy	349.00
9788126533589	**Job Searching With Social Media For Dummies**	Joshua Waldman	349.00
9788126533534	**Yoga For Dummies, 2nd Edition**	Georg Feuerstein, Larry Payne	399.00
9788126533565	**Work/Life Balance For Dummies**	Katherine Lockett, Jeni Mumford	349.00
9788126533541	**Facebook Marketing For Dummies, 2nd Edition**	Paul Dunay, Richard Krueger	349.00
9788126533725	**Leadership For Dummies**	Dr John Marrin	349.00
9788126533749	**Life Coaching For Dummies, 2nd Edition**	Jeni Purdie	349.00
9788126533688	**Professional Blogging For Dummies**	Susan J. Getgood	349.00
9788126533572	**Self-Hypnosis For Dummies**	Mike Bryant, Peter Mabbutt	349.00
9788126533558	**Social Media Marketing All-In-One For Dummies**	Jan Zimmerman, Doug Sahlin	499.00
9788126534661	**French For Dummies, 2nd Edition**	Dodi-Katrin Schmidt, Michelle M. Williams, Dominique Wenzel, Zoe Erotopoulos	399.00 w/CD
9788126534647	**German For Dummies, 2nd Edition**	Paulina Christensen, Anne Fox, Wendy Foster	399.00 w/CD
9788126534685	**Flirting For Dummies**	Elizabeth Clark	199.00
9788126534654	**Spanish For Dummies, 2nd Edition**	Susana Wald, Cecie Kraynak	399.00 w/CD
9788126534708	**Chinese For Dummies, Revised Edition**	Dr. Wendy Abraham	349.00 w/CD
9788126535873	**Dad's Guide To Pregnancy For Dummies**	Dr. Roger Henderson, Matthew M.F. Miller, Sharon Perkins	349.00
9788126535880	**Pregnancy For Dummies, 2nd Edition**	Dr. Sarah Jarvis, Dr Roger Henderson, Joanne Stone, Keith Eddleman, Mary Duenwald	349.00
9788126536498	**Confidence For Dummies, 2nd Edition**	Kate Burton, Brinley Platts	249.00
9788126536504	**Body Language For Dummies, 2nd Edition**	Elizabeth Kuhnke	349.00
9788126536511	**Excel 2010 For Dummies, Pocket Edition**	Greg Harvey	99.00
9788126536528	**Twitter For Dummies, Pocket Edition**	Laura Fitton, Michael E. Gruen, Leslie Poston	99.00
9788126538331	**Windows 8 For Dummies**	Andy Rathbone	349.00
9788126538744	**Meditation For Dummies, 3rd Edition**	Stephan Bodian	399.00
9788126538737	**Personal Branding For Dummies**	Susan Chritton	349.00
9788126538690	**Voice & Speaking Skills For Dummies**	Judy Apps	399.00
9788126538720	**Social Media Metrics For Dummies**	Leslie Poston	349.00
9788126538751	**Marketing For Dummies, 3rd Edition**	Ruth Mortimer, Greg Brooks, Craig Smith, Alexander Hiam	349.00
9788126538713	**Social Media Marketing For Dummies, 2nd Ed.**	Shiv Singh, Stephanie Diamond	349.00
9788126538768	**Performance Appraisals & Phrases For Dummies**	Ken Lloyd	199.00
9788126539109	**Social Media Marketing All-In-One For Dummies, 2nd Edition**	Jan Zimmerman, Deborah Ng	499.00
9788126538775	**Android Application Development For Dummies, 2nd Edition**	Michael Burton, Donn Felker	399.00

ISBN	Name	Author	Price
9788126538706	**Persuasion & Influence For Dummies**	Elizabeth Kuhnke	349.00
9788126539697	**Japanese For Dummies, 2nd Edition**	Eriko Sato	499.00 w/CD
9788126539093	**Six Sigma For Dummies, 2nd Edition**	Craig Gygi, Bruce Williams, Neil Decarlo	399.00
9788126539574	**Online Reputation Management For Dummies**	Lori Randall Stradtman	399.00
9788126541348	**Guitar For Dummies**	Mark Phillips, Jon Chappell	399.00 w/DVD
9788126541331	**Mind Mapping For Dummies**	Florian Rustler	399.00
9788126541355	**Success as a Mediator For Dummies**	Victoria Pynchon, Joe Kraynak	399.00
9788126541775	**Microsoft Excell 2013 All-in-One For Dummies**	Greg Harvey, Phd	499.00
9788126541751	**Microsoft Office 2013 All-in-One For Dummies**	Peter Weverka	499.00
9788126541768	**Microsoft Office 2013 For Dummies**	Wallace Wang	399.00
9788126542550	**Networking For Dummies, 10th Edition**	Lowe	399.00
9788126542567	**Excel Formulas and Functions For Dummies, 3rd Edition**	Bluttman	399.00
9788126542574	**Project Management For Dummies, 4th Edition**	Portny	399.00
9788126542475	**Critical Conversations For Dummies**	Schlachter	249.00
9788126542550	**Networking For Dummies**	Doug Lowe	399.00
9788126542574	**Project Management For Dummies**	Stanley E. Portny, PMP®	399.00
9788126542871	**Project 2013 For Dummies**	Cynthia snyder, Nancy Muir	449.00
9788126542918	**Hybrid Cloud For Dummies**	Judith Hurwitz, Marcia Kaufman Dr. Fern Halper, Daniel Kirsch	449.00
9788126543021	**Stress Management For Dummies**	Allen Elkin	399.00
9788126543014	**Mobile Marketing For Dummies**	Michael Becker, John Arnold	399.00
9788126542963	**Microsoft Office 2013 For Dummies with DVD Bundle**	Wallace Wang	599.00
9788126542970	**Microsoft Excel 2013 For Dummies with DVD Bundle**	Greg Harvey	599.00
9788126543281	**Big Data For Dummies**	Judith Hurwitz, Alan Nugent, Dr. Fern Halper, Marcia Kaufman	399.00
9788126543762	**Job Search Letters For Dummies**	Joyce Lain Kennedy	399.00
9788126543779	**Business Models For Dummies**	Jim Muehlhausen JD	399.00
9788126543786	**Hacking For Dummies, 4th Edition**	Kevin Beaver	399.00
9788126543793	**Business Analysis For Dummies**	Paul Mulvey, Kate McGoey, Kupe Kupersmith	449.00
9788126543809	**Psychology For Dummies, 2nd Edition**	Adam Cash	399.00
9788126543816	**Codependency For Dummies**	Darlene Lancer	399.00
9788126543977	**Competitive Intelligence For Dummies**	Jim Underwood	449.00
9788126544394	**Facebook For Dummies**	Carolyn Abram	399.00
9788126544387	**Neuromarketing For Dummies**	Stephen J. Genco, Andrew P. Pohlmann, Peter Steidl	499.00
9788126544776	**PMP Certification All-in-One For Dummies**	Cynthia Snyder	599.00
9788126544769	**Wine For Dummies, 5th Edition**	McCarthy, Mary Ewing-Mulligan	399.00